Ken Russell

Ken Russell

Ken Russell

The Adaptor as Creator

Joseph A. Gomez

Frederick Muller Limited · London

First published in Great Britain 1976
by Frederick Muller Limited, London NW2 6LE

ISBN 0 584 10203 8

Printed in Great Britain by The Anchor Press Ltd
and bound by Wm Brendon & Son Ltd
both of Tiptree, Essex

To Andrea who provided the inspiration
and to Jodi and Jason whom I wish to inspire.

Acknowledgements

This book could not have been written without the assistance of Ken Russell, John Baxter, and Richard Gollin. Ken Russell not only patiently answered my many questions and allowed me to watch him at work filming *Tommy*, but he gave me complete access to his own collection of 16 mm prints. John Baxter offered friendship and advice, as well as generously sharing the fruits of months of research with me. Richard Gollin weathered the many detours this project took, encouraged me in moments of despair, and provided penetrating criticism and insight. I owe these individuals more thanks than this brief acknowledgement allows.

I would also like to thank Prue Hazledine, who supplied me with a different perspective and with copies of the early drafts of *Mahler* and *Tommy*; Rev. Gene Phillips, who wrote to Ken Russell on my behalf; Andrea Sharf, who challenged my ideas with a number of shrewd observations; Liz Welch, who conscientiously typed my manuscript; and James Gifford, who shared my enthusiasm.

Finally, early versions of sections of Chapters 3, 8, 9 and 10 appeared in the following essays: "*Dante's Inferno*: Seeing Ken Russell Through Dante Gabriel Rossetti", *Literature/Film Quarterly*; "*Mahler* and the Methods of Ken Russell's Films on Composers", *The Velvet Light Trap*; "Ken Russell Meets *Tommy*", *Concert*; "Russell's Methods of Adaptation: *Savage Messiah* and *Tommy*", *Ken Russell*, edited by Thomas Atkins and published by Simon and Schuster.

Grateful acknowledgement is made to the following for permission to quote copyrighted material: John Baxter for *An Appalling Talent/Ken Russell*; H. S. Ede for *Savage Messiah*; Faber and Faber Ltd. for *Henri Gaudier-Brzeska 1891–1915* by Horace Brodzky; Chatto and Windus Ltd. and Mrs. Laura Huxley for *The Devils of Loudun* by Aldous Huxley; Chatto and Windus Ltd. and Grover Smith for *Letters of Aldous Huxley*; Harold Ober Associates Inc. for *Beloved Friend: The Story of Tchaikovsky and Nadejda von Meck* by Catherine Drinker Bowen and Barbara von Meck. Copyright 1937 by Random House, Inc. Renewed; A. D. Peters and Co. Ltd. for *The Devils* by John Whiting; Playboy Publications, Inc. for "Conversation with Ken Russell" by Terry Curtis Fox. Originally appeared in *Oui* Magazine. Copyright 1973 by Playboy Publications; Laurence Pollinger Ltd. and the Estate of Frieda Lawrence for *Women in Love* by D. H. Lawrence.

Unless otherwise specified all illustrations appear with the kind permission of Ken Russell.

Contents

Foreword

Here are a few extracts from some of my favourite reviews:

A psychologist of the uglier emotions.
Hatred, contempt, rage, disgust, despair, mockery and defiance serve as models for his moods.
Delights in outraging our sensibilities.
Should be banned on the grounds of indecency.
A thoroughly vicious work full of chaos and bad taste.
Crazy pursuit of novelty, decadence and death.
Erratic and erotic spasms of ugliness.
Ideas as pretentious as they are bizarre.
The extreme ecstasy is forced, unnatural and hysterical.
Chaotic, meaningless, ungrammatical stuff.
A sentimental voluptuary wallowing in nature.
If you are perverse enough to endure over an hour of masochistic flagellation, here's your chance.
Fatuous mysticism and screaming hysteria adding up to a sublimely ridiculous minus zero.
Threads all the foul ditches and sewers of human despair, vulgar and obscene.

You can almost see them running home to their typewriters fearful lest their outrage might cool before they can immortalize their judgement in print.

How important they felt as they wrote off a year's hard work in half an hour.

Bellaigue, Aldrich, Darrell, Elson, Marchesi, Scudo, Apthorp—do these names mean anything to you? They are some of the critics responsible for the fragments of hate listed above – not written about me but some people very dear to me – namely Bartók, Delius, Prokofiev, Liszt, Debussy, Mahler and Tchaikovsky.

Don't worry, I'm not setting myself up in the Hall of Fame along with these geniuses, but if I've nothing in common with them other than these notices (most of which have been applied to my work) then that at least is some comfort.

To expect the same thought, energy, love, anguish, knowledge, understanding, research, laughter, vision, excitement, blood, sweat and tears to go into the criticism of a work as went into its creation would simply not be possible – it would be crying for the moon.

Yet by the time I turned the last page of this book I *was* crying – with joy. I was holding the moon in my hands.

Ken Russell, 1976

1

Introduction

A book on the sources and films of Ken Russell needs if not justification at least some explanation. Although a lengthy theoretical discussion on the differences and similarities between the print and film media would be out of place, a few basic questions concerning the more limited area of film adaptation should be considered briefly in this introduction. For instance, what constitutes a successful adaptation from literature to film? How will the study of a single director's canon contribute to a better understanding of the adaptation process? And finally, why an analysis of the films of Ken Russell?

There have been recently some books, like Robert Richardson's *Literature and Film*,[1] which have attempted to expand the subject area of literature to include film scripts. Such attempts are ill-fated, but the validity of literature/film discussions cannot be doubted. Analysis of these two modes of expression goes back to the early days of filmmaking, when movies were frequently conceived in theatrical terms and when "classics" from literature were often presented in film form.[2] Since then, the trend of adapting material from other media has expanded to the point where, at present, some authors consider screen rights when they are still in the process of writing a play or novel. About one-fourth of all films made are adaptations,[3] and the percentage is probably much higher in England and the United States. Considering the economic realities of the film industry, one can only predict that the rate will even increase in the future. After all, a book which achieves some measure of success assures the producer of a ready-made audience for the film.[4]

Similar as these media may be at times, the differences are fundamental, lasting, and obvious. Words are the building blocks of all literary genres, while the photographic image is the foundation of film. The distinction is crucial: mental images generated by patterns of words versus a series of actual images on celluloid projected in a darkened room. Of course, one may use similar methods of analysis when dealing with fictional narrative, or one may even suggest the two have similar grammatical modes (if the shot equals the word, the movements from shot to shot are analogous to various types of punctuation), but the basic modes of apprehension remain different.

Even so, some of the basic techniques of filmmaking were still influenced by literature, as Sergei Eisenstein, the noted Russian director and theorist, suggested in "Dickens, Griffith and the Film Today". According to Eisenstein, D. W. Griffith derived many of his techniques, including the close-up, cross-cutting, and montage effects, from Victorian literature, most notably from the novels of Charles Dickens.

> I don't know how my readers feel about this but for me personally it is always pleasing to recognize again and again the fact that our cinema is not altogether without parents and without pedigree, without a past, without the traditions and rich cultural heritage of the past epochs. It is only very thoughtless and presumptuous people who can erect laws and an esthetic for cinema, proceeding from premises of some incredible virgin-birth of this art.
>
> Let Dickens and the whole ancestral array, going back as far as the Greeks and Shakespeare, be superfluous reminders that both Griffith and our cinema prove our origins to be not solely cultured past; each part of his past in its own moment of world history has moved forward the great art of cinematography. Let this past be a reproach to those thoughtless people who have displayed arrogance in reference to literature, which has contributed so much to this apparently unprecedented art.[5]

Much recent critical writing suggests, however, that the idea of debt or influence is not one-sided; many commentators discuss, for instance, the cinematic qualities of such literary works as John Dos Passos' *U.S.A.*, West's *The Day of the Locust*, Joyce's *Ulysses* and T. S. Eliot's "The Love Song of J. Alfred Prufrock". The results of such observations, however, are frequently valueless. Again, Robert Richardson's simplistic *Literature and Film* is a prime example; it gingerly moves through a series of dubious comparisons and references ("In retrospect, *The Dynasts* suggests that the form Hardy wanted for his Napoleonic work was quite close to what came to be known as the scenario") only to drown finally in a gratuitous conclusion about the survival of humanism in the arts. ("And it has taken the combined efforts of modern poetry and film to show us that when we find an order that is useful and livable, that order will have a human face.")[6] Charles Eidsvik in an article entitled "Demonstrating Film Influence" suggests that this increased critical discussion of film influence has taken criticism out "of the media-naïveté which made literary critics merely print-critics",[7] but he also notes that the lack of critical precision and the frequent misuse of the term "cinematic" make many critical speculations highly suspect.

Even so, the conventional study of the metamorphosis of literary works into films still allows the best approach to an understanding of the differences and similarities between these forms, and it is in this particular area that some of the best theoretical and practical film criticism has been written—e.g. George Bluestone's *Novels into Film*, André Bazin's *What Is Cinema?*, J. Blumenthal's "*Macbeth* into *Throne of Blood*" and Martin C. Battestin's "Osborne's *Tom Jones*: Adapting a Classic".[8]

Bluestone's work, already 19 years old, remains the most important book in this field, but only because his lengthy first chapter remains an impressive theoretical statement about the limits of the novel and film. The actual analysis of the six films presented in the book is disappointing, in part because the selection stems from an awkward marriage between preference and necessity.

In contrast to André Bazin's view that the faithful adaptation is a translation, Bluestone discusses the serious adaptor as a creator in his own right.

> We discover, therefore, in film versions of the novel an inevitable abandonment of the novelistic elements. This abandonment is so severe that, in a strict sense, the new creation has little resemblance to the original. With the abandonment of language as the sole and primary element, the film necessarily leaves behind those characteristic contents of thought which only language can approximate: hopes, dreams, memories, conceptual consciousness. In their stead, the film supplies endless spatial variations, photographic images of physical reality, and the principles of montage and editing. All these differences derive from the contrast between the novel as a conceptual and discursive form. In these terms, the film-maker merely treats the novel as a raw material and ultimately creates his own structure.[9]

What we have in a film adaptation is a transformation from one way of seeing to another. "And between the percept of the visual image and the concept of the mental image lies the real difference between the two media."[10] This does not mean, however, that the act of perception is an entirely passive one. Charles Eidsvik, for instance, notes that vision is also a selective process of "reaching out for visual objects, separating them from their contexts, and observing their characteristics while watching how they interrelate with their surroundings".[11] Still, the immediacy of impact of the visual medium affects both audiences and the ways in which time, space, structure, and states of consciousness can be handled by the filmmaker. As Bluestone notes: "changes are *inevitable* the moment one abandons the linguistic for the visual medium".[12] It becomes impossible then to say that a film is better or worse than a novel, but the critic can and must analyze the properties unique to each, so that finally he can make a judgment about the nature of the adaptation. Films taken from literary sources which attempt in some way to remain faithful to the original material must capture what George W. Linden calls "visual analogues", or what might even be better expressed as the visual essence of literary conception. The film should preserve the theme and tone of the original, but through "aural/visual" patterning,[13] rather then through devices peculiar to another medium.

Martin Battestin's essay on *Tom Jones* proved convincingly that this film is almost universally accepted as an intelligent film adaptation because Osborne and Richardson succeed in capturing analogous attitudes and rhetorical techniques. Other films, however, even those by the same director and scriptwriter, have not been analyzed from this perspective. As a result, they have often been misunderstood by critics. *The Entertainer* (1960), for instance, was attacked by Penelope Houston because the film as she saw it "blurred the impact of the play",[14] and John Russell Taylor declared the "film version scripted by Osborne himself" totally misconceived, because it "tries to transplant the least realistic sections unchanged into a setting of documentary realism".[15] Richardson, however, was quite aware of the differences between film and theatre in this particular instance, and made significant changes in the structure which, in turn, allowed for "aural/visual" patterning appropriate to film, and a manipulation of the music-hall sequences to correspond, rather than conflict, with the naturalistic delineation of the seaside resort.[16]

The study of adaptations from literature to film serves a number of functions. Most significantly, it provides the most meaningful method of seeing the similarities and differences between film and literature, and it also offers a valuable and, at times, even necessary aid in the evaluation of a film. However, to date, one important area of investigation has been largely ignored: little has been written on a director's particular method or style of adaptation.

The value of a lengthy study of a director's conception of adaptation should be obvious. First of all, it allows us to test Bluestone's contention that the adaptor becomes a creator, not with a random sampling of films, but with a coherent body of work from a figure concerned with both a personal vision of the universe and being faithful to his original sources. This, in turn, should provide insight into the heart of the process of adaptation. We can examine the adaptor as juggler—one who must achieve a balance between fidelity to the theme and tone of the original work and to the expression of his own concerns.

Leo Braudy, in his superb book *Jean Renoir: The World of His Films*, describes when an artist should become the subject of such a study.

> The need to write a book about any creative artist begins in one's first feelings that the subject is separate from other artists with whom he may share superficial similarities, that he has passed through that unspecifiable boundary beyond which a writer, composer, sculptor, painter, or film director becomes a country unto himself.[17]

Ken Russell, although he has been making feature films for only a short period of time, and though his significance and stature as filmmaker depend on a prolific output within a somewhat limited area of exploration, has already passed beyond "that unspecifiable boundary" which allows one to make the designation "the world of his films". His canon also allows for ample discussion of the issues raised by this chapter. Russell possesses a unique style and personal vision which stamps nearly every frame of his films, and he also depends almost exclusively on adapting his films from literary sources. In a sense, he is the film world's adaptor-creator *par excellence*.

A number of critics are only too willing to acknowledge that Ken Russell has become, to use Braudy's term, "a country unto himself", but unfortunately they see him as a bizarre, excessive showman who should be expelled from any brotherhood of artists. Pauline Kael, for instance, claims that he is the "most recklessly eclectic movie director now at work" and adds in her review of *Savage Messiah*:

> What is the sum total of his vision but a sham superiority to simple human needs, a camp put-down of everything? . . . One can't just dismiss Russell's movies, because they have an influence. They cheapen everything they touch—not consciously, I think, but instinctively.[18]

Ms. Kael, however, like most critics in the U.S.A., lacks the proper vantage point from which to assess Russell's specific concerns and the nature of his recent experiments.

Although Russell has drawn material from novels, plays and even a rock opera for his films, his forte is clearly that of the biography film or "biopic". This special interest, however, is probably yet another reason why so many critics unfairly dismiss him. Gary Arnold of *The Washington Post*, for instance, not only viciously ridiculed *The Music Lovers* but insisted that the composer biography was "one of the silliest of movie genres".[19] Unlike the other major film genres, little has been written on the biopic, and nothing of any consequence has been written concerning the problems involved with the adaptation of biography. This book then can provide not only a proper perspective from which to examine Russell's films and a means of evaluating Bluestone's assumptions on the movement from prose to film, but hopefully it will also supply insights peculiar to film adaptations from this type of literature.

The old notion that non-fiction is instructive while fiction is merely entertaining has thankfully lost authority, but occasionally one still encounters the lingering bias that biography is more valuable than fiction because it is true. The biography, however, like fiction, must be shaped by the author and thus can never be totally objective; they are both part of one mode of art. Catherine Drinker Bowen, in *Biography: The Craft and the Calling*, disputes a novelist friend's claim "that compared to fiction writers, biographers have an easy time. Their plot is ready to hand before they even begin to write."[20] Ms. Bowen counters that chronology is ready rather than plot. The writer of biography draws from "ready-made" factual material, but he must organize his account. He makes choices concerning the selection of details, employs functional description to capture both atmosphere and scene, devises techniques to reveal his characters' thoughts, and creates a pattern of explanation which embodies theme and symbol. As such, for André Maurois, the biographer

> has greater difficulty than the novelist in composition. But he has one compensation: to be compelled to take over the form of a work ready-made is almost always a source of power to the artist. It is painful, it makes his task more difficult; but at the same time it is from this struggle between the mind and the matter that resists it that a masterpiece is born.[21]

Just as the genre of the novel has undergone a number of changes since the eighteenth century, the nature, concerns, and methods of Boswell's *Life of Johnson* are quite different from Erik Erikson's *Young Man Luther* or George Painter's biography of Proust. In his inaugural lecture at Oxford in 1971, Richard Ellmann noted that "the form of biography . . . is countenancing experiments comparable to those of the novel and poem". Of course, biography is usually limited to some extent in that it retains some vestiges of a chronological pattern, but according to Ellmann, the best biographies "will offer speculations, conjectures, hypotheses. The attempt to connect disparate elements, to describe the movements within the mind as if they were movements within the atom, to label the most elusive particles, will become more venturesome."[22] Ellmann's observations, of course, relate directly to literary biography, but they are not unrelated to experimentation in the genre of filmed biography.

Film biographies are almost universally pigeonholed into two separate categories: the Hollywood romantic popularization and the faithful, factual reconstruction. The best of the first type is epitomized in the numerous biopics (*The Story of Louis Pasteur* (1936), *The Life of Emile Zola* (1937), *Juarez* (1939), *Dr. Ehrlich's Magic Bullet* (1940), etc.) directed by William Dieterle for Warner Brothers, but all Hollywood biopics must falsify fact in order to heighten the dramatic impact, to soften character faults, or to allow for moments of inspirational creation. At the other end of the scale is the factual presentation, perhaps best represented by some of the films of Charles Frend, *The Foreman Went to France* (1942), *San Demetrio, London* (1943) and *Scott of The Antarctic* (1949), and the British TV documentaries of the fifties and the early sixties. Here the emphasis was on factual re-enactment and concern for accurate detail.

Although Ken Russell grew out of this latter tradition, his feature length TV biographies and his later feature films should not be linked to either of these two approaches. His films are complex experiments involving form and structure which force the viewer to reconsider the very nature of the biopic genre, and thus any attempt by misguided critics to force his films into a Procrustean bed of simplistic categorization is both unfortunate and unjust.[23]

Russell claims that "artists are explainable by what they produce",[24] but his own film biographies also show that what an artist produces can, in part, be explained by what he is. Certainly in his own case, his life as a child and young man provides a key to understanding his artistic methods and vision, and perhaps unconsciously he reveals this by the way in which he frequently discusses his past life in interview situations. Time is compressed in his responses, and when occasionally dates are cited in different interviews, they frequently contradict each other. Also, his memories are impressionistic descriptions of particular incidents, chiefly those of flights of imagination or the discovery of "art" in rather mundane or dreary circumstances.[25]

John Baxter's long delayed *An Appalling Talent/Ken Russell* finally clears up much of the elusiveness concerning the facts of the director's life, but since much of the book derives from taped conversation with Russell, the impressionism and preoccupation with the past are even heightened. "I'm a very nostalgic person," Russell says, "but I hope to derive ideas and strength from the past rather than wallow in it."[26]

Russell was born on July 3, 1927, and grew up in the port town of Southampton. His father, a lower-middle-class merchant, owned a boot-and-shoe shop, and his mother passed most of her afternoons at the movie palaces on the High Street. Russell's childhood was noticeably lonely—an unvarying pattern, as he describes it, of staying at his grandmother's house, staring vacantly out of the front window at nothing or accompanying his mother on her jaunts to the movies.[27] His older cousin Marion provided some of the few variations of this cycle.

> Every summer we used to go to this place called Highcliffe. There were bungalows around a field, and you went down a steep cliff to the beach. We had marvelous adventures. She was a sort of ideal character. She was like a boy and a girl at the same time, fantastically beautiful. She was too good to live, practically . . . and she didn't. When the war came, she went to Highcliffe one day—she was twelve or thirteen—and the army had mined the field, and she trod on a mine and was blown to pieces.[28]

Closed off from friends and other outlets from boredom, Russell created a fantasy world. He spent hours alone sitting in his favorite tree inventing playmates or acting out scenes from the movie that he had just seen at the Picture House or on his own 9·5 mm Pathescope projector. He was especially attracted to fire and water and used these elements extensively in his fantasy world, as he was to use them later in his films. "I remember looking at clouds reflected in rain puddles and trying to jump down into them, into the blue shining depths." Reading and the arts, however, had little impact in the cultivation of his imagination at that time. "I had never seen a painting . . . till I went to school. I don't recall *ever* reading a book as a child."[29]

Russell's education consisted of attending a series of mediocre schools, but in 1941, at the age of 14, he became a cadet at the Royal Naval College at Pangbourne. The romantic lure of the sea was obviously an inducement, but the discipline, class snobbery, and rigidity of behavior patterns at nautical school were not much to his liking, and it was only in directing one of the performances of the annual concert that he was finally able to give substance to some of his fantasies.

> I spent three years breaking bounds to see Betty Grable and Dorothy Lamour movies, for which I was caned unmercifully upon my return. The shows were mostly dull affairs, but when *I* directed a show, it was lovely, because I dressed them all up in drag and made Carmen Mirandas out of them.[30]

Using some of the cadets and the camera of a fellow student, he also made his first film—a crazy hodge-podge of gags and plot gimmicks which grew out of his familiarity with slap-stick comedies and horror movies.[31]

Later, after leaving Pangbourne and going to sea with a modern day Captain Bligh, Russell suffered a nervous breakdown and was released from the Navy. During his period of recovery, he discovered classical music.

I just happened to be listening to the radio, and I heard some music I couldn't believe. The man announced that it was Tchaikovsky's *First Piano Concerto*. I rushed out and bought the records. From then on, I couldn't have enough music. I would buy every record I could afford.[32]

Not knowing what to do with his life, Russell joined the R.A.F., but he soon found that he disliked the Air Force about as much as he disliked the Navy. During these wasted years, however, he ran a music circle with a sailor named Bert Woodfield, a 15-stone eccentric who introduced him to ballet one day by suddenly jumping up and doing the male bluebird variation from *Sleeping Beauty*. After being demobbed, Russell unsuccessfully attempted to break into the film industry, and finally at Woodfield's suggestion, he went to the Hampstead Ballet Club, where he studied at night after working days at the Lefévre Art Gallery. He then became a student at the International Ballet School, later toured with the Norwegian Ballet, and danced with a small company called the London Theatre Ballet, when it did *Dr. Coppelius* off-season at a tatty seaside resort. His longest dancing job, however, came as part of the chorus line of a touring production of *Annie Get Your Gun*.

After experience with ballet came an acting stint, but Russell was so hopelessly inept that he lasted only three weeks with a group called the Garrick Players, at Newton Poppleford, South Devon. He then decided that since actors and dancers always wanted portraits he could earn a living as a photographer. So he went off to technical college to study photography, and it was here that he met Shirley Kingdon, his future wife and costume designer for all his major films. At first, he thought of making his living as a fashion photographer, but after completing his schooling he worked as a magazine features photographer.[33]

It was during this period that Russell converted to Roman Catholicism, an act as significant as his discovery of painting, ballet, music, and photography in providing the groundwork for his artistic development as a filmmaker. "I was converted, and I suddenly found a direction. I've known exactly what I've been trying to do ever since."[34]

Soon after becoming a Roman Catholic, he married Shirley, also a convert, and began working for such magazines as *Illustrated* and *Picture Post*.

I did feature work then, but the things I liked best were the things we did on our honeymoon. We had our honeymoon at Howarth, where the Bronte sisters lived. I dressed Shirley up in Victorian gear, and we tramped all over the moors, evoking the spirit of the Brontes, against the backlit grass and mud. I photographed the churchyard, the couch where Charlotte died, and so forth. They were evocative, moody atmospheric things, but there wasn't much call for them.[35]

As the years passed, Russell managed to save enough money to make three amateur films: *Peepshow* (1956), *Amelia and the Angel* (1957) and *Lourdes* (1958). These were then submitted to Huw Wheldon of the BBC, and Russell was hired on a trial basis to replace John Schlesinger as one of the filmmakers for the bi-weekly *Monitor* arts program.

Between 1959 and 1962, Russell made 20 films for *Monitor*. Many of them were short, often about 15 minutes in length, and the subjects ranged from guitars, dancing, and brass bands to Shelagh Delaney, John Betjeman, and Spike Milligan. In 1961, he attempted his first biography-documentary, a portrait of Sergei Prokofiev, but it was his film on Edward Elgar (first telecast on November 11, 1962) that achieved his nation-wide recognition. In fact, the film became one of England's most popular TV films, and a number of music historians credit it with a significant role in the revival of interest in the composer during the sixties.[36]

Soon after *Elgar*, Russell left his sheltered world at the BBC for a brief excursion into the world of feature films to make *French Dressing* (1963). Although now considered by some to be far ahead of its time, the film is actually a lack-luster British imitation of Jacques Tati's early films which wastes the comic talents of James Booth, Roy Kinnear, and Bryan Pringle. There are some memorable moments: a fight in a theater in front of the screen on which is projected the large mouth of a woman who appears about to devour the Lilliputian figures around her, and a sequence of encounters with plastic dummies which are finally burned in a pit. For the most part, however, these are more ominous than humorous. The film, given a limited release in Britain, was considered a "disaster" by those involved with it, and Russell fled back to the BBC. He then made two more short films, *Watch the Birdie* (1963) and *Lonely Shore* (1964), before embarking on his next biopic.

In *Bartók* (1964), Russell was allowed to use Boris Renevsky in close-up to portray the lonely Hungarian composer, but the BBC would still not allow an actor to speak any lines on camera. In *The Debussy Film* (1965), however, Russell solved this difficulty by having the film center on the activities of a TV director as he works on a film about the composer. *The Debussy Film* was also the first of his four collaborations with Melvyn Bragg, the novelist/filmmaker who still works for the BBC. Bragg also acted as co-scriptwriter on Russell's next project, *Always on Sunday* (1965), a film about Henri Rousseau narrated by Oliver Reed and starring James Lloyd, the primitive painter who was the subject of an earlier Russell work for *Monitor* entitled *The Dotty World of James Lloyd* (1964).

After *Don't Shoot the Composer* (1966), a film on his friend Georges Delerue,[37] Russell turned his attention to *Isadora Duncan, The Biggest*

Dancer in the World (1966), a work which he still regards as one of his best TV films. This was the first of Russell's BBC biopics to be seen in the United States, and a number of critics, including Andrew Sarris, considered the film to be "far more responsive to the subject" than Karel Reisz's more widely seen *The Loves of Isadora* (1968).[38]

It was also at this time that producer Harry Saltzman invited Russell to join a consortium of directors who would be able to make the feature films of their choice. In keeping with this offer, Russell and Melvyn Bragg began work on a script dealing with the life of Nijinsky, but when the screenplay was near completion, Saltzman proposed that Russell direct *Billion Dollar Brain* (1967) as a warm-up exercise.[39] Before taking over this underfinanced film, however, he finished a feature-length biography film for the BBC on Dante Gabriel Rossetti and the Pre-Raphaelite circle. *Dante's Inferno* (1967) starred Oliver Reed as the tormented poet-painter and included a cast of amateurs who bore striking physical resemblances to the people they portrayed. Saltzman's consortium never did come into existence. So after his second unhappy experience directing a feature film, Russell again returned to the BBC where he made *Song of Summer* (1968), a subtle chamber film which focuses on the last years of Frederick Delius and the remarkable relationship that the blind, paralyzed composer established with his amanuensis, Eric Fenby.

The opportunity to direct *Women in Love* (1969) came about, strangely enough, because the people in the British office of United Artists thought that *Billion Dollar Brain* deserved much more than the lukewarm critical and box-office receptions it received,[40] and it was the success of this screen adaptation of Lawrence's novel that at long last established a place for Russell in the world of feature filmmaking. Before devoting his energies exclusively to features, however, Russell made one last biopic for the BBC. His controversial comic-strip life of Richard Strauss *(The Dance of the Seven Veils)* was telecast on February 15, 1970, and was promptly banned from any other public showings.

Russell's irreverent approach to his subject matter continued in his next film, a feature biography on the life of Peter Ilyich Tchaikovsky adapted from *Beloved Friend* by Catherine Drinker Bowen and Barbara von Meck. Unfortunately, *The Music Lovers* (1970) never found a substantial audience outside England, perhaps in part because it is a complex and subtle film which confused and disappointed those who expected a film in the same vein as *Women in Love*.

Even before Russell began directing *The Music Lovers*, United Artists approached him about making a film version of *The Devils of Loudun*, Aldous Huxley's biographical account of the most famous sorcery trial in seventeenth century France, but because of a shift in policy and personnel at U.A., Warner Brothers finally took over the production of *The Devils* (1971). The film, especially in the British version, is not merely a brilliant historical re-creation of the last years of Urbain Grandier; it is also an aesthetically powerful, visionary film about our own time. As such, Russell believes it to be his best work to date, even though it is often the object of his detractors' most vociferous condemnations.

The strain of making a film about events as brutal as those depicted in *The Devils* was one of the reasons why Russell, after finishing this project, turned almost immediately to making a screen version of *The Boy Friend*, Sandy Wilson's gentle parody of musical comedies of the twenties. *The Boy Friend* (1971), however, proved to be no pleasant diversion for the director, for although it received generally favorable critical notices, the actual filming was fraught with personal squabbles among the cast members and difficulties involving the lack of facilities and the inexperience of British technicians in making a musical with such large-scale production numbers.[41]

Perhaps because of these difficulties, Russell, for his next film, turned to a low-budget adaptation of H. S. Ede's biography *Savage Messiah*. *Savage Messiah* (1972), like *Song of Summer*, is a chamber film concentrating on the unique relationship of two people, in this case the Platonic friendship of Henri Gaudier, the Vorticist sculptor, and Sophie Brzeska, a Polish woman twenty years his senior. After this film, a period of aborted scripts and failed projects followed, until Russell finally made *Mahler* (1974), an adventurous work which is just the first of six features on composers to be made for Goodtimes Enterprises. This recent film seems to have signalled another period of intense activity, for since its completion, Russell has made *Tommy* (1975), a screen adaptation of the rock-opera by The Who, and *Lisztomania*, a film based on the life of Franz Liszt.

When discussing Russell's films in depth, one cannot, like most critics today, simply beg the question of authorship and assume that the director is ultimately responsible for everything on the screen. Andrew Sarris, in one of his numerous defenses of the *auteur* theory, acknowledges that directorial domination has not always been permitted in England and the United States, but nevertheless he claims that the script writer has been victimized more than the director, in part because producers are more apt to tamper with the story than with visual style.[42] Such, however, is not always the case, as *Memo from David O. Selznick* testifies.[43] Moreover, commentary from people directly involved in filmmaking casts some doubt on Sarris' defense of the *auteur* theory. Joan Didion, for instance, lashes out against the whole idea of film reviewing and critical analysis.

> A finished picture defies all attempts to analyze what makes it work or not work: the responsibility for its every frame is clouded not only in

> the accidents and compromises of production but in the clauses of its financing. . . .
>
> About the best a writer on film can hope to do, then, is to bring an engaging or interesting intelligence to bear upon the subject, a kind of *petit-point*-on-kleenex effect which rarely stands much scrutiny. "Motives" are inferred where none existed; allegations spun out of thin speculation. Perhaps the difficulty of knowing who made which choices in a picture makes this airiness so expedient that it eventually infects any writer who makes a career of reviewing; perhaps the initial error is in making a career of it.[44]

Nat Boxer, a sound production chief who has worked on such films as *Bananas, They Might Be Giants, The Conversation*, and *The Godfather Part II,* disagrees with Ms. Didion's appraisal of the possibilities of film criticism, but argues that one must take great care in attributing to the director a particular vision, since even visual style can be determined by the art director rather than the cameraman or director.[45]

The validity of *auteur* studies dealing with the films of Jean Renoir, Ingmar Bergman, Federico Fellini, or François Truffaut is rarely questioned; conditions within those national film industries differ from conditions in the United States and England. These directors have almost total control over their work. But what of Ken Russell?

Russell, along with Stanley Kubrick, is a man who has managed to combine the "functions of artist, technician, showman and business man". These two filmmakers were both originally still photographers. They know about lenses and emulsions; they can operate cameras, splicers, and Moviolas; and they often do so (as far as trade union rules permit).[46] Most significantly, however, they are often their own producers.

> They not only select their own subjects but are the authors and co-authors of their own screenplays. They hire their own actors and technicians. They supervise the editing right down to the last frame. They choose their own music . . .
>
> They even exercise a considerable influence over the presentation of the end product. When one of his films was transmitted on television, Russell was the scourge of the electronic experts who control the density and contrast of the image from scene to scene.[47]

Ken Russell's "stock company" goes back to his BBC days, and should be the envy of most directors working in England and America. It includes not only particular experienced actors, but a sizable portion of the crew.[48] Neither chance nor compromise governs his choices of material, thematic concerns, treatment, visual style and technical method. The world of Ken Russell's films exists. We must now describe it and discuss the principles supporting it.

NOTES

[1]Robert Richardson, *Literature and Film* (Bloomington: Indiana University Press, 1972).

[2]See Vachel Lindsay, *The Art of the Moving Picture* (New York: Macmillan, 1915).

[3]Louis D. Giannetti, *Understanding Movies* (Englewood, N. J.: Prentice Hall, 1972), p. 161.

[4]Recently, Warner Brothers carried this idea to an extreme by suggesting that Herman Roucher turn his screenplay of *Summer of '42* into a novel before the film was released, so that the novel would promote the film. See "For Herman Raucher", *Family Weekly*, 29 July 1973, p. 2.

Of course, sales of books also increase with the release of the film, and the popular successes of such controversial films as *I Am Curious Yellow* and *Last Tango in Paris* almost always guarantee paperback publication of the script with profuse illustrations or at least a novelized version of the screenplay. See Vilgot Sjoman, *I am Curious (Yellow)* (New York: Grove Press, Inc., 1968) and Bernardo Bertolucci, *Last Tango in Paris* (New York: Dell Publishing Co., 1973).

[5]Sergei Eisenstein, "Dickens, Griffith, and the Film Today", *Film Form* (New York: Harcourt, Brace and World, *c.* 1949), pp. 232–3. For a different version of how Griffith devised many of his techniques, see Robert M. Henderson, *D. W. Griffith: The Years at Biograph* (New York: Farrar, Straus and Giroux, 1970, London: O.U.P., 1972), especially Chapter 11.

[6]Robert Richardson, *Literature and Film,* pp. 23 and 132.

[7]Charles Eidsvik, "Demonstrating Film Influence", *Literature/Film Quarterly* 1 (1973), p. 120.

[8]See George Bluestone, *Novels into Film* (Berkeley: University of California Press, 1961); André Bazin, *What Is Cinema?* (Berkeley: University of California Press, 1967); J. Blumenthal, "*Macbeth* into *Throne of Blood*", *Sight and Sound,* 34 (1965), pp. 190–5; and Martin C. Battestin, "Osborne's *Tom Jones*: Adapting a Classic", *Man and the Movies,* ed. W. R. Robinson (Baltimore: Penguin Books, 1969), pp. 31–45.

[9]George Bluestone, *Novels into Film,* pp. viii–ix.

[10]*Ibid.*, p. 1.

[11]Charles Eidsvik, "Soft Edges: the Art of Literature, the Medium of Film", *Literature/Film Quarterly,* 2 (1974), p. 19.

[12]Bluestone, p. 5.

[13]George W. Linden, *Reflections on the Screen* (Belmont, California: Wadsworth, 1970), p. 49.

[14]Penelope Houston, *The Contemporary Cinema* (Harmondsworth, England: Penguin Books, 1964), p. 121.

[15]John Russell Taylor, *Anger and After* (Harmondsworth, England: Penguin Books, 1966), p. 45.

[16]Still, Miss Houston and Mr. Taylor at least pay lip service to the literary origins of many films, which is more than many film critics bother to do. An understanding of the adaptation of a literary work into a film is not a pedantic exercise; it is often crucial to an evaluation of the film, and all too often this kind of analysis

is done only by academics who write criticism for journals like *Literature/Film Quarterly* and *Film Heritage.*

In their first issue (September–October 1972) the editors of *Film Critic,* the journal of the American Federation of Film Societies, attacked such criticism as being so many mouldy tales from a Ph.D. program's crypt and pleaded instead for relevant criticism which "deals with cinema in the social, political and cultural context of its time. Not just social, political and cultural issues and ideas, but the institutions that embody and affect them". This kind of attack, and the misuse of the *auteur* concept as a tennis ball to be slammed back and forth between opposing schools of criticism, serves as an indication that film criticism, although in transition, is often close to chaos.

The special problems which haunt the criticism of films also add to the situation. Some reviews still misassign contribution in a film, and this kind of lapse raises the question as to whether or not most reviewers really understand who does what on a film. Of course, in many cases the credits themselves are not always accurate. Too, there is the question of final cut. Even if we assume that the director is the strongest creative force in the film (and this is not always the case), what about the right to final cut, which most American directors do not have? How do we or the reviewer know when we are not seeing the film as the director wished it to be released? Too many critics simply beg the question and accept the film as the director's own. In a series of letters between Seymour Peck, former Arts and Leisure Editor of the *New York Times,* and the writer of this book, Mr. Peck quoted Vincent Canby, the *Times* film reviewer, as contending "that basically a critic must evaluate what he sees on the screen and cannot probe constantly for the background.... Certainly, the general reader wants an evaluation of the final film to determine whether or not it is worth his time and money."

On the contrary, if film criticism is to ascend from its present state of mediocrity, we must expect the good critic (as distinguished from local movie reviewer) to assume the Herculean tasks of providing background about cutting, editing, and even sources of films. This is where the study of adaptations can be of significant value. Adaptations, however, should not be limited merely to a study of novels and plays as sources. Only a few critics, for instance, bothered to note that Sam Peckinpah's *Pat Garrett and Billy the Kid* (1973) was cut by some 18 minutes and rescored by MGM, and only one bothered to examine such works as Pat Garrett's *The Authentic Life of Billy the Kid* or any other biographies to see when Peckinpah was historically accurate and when he consciously attempted to make Billy the mythic embodiment of his own value structure. In this particular case, such an analysis helps to provide a rationale for the structure of the film, whether the director's film or the studio's.

[17]Leo Braudy, *Jean Renoir: The World of His Films* (Garden City, New York: Doubleday, 1972), p. 13.

[18]See Pauline Kael, "Pleasing and Punishing", *New Yorker,* 8 January 1972, p. 74; and Pauline Kael, "Hyperbole and Narcissus", *New Yorker* 18 November 1972, p. 232.

[19]Gary Arnold, "Music Lovers", *Washington Post,* 25 February 1971, Section C, p. 14, cols. 1–2.

[20]Catherine Drinker Bowen, *Biography: The Craft and the Calling* (Boston: Little, Brown and Co., 1969), p. 3.

[21]*Ibid.,* p. 4.

[22]Richard Ellmann, "Literary Biography", *Golden Codgers: Biographical Speculations* (New York: Oxford University Press, 1973), p. 15.

[23]Although Russell is the foremost experimenter in the biopic genre, he is not the only one. Peter Watkins, another director who grew out of the BBC approach to factual reconstruction, has recently completed a 3½-hour film biography of Edvard Munch which deals only with ten years of the expressionist painter's life. The film dispenses with the usual chronological structure and offers instead an involved pattern of image clusters and complex time relationships which make multiple viewings a necessity.

[24]Cited in "Director in a Caftan", *Time*, 13 September 1973, p. 53.

[25]See Lee Langley, "Ken Russell: A Director Who Demands the Right to be Outrageous", *Show*, October 1971, pp. 34–8; Guy Flatley, "I'm Surprised My Films Shock People", *New York Times*, 15 October 1972, Arts and Leisure Section, p. 15; Glen O'Brien, "Ken Russell in the Port of New York", *Interview*, 27 November 1973, pp. 9–11; Peter Mezan, "Relax, It's only a Ken Russell Movie", *Esquire*, May 1973, pp. 167–71 and 198–202; Fred Robbins, "The Savage Russell", *Gallery*, May 1973, pp. 105–6 and 126–7; Terry Curtis Fox, "Conversations with Ken Russell", *Oui*, June 1973, pp. 63–4 and 102–8. When talking to Ken Russell about his past life, one is perhaps most struck by the same telescoping of events and juxtaposition of radically different perceptions which are so much a part of his methods as a film-maker.

[26]John Baxter, *An Appalling Talent/Ken Russell* (London: Michael Joseph, 1973), p. 43. Publication of Baxter's book was held up for almost a year because of a threatened law suit by producer Harry Saltzman.

[27]*Ibid.*, pp. 41–9.

[28]Cited in Mezan, p. 200.

[29]Cited in Langley, p. 38. Also see Baxter, *An Appalling Talent*, pp. 59–61.

[30]Cited in Flatley, p. 15.

[31]See Baxter, *An Appalling Talent*, pp. 61–70.

[32]Cited in Fox, p. 63.

[33]See Baxter, *An Appalling Talent*, pp. 77–90.

[34]Cited in Fox, p. 106. Although he is no longer a practicing Catholic, the importance of ritual and the consequences of guilt, two very Catholic concerns, still determine much of the style and the content of his films.

[35]*Ibid.*, p. 64.

[36]Baxter, *An Appalling Talent*, p. 18.

[37]Delerue composed the music scores for *French Dressing* and *Women in Love*. The title of Russell's film is an allusion to François Truffaut's *Shoot the Piano Player*, for which Delerue also wrote the music.

[38]Andrew Sarris, cited in his review of *Savage Messiah*. See "*Savage Messiah*", *Filmfacts*, 15 (1972), p. 582.

[39]See Baxter, *An Appalling Talent*, pp. 152–60; and Fox, p. 102.

[40]Baxter, *An Appalling Talent*, p. 167. Also see Fox, pp. 102–3.

[41]Baxter, *An Appalling Talent*, pp. 211–19.

[42]Andrew Sarris, *The American Cinema: Directors and Directions 1929–1968* (New York: E. P. Dutton & Co., 1968), pp. 29–34.

[43]See David O. Selznick, *Memo From David O. Selznick*, ed. Rudy Behlmer (New York: Viking, 1972)—especially the chapters dealing with *Gone With the Wind* and *Rebecca*. Also see Charles Thomas Samuels (ed.) *Encountering Directors* (New York: Putnams, 1972), especially the interviews with Carol Reed and Vittorio DeSica.

[44]Joan Didion, "Hollywood: Having Fun", *New York Review of Books*, 22 March 1973, p. 17, col 2.

[45]Nat Boxer in a lecture-discussion entitled "Technical Contributions of a Film Crew in the Making of Feature Films", delivered on April 9, 1973 at Mohawk Valley Community College as part of the First Utica Film Symposium.

[46]In an interview with Fred Robbins, Russell notes that he works "very closely with the cinematographers on the film, perhaps more closely than most directors. I even light certain scenes and I certainly operate the camera at times, so I suppose a particular style is bound to come out." See "The Savage Russell", *Gallery*, pp. 105–6. My own observations of the director at work on the set of *Tommy* verify these claims.

[47]Tony Rose, "Other People's Pictures", *Movie Maker*, April 1972, p. 245. It must be noted in fairness, however, that Russell's films do not always appear on the screen in the form he desires. Prior to the première of *The Devils* in England, Russell was forced to make a few cuts to please the censors, and Warner Brothers further trimmed the film in an effort to avoid an *X* rating in the United States. MGM also lopped off over 15 minutes of the print of *The Boy Friend* distributed in the United States, but Russell managed to have final cut of the print distributed in England and Europe.

[48]Shirley Russell serves as costume designer for nearly all of her husband's films; Michael Bradsell edited most of the major TV films and all of the features with the exception of *French Dressing, Billion Dollar Brain,* and *Tommy*; Luciana Arrighi worked on the TV films and decorated the set of *Women in Love*, but Ian Whittaker has since replaced her in this role. Terry Rawlings, Maurice Askew and Brian Simmons have been in charge of sound, and Terry Gilbert, an old friend from Russell's ballet days, served as choreographer until being replaced by Gillian Gregory. Roy Baird is often the associate producer; Harry Benn is in control of production on most films; Melvyn Bragg still works on scripts, and Dick Bush, who served as director of photography on *Isadora Duncan* and *Song of Summer*, has since shot three of Russell's features. Those in the "stock company" of actors and actresses who have worked with him include: Oliver Reed, Glenda Jackson, Max Adrian, Judith Paris, Christopher Gable, Vladek Sheybal, Andrew Faulds, Kenneth Colley, Catherine Wilmer, Georgina Hale, Murray Melvin, Ben Aris, and Iza Teller.

2

From Amateur Films to *Isadora Duncan*

Russell's Approach to Biographical Films and the Development of a Personal Style

> Biographies seem to me rather like detective stories. You're given the clues of a man's life and you supply the motive for the crime, the crime being the work of art or the body of art produced by the man.
>
> Ken Russell[1]

Ken Russell's career as a filmmaker began with three amateur films. More than mere exercises with a camera, these films foreshadow some of the hallmarks of his mature style and present in embryonic form a number of the themes embodied in his feature films. *Peepshow* (1956), a film in which Russell and his friends dressed up in old costumes and portrayed puppets who come to life, has been described as being "something of a metaphorical statement about the relationship of art and magic".[2] *Amelia and the Angel* (1957), seemingly a charming children's film, on another level allows the viewer a glimpse of an almost religious attitude towards the artist, and finally in *Lourdes* (1958), Benjamin Britten's music from the ballet *The Prince of the Pagodas* provides a sense of form and structure.

> Even then I liked to find something—music, poems—that imposed not only a form and a style but a definite cutting sequence. You find, because music is mathematics, that whether you want to or not you're cutting your film with the music, and imposing a logical form—an A-B-A-C form, a rondo form, a sonata form—so you've got a good ground plan on which to build your film.[3]

Even Russell's plans for amateur films which were never made serve as signposts for things to come in his later BBC work and the feature films. In an article entitled "Ideas for Films" published in *Film* (the journal of the Federation of Film Societies), he described plans for two amateur films, both of which harken back to the concerns of *Peepshow* and *Amelia and the Angel*. The first project concerns a Punch and Judy man whose pitch is taken away from him. He learns his fate in the middle of a performance and uses his puppets to debate with the police officer who has come to remove him. The merging of art and life is further suggested when we later learn that the showman's nagging wife is named Judy. The second proposed film also presents the fantasy and real worlds of a pavement artist and uses this juxtaposition for full effect.[4] Variations on this theme are basic to a number of Russell's later films, including *The Debussy Film, The Music Lovers,* and even *The Boy Friend*.

Of Russell's early amateur films, one would suspect that *Lourdes*, since it was a documentary, played the most important role in helping him to get a job at the BBC, but Huw Wheldon of the *Monitor* arts program claims that he saw only *Amelia and the Angel*.[5] This film, made on accumulated savings and a small loan from the British Film Institute, was strongly influenced by *The Red Balloon,* but it still possesses more imagination, energy, and vitality than some of Russell's more polished early BBC shorts. Briefly, the plot concerns a young girl who will dance the role of an angel in an upcoming school program. Unable to wait until her mother can see her costume at the performance, Amelia takes her wings home, even though her teacher has warned all the children not to do so, since "there's not a single pair more to be found this side of heaven". Once home, her thoughtless brother takes the wings for a romp through the local playground and destroys them. As the hour of the performance grows nearer, Amelia begins a search for another pair of wings. Her quest takes her to the Portobello Road Market, an abandoned railway station which also serves as the home of Mike Sniver, "trainer of wild animals", and his dog "Rock", and finally to the base of a stone angel in the park. Amelia then looks up to see a woman with a pair of wings running through the park, and in a sequence probably derived from Cocteau's *Orphée*, she pursues the elusive figure. Finally, after losing sight of the woman, a feather on the sidewalk indicates to Amelia that she has entered a sinister house. Amelia cautiously enters the house, and after being frightened by a fashion designer's mannequin, which appears suddenly as a headless woman, she discovers her "angel" who is modelling for a painting. The painter, a bearded Christ figure in monk's robes and sandals, then climbs up a long ladder and returns from "heaven" with a set of wings for the happy child.

Russell's preoccupation with the choreography of cinema (the movement of actors and camera), his making do with what is available, and his emphasis on the image rather than the word are all found here. More importantly, however, the film demonstrates his earliest experiments with the use of music to define mood and with the image to create meaning. Also, some of the rhythm of the editing seems to be determined by the soundtrack, which, for the most part, consists of Victorian melodies played by a "polyphon" and an "ariston" (precursors to the modern phonograph and operated through the use of perforated discs). However, once Amelia reaches the artist's home, the simple melodies are replaced by the beautiful and complex sounds of the Vivaldi-Bach *Concerto for Four Harpsichords*. This music, in turn, supports the visual metaphor which suggests that the artist possesses god-like powers and is capable of the highest form of revelation.[6]

In a number of interviews, Russell has claimed that for him music is probably "the most incredible event in human history" and that if he could compose he wouldn't make films.[7] Evidence of this love of music goes far beyond the fact that composers are often the subjects of his film biographies. He frequently plays recordings on the sets of his films, so that music can act as a catalyst for his imagination. Also, he uses it to plunge himself, his actors, and often the audience of the film into a particular mood.[8]

It is the final effect in the film, however, that is of major concern, since more than merely supplying a mood, music in a Russell film is an integral part of the director's vision. Music frequently provides an aural rhythm to complement the dominant visual rhythms created through camera movement and editing. It also supplies means for ironic commentary and disorientation of the audience as well as a rich context for allusion. The context for allusion is especially important, since it can suggest and guide how a sequence should be interpreted or even underscore the psychological progression in a character.

This complex use of music, however, emerged gradually in Russell's "apprenticeship" films, but as early as *Gordon Jacob* (1959), his second film for the BBC, one finds him hard at work trying to develop visual patterns and relationships to accompany music. The result is a rather crude literal translation: images of pigs rooting through a forest edited to the "Pannage" movement of Jacob's "New Forest Suite". This is the only section of the film, however, to manifest the creativity of the director; the remainder fits snugly into the established format for BBC documentaries.

Although unable, for the most part, to experiment with form, the filmmakers on *Monitor* at least pursued their own interests, and thus a number of Russell's early films reflect his many enthusiasms:

mechanical musical instruments (*Variations on a Mechanical Theme*—1959), two favorite painters whom he met when he worked at the Lefévre Art Gallery (*Colquhoun and McBryde*—1959), ballet and the role of the Ballet Rambert Company (*Marie Rambert*—1959), the various kinds of dancing in England (*The Light Fantastic*—1960), the brass band competition at Bedlington (*The Miner's Picnic*—1960), a Pre-Raphaelite "shrine" presided over by the ninety-nine-year-old sister of Evelyn de Morgan (*Old Battersea House*—1961), and the strange contrasting worlds of fashion, news, and feature photography (*Watch the Birdie: David Hurn*—1963).[9]

Russell had attempted to use actors in his first BBC film *Poet's London* (1959) in order to suggest the Edwardian atmosphere of John Betjeman's childhood, but he was made to remove the sequence for fear of offending Betjeman.[10] For some time, Russell was forced to abide by the archaic policy which frowned on the use of actors to impersonate people who had actually lived, but little by little, he managed to change all of this. Three years after coming to the BBC, Russell made his first biographical film, *Portrait of a Soviet Composer* (1961), in which he experiments further with the editing of images (mostly newsreel footage) to reflect the music. This brief biography of Sergei Prokofiev, however, with its awkward compilation of stock footage, stills, and live action shots lacks structure, atmosphere (a key word for the discussion of the later Russell films) and any kind of insight, beyond the most superficial, into the composer's life and work. The importance of the film then rests not with the finished work that one sees on the screen, but with the way in which Russell managed to handle the people at the BBC in bringing about the few minor shifts in policy evidenced in the film.

First of all, Russell had to overcome questions concerning the subject matter and his ability to deal with it. Was Prokofiev a "big enough" composer to be the focus of a film? Was he a bit too much outside the understanding of a "normal" audience? Did Russell himself have enough authority to tell this story? Much consideration was given to these questions, but finally he was allowed to do the film. The other issue of the use of actors, however, was more difficult to resolve.

> We also needed Prokofiev in the film and that the BBC wouldn't allow. First of all they let us show a pair of hands playing the piano, though they didn't like that too much. "If you say they're Prokofiev's hands you're cheating." Then I said, "There's a scene where we should see him." "No!" "What about a reflection in a pond?" "Well if it's a *murky* pond!" There was a great soul-searching about this. It wasn't said lightly. "OK" I said. "I'll shoot the pond. But there's a scene where I should show his back, just going out of the room." "No. Can't *possibly* do that." "Just let me shoot it," I said. "If you don't

> like it we can take it out. It's a simple thing." "Well" . . . "Then," I said "I also want to shoot him as a child." "A CHILD?!!! You want to shoot him as a *what*?" So when I showed him as a child it had to be very abstract, rather Impressionistic, just glimpses. We saw photographs of him and occasionally a back view of one of the three or four people we used, or a silhouette, always subsidiary to the music. . . . And from then on it was a question of advancing step by step.[11]

The gradual advancement in terms of experimental approaches and length of films continued, and for *Monitor*'s hundredth program, Russell got the go-ahead to do a full 50-minute evocation of Edward Elgar and his music. Actors were to be used to portray Elgar and his wife in medium and long shot, but, of course, it was understood that they would not speak. They didn't have to, however, since what appealed to Russell most about the project was the idea of "the man in the landscape".[12] The narrator (Huw Wheldon) informed the audience of events in the composer's life, while Russell attempted to present the man through an interpretation of his music set to the appropriate corresponding images. As a result, *Elgar* (1962) offers a one-dimensional portrait of the composer in that the narrator, music, and lyrical images work together to establish what Russell now considers a false public relations job. Still, it is a lush, romantic film filled with memorable sequences which depict a variety of moods: a pony ride through the hills of Malvern, a bicycle ride across the hills at sunset, a playful flying of kites, and the composer's last car ride with his numerous dogs.

Given the staid world of documentaries on British TV at this time, it is easy to understand why this film was shown four times throughout the sixties, and why polls indicated it to be the second favorite TV program of the decade in Britain.[13] Perhaps at least part of the extraordinary popularity of the film derives from the fact that it is a safe film, and Russell himself sees this as being responsible for much of its success. He suggests that Elgar looked more like a cavalry officer than the stereotyped aesthete artist; he was someone who bettered himself, overcame his failures, and finally rose to become "the poet laureate" of English music. People could respond and perhaps even identify with this romantic hero.[14] The film was also safe in that everything was carefully documented, and often location sites were used where the actual events took place.[15] The only experimental aspect (if one can call it that) of the film was the juxtaposition of sections of *Pomp and Circumstance March No. 1* to particularly gruesome World War I footage for ironic effect, but an editorial row developed between Russell and Wheldon over this sequence and its validity. Wheldon's position stemmed from the "established" view of documentary at the BBC, while Russell's clearly showed his growing interest in presenting his own views

Ken Russell ready to conquer the world as a feature photographer in the offices of "Illustrated".

Vivien Pickles as Isadora, Alexei Jawdokimov as Yersemin, from the BBC film *Isadora Duncan*

Shirley Russell as Emily Brontë – taken by Ken Russell in 1957 on their honeymoon.

Ken Russell with his daughter, Victoria, who plays William Morris's daughter in the BBC film *Dante's Inferno*

Oliver Reed as Rossetti from the BBC film *Dante's Inferno*

Oliver Reed as Rossetti and Judith Paris as the reincarnation of his dead wife in a dream sequence from the BBC film *Dante's Inferno* (Gomez)

Oliver Reed as Rossetti and Judith Paris as his fiancée Elizabeth Siddall in a scene from the BBC film *Dante's Inferno*

Sally Bryant as the spirit of "Life" in a dance sequence from the BBC film *Dance of the Seven Veils*

Max Adrian as Delius from the BBC film *Song of Summer*

Strauss presents Hitler with a record of "A Hero's Life" in the BBC film *Dance of the Seven Veils*

Strauss dances to Hitler's tune in the BBC film *Dance of the Seven Veils*

"End of the Old Religion" – from the BBC film *Dance of the Seven Veils*

Michael Caine struggles for his life in *Billion Dollar Brain*

Alan Bates as Rupert Birkin pays Jennie Linden as Ursula Brangwen an impromptu visit in *Women in Love*

Oliver Reed as Gerald Crich, Glenda Jackson as Gudrun Brangwen in *Women in Love*

Alan Bates as Rupert Birkin, Jennie Linden as Ursula Brangwen in *Women in Love*

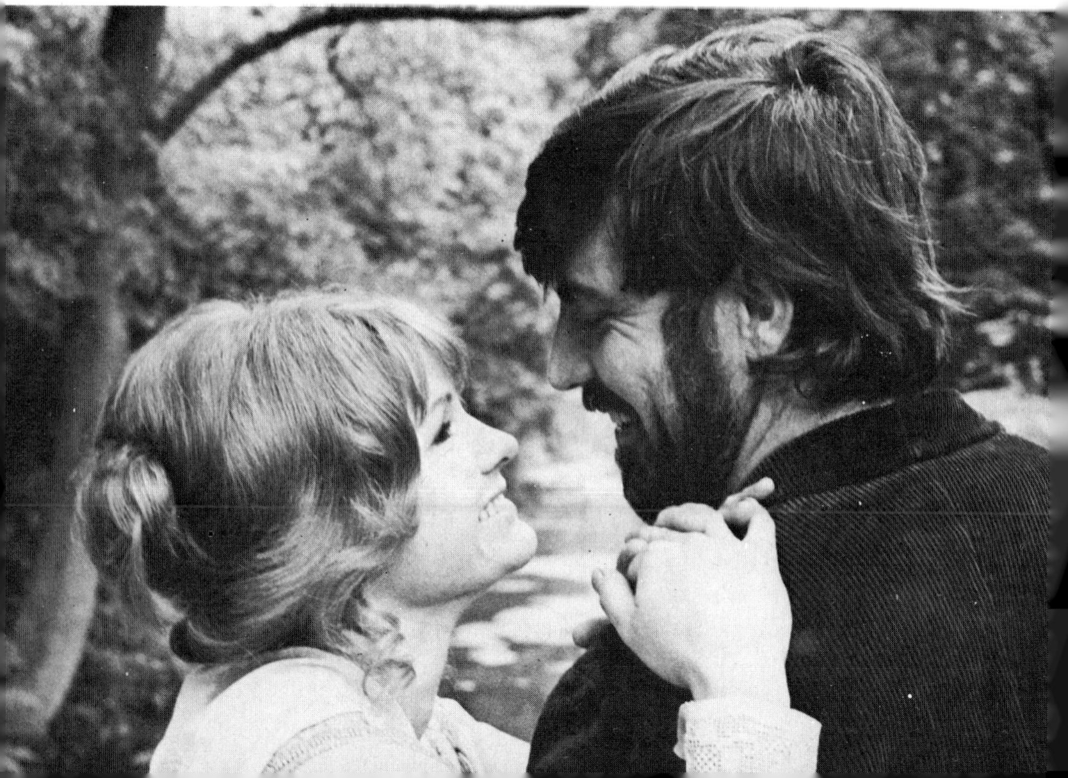

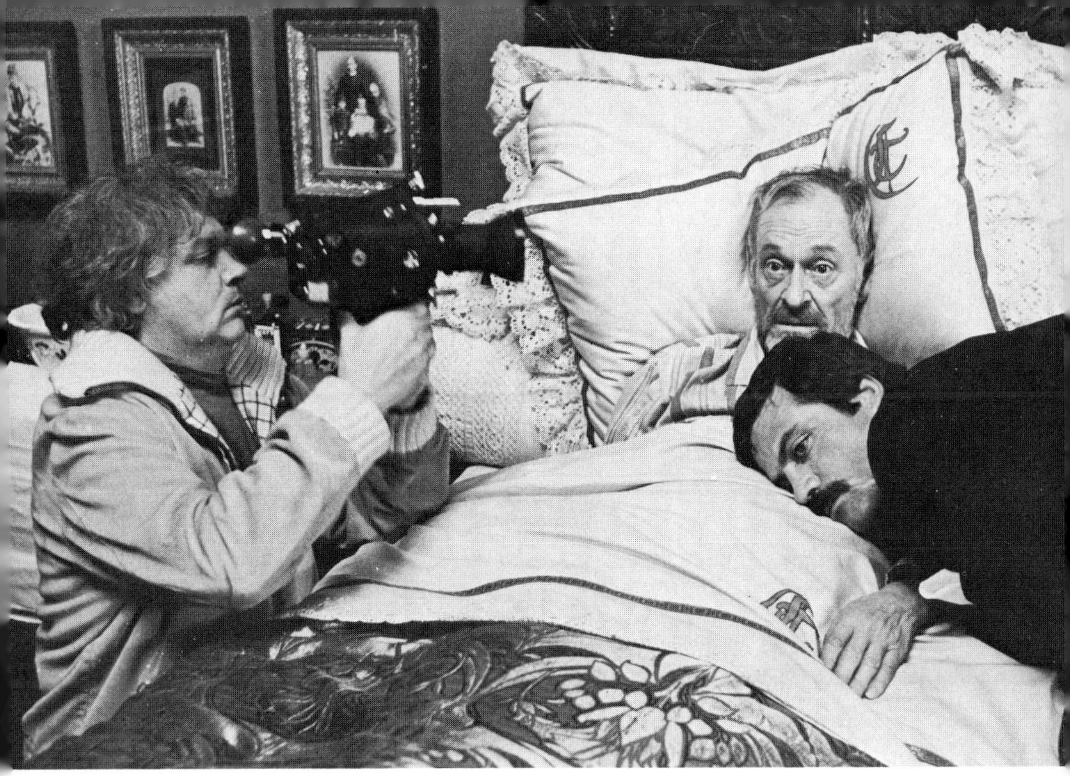

Ken Russell lines up a death scene in *Women in Love*

Alan Bates as Rupert Birkin rescues Oliver Reed (Gerald Crich) from drowning in *Women in Love*

Gerald (Oliver Reed) meets the girlfriend's family at the Crich picnic in *Women in Love*

Nina (Glenda Jackson) abandoned by her husband Tchaikovsky ends her days in a madhouse – *Music Lovers*

The doomed marriage – *The Music Lovers* (Gomez)

Tchaikovsky and his sister enjoying a musical evening – *The Music Lovers*

Father of five teaches extra how to use pram – *The Music Lovers*

and/or interpretations of events and attitudes. Wheldon questioned the sequence for presenting not only Russell's "searing comment" but an attitude attributed to Elgar with "Ken speaking on his behalf".

> If we were making a programme about Elgar's beliefs it was Elgar's beliefs that counted and the authority his beliefs had over our mind, not Ken's or mine. . . . The result of that argument was a compromise: the war sequence, including "Land of Hope and Glory", was cut exactly in half.[16]

In *Bartók* (1964), his next biographical film, Russell was at last allowed to use an actor to play the composer in close-up. Of much more significance, however, is the structure of the work, which depends so heavily on counterpointing shots of the isolated Bartók in his somber, sparsely furnished room in New York City, with the long sensuous and terrifying dramatizations of sections from *The Miraculous Mandarin* and *Bluebeard's Castle*—dramatizations which although rooted in the works themselves also reflect Russell's highly personal responses to them. The narrative line of the ballet and opera is preserved, but the visuals are not literal translations of the action. At one point, for instance, in the Bluebeard section, an acetylene torch, fire from a steel mill furnace, a rocket blast-off, and plaster facial masks become appropriate metaphors to reflect the music. The visuals and the music work together in suggesting that these Bartók compositions mirror the violence and alienation of the contemporary world—and through the structure of the film and the chillingly sterile skyscraper settings, Russell emphasizes Bartók's view of himself as an alien in a hostile world.[17]

Much of Bartók's music is rooted in ancient rhythms because of his belief that "only through the entirely old can the entirely new be born".[18] Yet the violence of the contemporary world constantly asserted itself in his life and music. Finally, shortly before he died, he again found the strength to compose a major work, *Concerto for Orchestra*, which derived its themes from his rural Hungarian heritage. This sequence, limited by *Monitor*'s low budget and short shooting schedule, unfortunately emerges as the weakest section of the film. After the opening dramatizations in which music and meaning are so stunningly matched, the stock footage of whirling gypsies and prancing horses edited to excerpts from Bartók's last music are disappointingly ineffective.

In his next biographical film, *The Debussy Film* (1965),[19] Russell and co-script writer Melvyn Bragg found an ingenious way of circumventing the limitations of the established BBC format. They structured the film around the activities of a film crew making a film on the life of Debussy and on the exact parallels between the lives of the actors and the people they were portraying. This framework, aside from finally allowing actors to talk, provided Russell with numerous opportunities to create sequences in which the music accompanies visuals which are metaphorical rather than literal programmatic representations. Finally, in a sense *The Debussy Film* is a self-reflexive work; that is, it not only seeks the essence of Debussy's complex, ambiguous character, but it also explores the various approaches and problems involved in the making of a biographical film. The film director (Vladek Sheybal), who also plays Pierre Louys in the film, discusses aspects of Debussy's life and character with the actor who plays Debussy (Oliver Reed); and he frequently poses problems of method which any maker of "biopics" must solve. "I don't know how to work it in. Gide, Oscar Wilde, Mallarmé, Rodin, Manet—all interacting, all so complicated. . . . There is so little evidence of what really happened."

As Huw Wheldon's comments on *Elgar* indicated, for the BBC the emphasis was clearly on the evidence of what did happen, and, therefore, it should come as no surprise that after the prologue to this film, a montage of Louys' photographs appear with a voice-over narration:

> Claude Debussy, born in poverty in 1862; died friendless in 1918. A film based on incidents in his life, his own words, and his relations with Gabrielle Dupont, attempted suicide; Lily Rosalie Texier, attempted suicide; "Chouchou", died at the age of 13; Madame Bardac, wife of a wealthy banker, and the man who took most of these pictures, Pierre Louys, pornographer, novelist, photographer.

Facts are important in Russell's film biographies, but with this film he attempted new methods of approaching his subjects. The character of the person himself influences the structure, and from this point forward, few of Russell's films are organized primarily through the chronological order of events. Debussy, for instance, was a man ultimately unconcerned with time, place, and the conventional modes of experience; and thus the film follows a dreamlike flow in which change is suggested through repetition, imagery, form, cutting, setting, and the relationship of sound to image. *The Debussy Film*, although embellished with layers of complexity in which story and reality merge,[20] possesses a rather obvious cyclical structure. The film begins and ends with the TV crew filming the funeral sequence, and it is that one line ("Il paraît que c'était un musicien") actually spoken by the children to the shopkeepers during Debussy's funeral procession in 1918 which becomes the key to the film.[21] Debussy was first and foremost a musician, and his music will reveal his life.

Russell uses letters, facts, and legends about the composer, but in order to suggest the emotional states of the historical figures rather than to depict the events that occurred. He depends on his own visual interpretations of Debussy's music to present the essence of his life and justifies the method, in part, with Debussy's own words put into the actor's mouth.

> Director: For 20 years he has been absorbed in composition, taking new ideas from poets and painters, slowly working out new patterns of music, ignoring his rejection. His work came out of this long day-dream.
>
> Actor playing Debussy: Music begins where words leave off. Music is made from the inexpressible. I would like it to appear that it comes from a shadow and from time to time will return there.

Music is a realm free from facts and the limitations of words, and in Russell's hands, the merging of image and music advances the narrative, delineates psychological nuances within the artist who composed it, and reflects responses to his work. The most notable sequence in this last area is the party at which the actor who portrays Debussy plays a recording of *Danse Sacré et Danse Profane* and his bored, philistine girlfriend (who also plays Gaby) responds by performing a strip-tease to the music.

> That was a specific example of where one was able to take a piece of music, do something totally different with it than Debussy intended but make a point about the public attitude to his work. I think it's one of the best examples I've done of an exposition of an idea in music.[22]

The Debussy Film marks the beginning of Russell's more adventurous methods of connecting divergent elements and of describing the inner movements of his characters. He weaves together facts, speculations, and conjectures into penetrating, visually stunning glimpses of his artist protagonists. These revealing, complex, frequently ambivalent portraits also derive from the manipulation of a tripartite perspective which incorporates the protagonist's own romantic self-image, a more objective view revealed by the perspective of time, and finally Russell's personal vision of his subject which is most strikingly presented in the editing, the patterns of aural/visual rhythms, and the structure. These three viewpoints are frequently played off against each other, and the importance of each aspect varies from film to film depending on the nature of the protagonist. It is this complex approach to the depiction of an individual's life, however, that stands as one of Russell's major contributions to the art of film biography.[23]

Shortly after *The Debussy Film* Russell and Bragg collaborated on the script of *Always on Sunday* (1965), a film portrait of Henri Rousseau, which although far less experimental than the film on Debussy, solidified the gains of that previous film in establishing Russell's particular form of personal dramatized-documentary biographies. James Lloyd, the primitive painter who plays Rousseau, not only speaks extracts from the painter's few extant letters, but he also speaks lines of dialogue in some of the film's dramatic sequences. Although the film follows a straightforward chronological development, the aural-visual patterning still allows for complexity and a rich, dense texture. The structure of the film, for instance, hinges on the seemingly endless shots of Rousseau wheeling his large canvases to the various salon shows and wheeling them back accompanied by the sounds of laughter and the repetition of unfavorable responses on the soundtrack. These sequences are then counterpointed by Oliver Reed's narration which reflects the perspective of history and the attitude towards Rousseau's work in the present day.

In a sense, of course, the film is yet another portrait of an artist misunderstood by the society of his own period. This time the artist-hero is a simple, naive man who sees himself as a "realist" painter and who is constantly duped by friends, scorned by the art establishment, and rejected by the "real" world outside his magnificent, nearly visionary paintings. Like Gustav Mahler, whose time of recognition has also arrived, Rousseau finally emerges triumphant—not in life, but in his art. In this context, the last sequence of the film is especially moving. After the camera dollies to a long shot of the dying Rousseau totally alone in an empty ward at a pauper's hospital, Russell cuts to the now familiar shot of Henri wheeling a canvas to a salon opening as the narrator's last line announces that Rousseau's "painting of *The Dream* is in the Museum of Modern Art in New York, valued at over a million dollars".[24]

Perhaps "everything fell together" in Russell's next film *Isadora Duncan, The Biggest Dancer in the World* (1966), in part, because he liked his subject so much.

> She did have genuine talent, some sort of mystical insight into things—and she was totally vulgar and very bad as well. . . . *She* was the art, and she affected and moved and meant a great deal to a lot of people. Everyone who saw or came in contact with her was a bit different when they left. I think she's one of my favourite artists.[25]

The success of this particular film, however, owes more to Russell's ability to make do with what's available than to his simple affection for the subject, and this becomes quite apparent on comparing it with Karel Reisz's unfortunate feature film *Isadora*, starring Vanessa Redgrave.[26]

First of all, Russell had a very small budget within which to work, since his film was only made for TV, and secondly, he had to overcome the fact that the Hakim brothers, who were financing the Reisz film, had managed to secure the rights to just about every book written on Isadora except "a very obscure book about Isadora's Russian days and journey to South America which had enough incidents in it to enable me to make my film without any recourse to the Hakims' material".[27] Russell also spoke with Sewell Stokes, who had given over the rights to his book to the Hakims for £100. The Hakims, however, didn't have the rights to the man, so Russell used Stokes in the beginning of his film to provide, along with his narration, the necessary historical perspective on Isadora.

The "legendary" view of Isadora, according to Russell, is found in the first minute of film—a capsule review of her life, which he confesses was filched from *Citizen Kane*—and what follows in the remainder of the film is an attempt to explore how Isadora saw herself and more significantly how Russell sees her. Isadora's self-image is captured in a lyrical moment from the opening of Leni Riefenstahl's *Olympia*.

> The extract from the Olympia film showed her as she saw herself, in a romantic Hellenic aura, a slim backlit silhouette against the sun, hands upraised in a libation to the gods. But she wasn't that at all. I thought Vivien Pickles caught the vulgarity of Isadora very well.[28]

Russell's attitude towards Isadora is best revealed by the structure of the film, the editing, the *mise-en-scène,* and rhythms established by aural/visual patterning. The extremes of Isadora's life are established early in the film, in part through lighting and choice of shots. In the lyrical sequences which depict her dancing, she is frequently seen in medium and long shot, and the rear lighting suggests a nearly mystical dimension to her personality; in her more sordid moments, the lighting is harsh and cruel, and Russell unsparingly assaults the viewer with unflattering close-ups of her dissipated features. As the film progresses, other "extreme" moments are further emphasized through effective cross-cutting that both builds towards and foreshadows the method of the final sequence.[29]

Isadora is a unique figure who embodies a number of contradictory qualities, but she never bows to the Establishment—be it Russian or American. First and foremost in her mind is her school of dance for the children of the world; this will be the way that her art will be kept alive after her death, and although Russell occasionally undercuts this dream by reminding us of her own dead children, this concern with the school dominates the film.

Isadora's dream of seeing all America dancing falls by the wayside early in the film, but her obsession with her school only becomes stronger. Its physical location simply shifts from country to country. First, there is France, and after that failure comes Mother Russia with her poverty and countless orphans. Her lack of a welcome to Russia is humorously portrayed at a lonely Moscow station, but

Isadora quickly accepts the situation and emerges triumphant by leading, in pied piper fashion, a group of homeless, hungry children in a spontaneous dance to the music of "The Stars and Stripes". Failure in Russia is followed by yet another unsuccessful attempt to begin a school in France and even by a suicide attempt. The scandal of her private life continues, but even in her decadence at Nice in 1927, she refuses to give up her vision of seeing 500 children dancing to the music of Beethoven's *Symphony No. 9*. This section of the film emerges as an amazing summation of the woman—a jumble of decadence, beauty, and vulgarity, who seemed forever caught between the dreams of the possible and the reality of the actual. Russell's view is detached and ironic as she poses for a photo as "one of the immortals" while a gramophone cranks out "Bye, Bye, Blackbird" just before the fatal accident. The epilogue, however, reflects his belief that Isadora Duncan transcends the limitations of her private life, but it also makes us only too aware of the nearly unfathomable gulf between the possible and the actual. At long last we see her leading hundreds of children in dance to the last movement of Beethoven's Ninth Symphony, but for the very last shot of the film, Russell returns to a close-up still of her grotesque face in death.[30]

> I just find I'm doing the films in the style I'm doing them. Before I start I immerse myself in the music of the period . . . in the iconography of the period, the photography, the painting, the literature, I absorb it like a piece of blotting paper and then I just go and do the film.
>
> Ken Russell[31]

Russell's exploration of a tripartite perspective and his other experiments within the genre of the biographical film reach artistic fruition in *Isadora Duncan*. Clearly, this film and *The Debussy Film* indicate that the life of the artist will be his most significant subject area and that his method of adaptation from prose account to film form will be one of metaphrase rather than paraphrase. His films will not simply restate facts or events culled from books; they will attempt to evoke a certain feeling, an attitude, and/or atmosphere which captures both the character of the subject under consideration and the period in which he lived.

Beyond its importance in revealing Russell's fundamental approach to the biopic genre, *Isadora Duncan* also displays the director in command of a mature style which will be in evidence in all his later films. This film, for instance, is not simply about dancing; the very way in which Russell directs the movement of the cameras and actors draws from a knowledge of and background in the art of dance.[32]

It does not suffice to describe his camera work as fluid, or to call his nearly non-stop camera movement non-functional, as many American film critics suggest. Just as ballet is a dance form employing steps and gestures in flowing, intricate patterns to accompanying music, Russell's camera work creates flowing, intricate patterns to accompany visual action and aural imagery. Russell knows the limitations of his medium and how and when to use the means at his disposal; yet he constantly strives, like Eisenstein and Visconti, to transcend the confines of a "pure cinema" and fuse together a cinema of various art forms, and in this context, dance is especially significant. Russell's camera choreography then is not simply a device to reduce the possibility of boredom; it attempts to develop a rhythm and a perspective appropriate to the subject matter being filmed.

The loud, physical, and flamboyant qualities of Isadora Duncan mirror the extravagance of Russell's method of filming her life, and from this point forward, most of his films will seek the baroque, or what could be called an operatic style not unlike that found in the later Visconti films.[33]

In Russell's films, close, tightly framed shots often of just two people in a room are juxtaposed with open, loosely framed natural scenes in such radical ways that sometimes audiences are unable to discern exactly what is happening. Russell also allows the fantasies of his characters free reign, and viewers occasionally are unable to distinguish fantasy from reality. Where does one approach end and another begin? What is serious and what is meant to be ironic or comic? Is there a meaningful pattern to this seemingly insane mixture? For Russell, theme, method, attitude and style merge together, and on a superficial level, seeing one of his films can be likened to a ride through a carnival funhouse—a controlled journey which jerks us back and forth and sideways as we catch glimpses of comic reproductions and grotesque or horrible images.

Russell, however, like Hamlet, is but mad north northwest. His sudden shifts in mood, perspective, and technique are more than mere devices to thrust an audience into some kind of awareness; in part, he makes use of this method of frontal assault and sudden shifts in mood and setting because he consciously imitates what he thinks is the manner of medieval drama.

> You see, I think of my films as sort of modern medieval mystery plays. In the days of mystery plays, they took religion, bashed it over the head, cocked a snook at it, blasphemed it, sent it up, treated it melodramatically, comically . . . all in one act. And people liked it.[34]

Like medieval mystery plays, his films mingle humor, horror, earthy details, and lyricism, and over the years he has managed to structure these aspects into patterns which often do not violate the themes, central situations, and spirit of his original sources. This is especially true of *The Devils*, for his conception, which has been misunderstood by most commentators on the film, is especially appropriate given the particular nature of the subject matter and Huxley's description of the chilling events at Loudun as a "grucsomc comedy".

Jean Cocteau always insisted that a filmmaker's signature was most clearly visible in his method of editing,[35] and shock editing permeates *Isadora Duncan* and all of Russell's later films, with the possible exceptions of *Song of Summer* and *Savage Messiah*. Russell's frequent use of shock techniques stems from his belief that most people have little or no conception of what they actually see on the screen, in part because of habits created by TV viewing during which they eat supper or talk while watching the news, and his first use of these devices can be traced back to the necessities of TV filming. The *Monitor* program followed the Sunday feature film on BBC 1, and thus Russell felt the urgency to startle the viewer immediately in order to keep his audience watching.[36]

Russell's use of impact or shock cutting has been misunderstood by some critics who see it as an alienation device. Rather it serves to force a passive viewer into activity. If the viewer fails to make immediate connections because of the intense concentration of material and the scrapping of conventional continuity, he must become further "involved" in the film in order to understand the relationship between the images. Witness the cut from the medium shot of Cardinal Richelieu praying for the demise of the Protestants in the opening of *The Devils* to the close-up of the maggot-ridden skull.

This method is just one of the techniques in Russell's lively visual assault on his audience. Many of the others, however, are far more subtle. One must become conscious of the shifting balance of images in each shot, the playing off of simple compositions with those of an embellished *mise-en-scène*, the emphatic use of close-ups to accompany ebullient acting, and the conscious manipulation of camera angles. All of these devices are part of a style which Raymond Durgnat has effectively dubbed "diagonalist", as opposed to the "Hawks'-eye-level" approach. "In a sense it's what's left of silent Eisenstein once you abolish the intellectual meaning of montage . . . gear it in with narrative or make drama out of documentary material."[37] Durgnat also notes that diagonalization runs the risk of connoting hysteria and of distracting the audience away from the action to the image itself; two faults which critics frequently attribute to Russell's films. What some of these critics fail to realize, however, is that the hysteria is intended at times and that often the importance of the image outweighs the action.

Finally, *Isadora Duncan,* like *The Debussy Film,* uses a number of water sequences, and from this point forward elements of nature become increasingly important in Russell's films. Fire, water, and mountains are, of course, stereotyped images, but in Russell's films, they take on additional significance as private symbols. These images which had stimulated and nursed his imagination in childhood serve as organizational patterns in individual films and offer a continuity of imagery throughout his canon.

Fire, for instance, aside from supplying visual excitement, usually signals an atmosphere of chaos. In such films as *Savage Messiah,* its use is minimal, but still reflects disorder; while in *Dante's Inferno* and *Women in Love,* it functions as a subtle visual leitmotif throughout the film. In *Mahler,* it becomes associated with the composer's death and the extermination of the Jews decades later. With *The Music Lovers* and *The Devils,* however, Russell's use of fire becomes so pervasive that one feels certain sequences could have been devised by a pyromaniac. Here, fire does not simply connote turmoil; it serves as a metaphor for demonic overtones. In *The Music Lovers,* fire is most frequently linked to Count Anton Chiluvsky, a Satanic figure, who during an elaborate birthday celebration marked by a showy display of fireworks, reveals to Madame von Meck her protégé's sexual preference. In a following sequence, Tchaikovsky returns to the palatial estate left at his disposal only to find that his patroness has withdrawn all support of him. The wheat fields have been set ablaze and the distraught composer runs from the locked house towards the now vacant home of Madame von Meck. He is finally subdued by his brother, Modeste, amidst the flames which intrude in all the shots—even medium close-ups. The use of fire here, on one level, is obvious. The action of Madame von Meck has thrust Tchaikovsky into a personal hell, but the image of the burning field and the verbal clue ("She loves me") push the perceptive viewer back to the fantasy of the first Piano Concerto where the composer and his sister, a "love" who also later "betrays" him, romp through the sunlit wheat fields.

The use of fire in *The Devils* is much more extreme. Its presence is justified on a literal level by the plague which necessitates the burning of contaminated objects, and as such, a sizable amount of the film is backlit with fire. The effect frequently makes Loudun into a "hell on earth", in which death and torture are so common that they become part of the lifestyle of the inhabitants. The burning of Grandier, which is treated as a carnival performance, reveals the decadence of the city, and the close-up of the city's inhabitants seen through the flames which consume Grandier show that they deserve their fate.

If fire establishes chaos and a hellish atmosphere, water, although it can lead to death (there are a number of deaths and attempted suicides by water in Russell's films), more often than not connotes tranquillity and serenity. In *The Music Lovers,* the intentionally banal lyricism of the first Piano Concerto fantasy sequence employs water as a stereotyped image to suggest a kind of sentimental romanticism, but at other times Russell uses water images to signal a genuinely lyrical moment. For instance, in *Savage Messiah,* the secular communion of Henri and Sophie which leads to the pledging of their troth is preceded by a number of shots of waterfowl and water as the Platonic lovers spend an afternoon sketching and writing near a pond.

Water is also basic to Russell's use of nature as a symbol of liberation from the ugliness and confinement of city environments. This kind of juxtaposition (release and spontaneity versus confinement and emotional imprisonment) is especially notable in *Dante's Inferno* and *Women in Love.* In the former, the Lake District, Oxford and Kelmscott Manor are set off against the decadence of London, as represented in the last half of the film by Rossetti's apartment and The Grand Turkish Rooms. In *Women in Love,* the coal mines and slums of Northern England contrast with the beauty of the country fields, Birkin's home, and the fatal pond at Shortlands. In *Savage Messiah,* the juxtaposition is even more obvious because of the squalor and prison-like setting of the Putney Arch studio. Even the motif of trains assists here. Early in the film, Sophie indicates her hatred of trains, and later, through much of the time at the studio, train noises punctuate the daily conversations. Only twice in the entire film do the Gaudier-Brzeskas free themselves from the confines of city life. The first takes place at Henri's parents, and the second occurs when, on holiday, they journey to the sea-coast where the exuberant Henri, high atop a cliff of marble slabs, looks at the sea and shouts about his genius and dreams.

Russell uses rocky cliffs and mountains in his films in an especially personal manner. Mountains appear to be as sacred to him as they were to the English Romantic poets. Byron, trying to be Wordsworthian in *Childe Harold,* claims that to him "High mountains are a feeling",[38] and the same might be said for Russell. In fact, one speculates that even the type of feeling is similar.

> As in youth, so in maturity, among the Cumberland hills or among the Alps, mountains remained symbols to Wordsworth and to his generation of that "more beyond" to which imagination persistently aspires, of the eternity and infinity that are the unattainable goals of the imagination.[39]

For Russell's characters, mountains seem to be equated, if not with a quest for the infinite, at least with a movement towards the transcendence of the ordinary self, and thus, mountains in his films frequently evoke moments of sublimity or ecstasy in which the self momentarily triumphs over the limitations and pressures of an oppressive world. The image is almost the same no matter what the specific context—a man or woman standing with arms outstretched at the base or the peak of a cliff or mountain. The examples become too numerous to catalogue, but one should at least note William Morris in *Dante's Inferno*, Delius in *Song of Summer*, Gudrun in *Women in Love*, Grandier in *The Devils*, and Gaudier-Brzeska in *Savage Messiah*. Finally, Russell even imposes this image on his treatment of *Tommy*. In the last sequence of the film, Tommy drags himself to the top of the mountain where he was conceived and sings his hymn of faith.

> The moisure [sic] in the early morning air halates and *Tommy's* shadow seems to rise up before him—glowing in the golden morning light. It is a shadow we have seen before in *Tommy's* mind—now we see it for the manifestation it is—an affirmation of Man's eternal divinity. *Tommy* raises his arms as if to embrace the life giving sun.[40]

Russell's style of filmmaking, which derives from his interest in other art forms and from his own personal vision, is characterized by flowing camera movements, shock editing, an embellished *mise-en-scène*, a flamboyant sense of humor, ebullient acting, and a dependence on elements of nature to function as private symbols. More than anything else, however, Russell is "*eaten up with the IMAGE*".[41] His great visual flair, an unusual quality for a British film director, has even been acknowledged by such an ardent defamer as Alexander Walker. Like many hostile critics, however, Walker argues that Russell's visual qualities "wear out their welcome when the content is shallow and the concept banal or vulgar".[42] *Isadora Duncan* and most of the later films reflect Russell's unique visual style, but they do not do so at the expense of content. The human aspect, which John Simon[43] claims is missing from much of Russell's work, exists and is recognizable, if one is willing to investigate the reasons why Russell so often selects artists as his subject matter and to study the methods of adaptation that he employs in his films.

NOTES

[1]Cited in the original draft of John Baxter's *An Appalling Talent/Ken Russell*, TS, p. 234.

[2]Terry Curtis Fox, "Conversations with Ken Russell", *Oui*, June 1973, p. 64.

[3]Cited in John Baxter, *An Appalling Talent/Ken Russell* (London: Michael Joseph, 1973), p. 106. Also see Tony Rose, "Other People's Pictures", *Movie Maker*, October

1971, pp. 650–3. In this brief article, Rose looks at *Lourdes* in terms of the juxtaposition of Russell's scornful attack on "the superstition element in Catholicism and more especially the commercial exploitation of it by gimcrack souvenir vendors" and his deep faith "in the central doctrine and possibility of present day miracles". Rose then makes interesting but not always convincing parallels to the methods used in *The Devils*.

[4]Ken Russell, "Ideas for Films", *Film*, No. 19 (January–February 1959), pp. 13–15.

[5]Baxter, *An Appalling Talent*, p. 118.

[6]This theme is presented in various guises throughout Russell's work. Its most recent manifestation is found in *Mahler*, both in the ending and throughout the dialogue of the film. For example, note this exchange taken from the post-production script.

> Max to Mahler: I thought all Jews were superstitious, oh, I beg your pardon, you're not a Jew now are you, not now you're successful. I can't remember what religion are you?
>
> Mahler to Max: I'm (pause) a composer.

[7]Lee Langley, "Ken Russell: A Director Who Demands the Right to be Outrageous", *Show*, October 1971, p. 38.

[8]In discussing, for instance, the use of Shostakovich's "The Execution of Stepan Razin" in the notorious carriage sequence in *The Music Lovers*, Russell claims:

> It was only a loop, a loop of the most barbaric fifteen-second section, and it was really . . . hypnotic. It was so loud, it became a solid entity. It even affected the men who were rocking the carriage. The cameraman was moving with it, the whole studio was possessed. And that comes off on the screen, somehow. Cited in Peter Mezan, "Relax, It's Only a Ken Russell Movie", *Esquire*, May 1973, p. 200.

[9]This particular film of a London photographer coming to a sense of social awareness hinges on the juxtaposition of opposites—especially the horrible with the lyrical and the real with the fabricated. Russell claims that Michelangelo Antonioni saw this film before making *Blow-Up* in order to get a basic understanding of the fashion milieu in "Swinging" London, and a few similarities in certain sequences from the film and some in *Blow-Up* tend to support Russell's contention.

[10]Baxter, *An Appalling Talent*, p. 114.

[11]This quotation is taken from John Baxter's original draft of *An Appalling Talent/Ken Russell*, TS, p. 132. Baxter himself deleted certain detailed sections (presumably the one cited above), but Russell also changed many of his comments and deleted large sections of the manuscript dealing with *The Boy Friend*. In view of the legal difficulties surrounding the publication of the book, perhaps it was a wise decision to cut out many of the very personal and often extremely candid comments found in this version of the book. As a result of these changes, however, for the purposes of this investigation, the original Baxter draft is frequently a valuable research source.

[12]Baxter, *An Appalling Talent*, p. 114.

[13]Richard Schickel, "Great Lives on TV", *Harper's*, January 1971, p. 31.

[14]Baxter's *An Appalling Talent*, p. 114.

[15]Russell's commentary from Baxter's original draft of *An Appalling Talent* is again revealing and worth citation.

> Actually, though a lot of people like *Elgar*, it's the least accurate of all my

biographies. I like the music and pictures in that film, but basically it isn't true. It's me hero-worshipping him, and it's what everyone wanted him to be like, what *I* wanted him to be like. Wheldon didn't mind at all, but he insisted on making the ingredients true even if the film itself wasn't accurate as a picture. (TS, p. 149).

[16]Baxter, *An Appalling Talent,* p. 122.

[17]The dramatization of the opening of *The Miraculous Mandarin* is especially stunning in its perverse mixture of alluring sexuality and sadistic violence. The narrative is simple enough: an attractive whore is forced to lure a young man to her room so that he might be robbed. The shots themselves and the editing to the music score, however, are complex and devastatingly effective. The close-ups of the whore's lips and her slow strip all lead up to a particularly sensuous series of shots of the lips of the woman and her client about to kiss. With a quick shock cut, Russell then shows the young man being viciously attacked by two thugs as the young woman sensuously licks her lips in delight (echoes of the theatre scene in *French Dressing*). It is the one sequence in the film of which Russell is still especially proud—and rightly so.

[18]This line is spoken by the narrator in the film.

[19]Between *Bartók* and *The Debussy Film,* Russell made a delightful adaptation of Grossmith's *Diary of a Nobody* (1964) with Bryan Pringle in the lead. Pringle narrates the film, and much of its charm derives from the contrast between the restraint of the narrator's account and the frequent slapstick visuals which draw from Russell's knowledge of the silent comedy tradition.

[20]"There are some points in the film, I think, where it doesn't matter if it's the director talking to the actor or Louys talking to Debussy—passages of intentional ambiguity." Russell, cited in Baxter, *An Appalling Talent,* p. 128.

[21]Edward Lockspeiser, *Debussy* (London: J. M. Dent, 1951), p. 106.

[22]Russell, cited in Baxter's first draft of *An Appalling Talent,* TS, p. 158.

[23]Robert Philip Kolker poses a similar analysis of Russell's method in "Ken Russell's Biopics: Grandier and Gaudier", *Film Comment,* 9, No. 3 (May–June 1973), pp. 42–45.

[24]Although in no sense "way out" (to use a Huw Wheldon term for some of Russell's TV films), *Always on Sunday* in a subtle fashion reflects Russell's growing concern over truth having more dimensions than simply the literal. This film takes great pains to show that there is a reality to Rousseau's paintings which was laughed at and misunderstood because the audience failed to see beyond the literal.

[25]Russell, cited in Baxter's first draft of *An Appalling Talent,* TS, pp. 163–4.

[26]Melvyn Bragg, interestingly enough, wrote the script for the feature film version of Isadora's life, but the film was never released in the form that Reisz desired. Although he is the author of the best textbook on film editing, *The Technique of Film Editing,* Reisz's film was re-edited by the studio, and as a result, it was cut by as much as thirty minutes.

[27]Russell, cited in Baxter's first draft of *An Appalling Talent,* TS, The following quotation which is not found in the final text of Baxter's book is noteworthy in this context. It also gives some indication of Russell's methods of making do with what's available and suggests much about how his mind works in finding "visual equivalents".

> The Hakim project and our own tiny budget caused endless troubles. For instance, when Paris Singer took Isadora on their honeymoon, he arranged for a fifty-piece orchestra to be ferried to a Greek island and hide in some ruins there. When the couple landed the orchestra was to play the *Pathetique* and Isadora would dance up the beach to the ruins. The boat was caught in a storm, apparently, and was five days late getting there, by which time the musicians didn't feel much like playing. But Singer took them on board his yacht and made them play on deck while Isadora danced among the rigging. This incident was in one of the books the Hakims owned, and I would have been in dead trouble if I used it, besides which there was no prospect of the BBC letting us go to a Greek island. I had to think of some similarly exotic present our budget could afford. So we got a wooden box, painted it gold, put six lady harpists in it and had her dance to that. Although it was supposed to be solid gold the box was plywood and wobbled a bit as it fell. Still, you can do a lot with sound. That's a good example of finding a parallel incident which, although it can't be as good as the truth, has some sort of flavour of the original. But I think that, because of the Hakims, it's a film of missed opportunities.

[28]See Baxter, *An Appalling Talent*, p. 131.

[29]See the sequence in which Isadora's dance of life is cross-cut with the children's ride to a watery death and edited to Satie's music. Also worthy of comment is the sequence in which her lunatic Russian husband sexually assaults their maid in the dressing room while Isadora performs her revolutionary dance for a hostile American audience.

[30]Russell's preoccupation with the artist's battle with the establishment is evident in nearly all of his films, but the theme of the artist's integrity versus the frequent necessity for compromise is especially important in the story treatment of his shelved script for *Music Music Music*. One of his techniques for this proposed film is to cross-cut between the possible and the actual in a way similar to that found at the end of *Isadora Duncan*. Witness the following description.

> He [Scriabin] is preaching about the harmony of the Universe which he is going to capture in his next great symphony to be performed by a thousand dancers, singers and musicians in the Taj Mahal to the accompaniment of coloured lights and fountains of perfume. At the climax of this psychedelic orgy Scriabin prophesied he would die in a passion of ecstasy. In reality he died of a gnat bite on the lip just before the Great War. His *Poem of Ecstasy* would be admirable for illustrating what might have been and what actually was.

[31]Cited in Fred Robbins, "The Savage Russell", *Gallery*, May 1973, p. 105.

[32]The influence of dance on Russell is superficially discernible by the fact that he draws many of his collaborators and performers from the world of dance. Judith Paris was a dancer before joining the Russell entourage, and Christopher Gable gave up a flourishing career with the Royal Ballet to act in Russell's films. Terry Gilbert, the choreographer for *Women in Love*, *The Music Lovers*, and *The Devils*, danced with Russell in his ballet days. Also, in every film since *Isadora Duncan*, there has been a dance sequence of some sort, and in *Women in Love*, dance becomes a major motif for character development and for the structure of the film.

[33]For most critics, this exuberance is a combination of vulgarity, bad taste, and commercialism, but one must remember Russell's reflections on the nature of vulgarity before responding to these accusations.

> It's strange that people can't reconcile vulgarity and artistry. They're the same thing to me. But don't get vulgarity mixed up with commercialism. By vulgarity

I mean an exuberant over-the-top larger-than-lifeslightly bad taste red-blooded thing. And if that's not anything to do with Art let's have nothing to do with Art. Let's have more of *that.*

See Baxter, *An Appalling Talent,* p. 131.

[34]Mezan, p. 202.

[35]See René Gilson, *Jean Cocteau* (New York: Crown Publishers, 1969), p. 115.

[36]See Fox, p. 64.

[37]Raymond Durgnat, "An Evening with Meyer and Masoch: Aspects of *Vixen* and *Venus in Furs*", *Film Comment,* 9, No. 1 (January–February 1973), p. 52.

[38]Lord Byron, "Childe Herold", *The Selected Poetry of Lord Byron,* ed. Leslie Marchand (New York: Random House, c. 1951), p. 90.

[39]Marjorie Hope Nicolson, *Mountain Gloom and Mountain Glory* (New York: Norton, 1963), p. 393.

[40]Ken Russell, *Tommy,* unpublished shooting script, p. 66.

[41]Baxter, *An Appalling Talent,* p. 38.

[42]Alexander Walker, *Hollywood UK: The British Film Industry in the Sixties* (New York: Stein and Day, 1974; London: Michael Joseph, 1974), p. 388.

[43]John Simon, "Citizen Ken", *Times Literary Supplement,* 8 November 1974, p. 1253.

3

Dante's Inferno, Song of Summer, and *The Dance of the Seven Veils*

Three Approaches to Adaptation

Rossetti used to be much delighted with an account a friend gave him of the peculiar biographical methods that obtain among the Kalmuk Tartars. . . . It seems that when a Kalmuk high priest dies, the reverend gentleman next in rank sets about composing his biography in this wise: first he burns his hero's body to ashes, and then, moistening the ashes with water and his own saliva, he kneads them into a dough—"the sacred dough"—and then kneads the dough into a statuette, taking care that the statuette's face shall suggest as far as possible a kind of amalgamated expression representing both artist and subject.

Anonymous Reviewer[1]

Let them give the creator the homage and gratitude he deserves for developing the powers that distinguish him from his fellows, and for the diligence with which he has turned that mysterious inner driving-power to beautiful account. But let them not make a God of him, for these creators are apt to turn out, after all, to be mere men, with the failings of men, like the rest of us.

Eric Fenby[2]

Over and over again I've had people saying I make everything up. No one believes what I show because it's so bizarre and shaking, but, in fact, it's all true . . . but I must be free to interpret the truth *as I see it.*

Ken Russell[3]

Ken Russell's own dramatic discovery of the arts certainly does much to explain his continued interest in the artist as the primary focus of his films. The exploration of the nature of the creative act, of the frequent juxtaposition of the truth and beauty of a creation with the egomania and the lack of human compassion, of the clash between the artist and society, and finally of the creative act as a means of self-transcendence serve to reveal Russell's own obsessions and struggles in some of these areas. In one sense, the majority of his films become autobiographical revelations manifested through the genre of the biographical film. The journey from *Portrait of a Soviet Composer* (1961) to *Lisztomania* (1975), however, also reflects consistent thematic preoccupations other than those mentioned above—stylistic unity and integrity, rapt experimentation and innovation in a cliché-ridden genre, and, most significantly for the purposes of this study, an evolving, yet consistently developed, means of adaptation which clearly illustrates his role as the adaptor-creator who maintains a kind of balance between fidelity and personal vision and who manipulates his raw materials in order to create a new structure which is uniquely appropriate to the medium of film.

The brief summary of Russell's BBC films contained in the previous chapter suggests that his methods of presenting the lives of his artist protagonists reached maturity in *Isadora Duncan, The Biggest Dancer in the World*. It is his last three films for the BBC, however, which most clearly demonstrate the complexities of his method. These films also best illustrate the changes in attitude which ultimately pushed him to a position singularly removed from the BBC concern with pedestrian faithfulness.

The first of these films, *Dante's Inferno* (1967), depicts the emotional turmoil of Dante Gabriel Rossetti's life from the singularly important "year of revolution", 1848, to his last years of physical and intellectual degeneration. The genesis of the film can be traced to a letter from Bryan Forbes, the scriptwriter and film director, saying that he had been given a script on the life of Dante Gabriel Rossetti written by Austin Frazer. Although he liked the idea, Forbes felt that the film couldn't be made as a feature, but he thought that Russell might consider it as a TV film for *Omnibus*.[4] Russell read the script, in part because he was already considering a film on the Pre-Raphaelites, immediately became interested in a film centering on Rossetti, and began substantially revising Frazer's script.

Russell claims that he approaches biography as a detective story, and Rossetti's life certainly contains enough loose ends and obscurities to satisfy the appetite of any sleuth. "It's an ambiguous story and I think it gives one more scope for suggesting things rather than saying them: that's what I like doing."[5]

The uncertainties in any account of Rossetti's life are mainly the result of his own efforts. During his lifetime, he expressed fears that "a biographical Devil . . . a scandal mongering Devil" would "scribble some malignity"[6]; and perhaps to frustrate future biographers, he destroyed much of his correspondence and private papers. He also left strict orders for members of the Rossetti family to destroy other material after his death. Thus any biography of Rossetti is limited, especially those written shortly after his death. Hall Caine's account stresses the sensational, while William Sharp's tends towards adulation. William Rossetti's discreet and defensive *Memoir* is supplemented by his brother's letters, but only carefully selected and censored ones. The revival of interest in Rossetti in the late twenties produced Evelyn Waugh's *Rossetti: His Life and Work*, which focuses on the poet-painter as "a Catholic without the discipline or consolation of the Church",[7] but like so many others, this work woefully lacks a sustained account of the declining years. Finally in 1949, Oswald Doughty wrote what still stands as the most comprehensive work on Rossetti, *Dante Gabriel Rossetti: A Victorian Romantic*. The book redefined the frame of reference for the sonnets from *The House of Life*, but more importantly it argued that the details of Rossetti's life suggested a pattern which led to two inescapable observations. One was that guilt or uncertainty over Lizzie's death "aggravated Rossetti's hereditary tendency to anxiety". The second was that a passion for Janey Morris, "which through its frustrations and complexities, together with the burden of debt, ill-health and demoralization through chloral, intensified his morbid tendency until it assumed at least some of the aspects of paranoia".[8]

These shared assumptions and such details as the alternative description of the first meeting with Janey Morris at Oxford strongly suggest that Doughty's book was used as the major source for the Russell–Frazer script of *Dante's Inferno*. Russell himself claims that they depended chiefly on one book (although "lots of research was involved") and it had "romantic something or other" in the title.[9]

Doughty's book, although frank and well-informed, is still essentially a conventional literary biography showing the chronological development of a man from cradle to grave. Russell's film biography of the figure whom Ruskin called "the great Italian lost in the Inferno of London",[10] may on first viewing appear wildly episodic, strangely disorientating, directorially self-indulgent, and extreme to the point of serious distortion. Yet with repeated viewings and research into Rossetti's life, the viewer should realize that this is a venturesome attempt to present a portrait of an ambiguous, extreme, and self-indulgent man.

Russell employs basically the same tripartite perspective that he used in *Isadora*, but *Dante's Inferno* is longer, more visually detailed, and more complex in patterning and structure. The subtle, cyclical structure of the film allows for chronological designation, mostly through casual references from the narrator, but more strongly suggests emotional change through the repetition of images, musical allusions, verbal links, form cutting, and even setting. Within this framework, Russell concentrates on what he sees as the central conflict of Rossetti's life—the discrepancy between his dreams of truth, chivalry, and beauty which form the basis of his idealism (one can hardly call it mysticism) and what might simply be described as his highly-sexed nature. This emphasis, in turn, reveals Rossetti's neurotic characteristics of repetitive, obsessional thoughts and feelings and further justifies the film's structure, since the content, to a great degree, dictates the form. Finally, even Doughty's observations help to support the basis for the structure of the film. He suggests that both Rossetti and Swinburne failed to develop with the years. For them, "life was but a series of emotional and intellectual cycles, of repetitions. And in time, when the wheel stopped . . . [both] became static, fell away from reality into retrospect, dream, disillusion, indifference, infantilism or despair."[11]

As should be clearly evident by now, Russell's approach to Rossetti is anything but an attempt at simplistic reduction. On one level, Rossetti as he is flamboyantly portrayed by Oliver Reed suggests a larger-than-life nearly legendary figure whose grand gestures only accentuate the melodrama of his life. This view, however, is superbly undercut by the narrator (Christopher Logue) who, from the near omniscient perspective of history, employs irony and sarcasm to puncture the visionary idealism of the protagonist. This counterpointing, in turn, creates that ambivalence so frequently found in Russell's films and further assists in establishing the multilevel view of the protagonist which is so much part of his method.

Perhaps it is a misunderstanding of this tripartite perspective which accounts for some of the damning accusations of inaccuracy in the film. A close analysis, however, of Doughty's biography, of earlier accounts, and of primary sources suggests that while all is not literally true in *Dante's Inferno*, even the most outlandish interpretations in the film have a factual basis. Indeed there were childish apple fights and endless examples of teasing "Topsy" Morris. Even the sequence depicting the major characters in suits of armour being led by a bicycling Rossetti in a "battle" against the evils of industrial progress was inspired by fact. The members of "The Jovial Campaign" (Morris, Burne-Jones, Swinburne, Rossetti, and a few others) actually did don medieval armour for occasional, playful escapades.[12]

The treatment of some of the characters who surround Rossetti might be objected to, but even here, Russell is usually not without some shred of support. He portrays Janey Morris, the "darling" of the Pre-Raphaelite Brotherhood, as a beautiful, bored, mindless woman who plays with a yo-yo while posing as Guinevere for Rossetti's fresco. Surely, the presentation is both comic and extreme, but to the modern scholar, the personality of the real Janey still remains elusive.[13]

The most obvious discrepancies in the film result from the condensing of Rossetti's two extended periods of residence at Kelmscott Manor into one in order, perhaps, to serve better the theme of the role of women in Rossetti's life and to downplay any other possible motives for his attempted suicide. Also, the sequences depicting Lizzie's visit to Oxford and the confrontation of Janey, Fanny, and Dante Gabriel after the suicide attempt can only be defended on aesthetic grounds. The first of these sequences, for example, is a visual working out of Rossetti's scarcely-conscious identification of life and art. His subject matter for the wall paintings at Oxford (the Lancelot–Arthur–Guinevere triangle) mirrors his own situation, and Topsy's Iseult-Tristram scene curiously enough also anticipates his own future emotional entanglement.[14] Russell underscores this motif through effective cross-cutting and aural-visual patterning and is, at this point, willing to sacrifice pedestrian faithfulness (the appearance of Lizzie) for the manipulation of one of his favorite themes, the ill-fated merging of life and art.

The more one knows about the Pre-Raphaelites, the more one can admire Russell's accomplishment. The actors and actresses look strikingly similar to the people they portray, and much of the dialogue in the film is taken from letters or journals, although often presented in altered contexts. Even the composition of many of Russell's shots is modeled after Pre-Raphaelite paintings. Occasionally, scenes which appear gratuitous or slightly ridiculous assume new meanings in the light of further knowledge of the subjects involved. When Dante Gabriel attempts to kill himself, he breaks through a glass window, stumbles through his weird menagerie, smashes into cages of doves and falls to the ground. The camera lingers on the swirling cages then cuts to a medium close-up of Rossetti as a snake crawls over his face. The phallic symbolism is obvious, but the lingering shots of the doves take on additional nuances with the knowledge that one of Rossetti's favorite names for Lizzie was "Dove", and in this context, the scene helps to prepare for the nature of the fantasy sequence to follow.

If much of the film is firmly grounded in probability, much is also constructed from Russell's imagination, and thus there are scenes consciously designed to jolt the passive viewer. The short prologue to the film, for instance, shows a casket being removed from a grave. The camera assumes the perspective of those about to open the casket, and when the lid is removed, the corpse of a woman is revealed. A hand reaches into the coffin and removes what appears to be a book. The camera then dollies in for a close-up of the decayed face of the corpse. Cut to the title *Dante's Inferno* followed by the sub-title "The Private Life of Dante Gabriel Rossetti". We immediately realize that the film will center on the man and not on the ideological concerns of the Pre-Raphaelite Brotherhood, but what we do not yet know is that the desecration of the grave of Rossetti's wife seen in the prologue is offered by Russell as the single most important act in the creation of Rossetti's guilt-ridden, self-created torment.

The shock element of the prologue is carried over into the first sequence, as Dante Gabriel leaps across a bonfire and out at the camera. The narrator sets the scene as the turbulent year of 1848 and briefly describes the concerns of the artists who formed the Pre-Raphaelite Brotherhood. This short introductory sequence then closes with a shot of Lizzie Siddal (Judith Paris) in the guise of Joan of Arc, one of the two women included in the Pre-Raphaelite Brotherhood's list of immortals. Lizzie is to be the inspiration of the Pre-Raphaelite Brotherhood, but Russell's chief interest is in the private man, and thus in the next sequence, we see Rossetti acquiring if not the method of painting then the model. Lizzie is posing as Ophelia for John Everett Millais, and although Dante Gabriel met Lizzie long before she modeled for this painting, Russell introduces them at this point to comment on the nature of their future relationship. Like Hamlet, Dante Gabriel will help to drive his Ophelia to the point of distraction and eventual suicide, and it is this image of Lizzie as Ophelia which continually haunts him—so much so that he too is tempted to death by drowning.

Just as Rossetti embellished his paintings with significant symbolic objects (cups, swords, bells, etc.), Russell adorns his film biography with appropriate objects that extend visual parallels much like ripples in a pool after being pierced by a stone. The tub in which Lizzie models as Ophelia serves as a counterpart to her casket, just as Ruskin's box of health-restoring ivory dust parallels Howell's case containing the volume of poetry ripped from Lizzie's grave. Russell also isolates the two extremes of Rossetti's personality in Ruskin and Howell. Ruskin, "The Great Prohibited", guides Rossetti during his more idealistic moods in the first half of the film, but he is replaced by the decadent, demonic Howell who acts as a governing force during the moods of guilt-ridden despair. This split is also suggested by the counterpointing of the idealized objects of the richly textured paintings with the details of the mundane world. Lizzie's sword of inspiration becomes the sewing needle she wields to ward off the amorous advances of a frustrated Dante Gabriel, and her golden chalice finds its counterpart in the glass of laudanum she drinks to take her own life.

This method of accumulating and paralleling visual images is also supported by the use of music in the film. Pleasant zither music serves as a leitmotif during the extended courtship of Dante Gabriel and Lizzie, but much later this music turns sinister when used in The Grand Turkish Rooms sequence to haunt the anxiety-ridden Rossetti. An interlude from Berg's *Wozzeck*, sections from Prokofiev's *Symphony No. 3*, and various excerpts from Holst's *The Planets* establish moods but also offer a rich context for allusion, and even pseudo-Eastern pieces provide musical satire on William Holman Hunt. The most intriguing use of music, however, is the bouncy calliope which belts out such tunes as "Ma, He's Making Eyes at Me", and which seems hopelessly out of place. Yet the short sequence of Rossetti chasing cows, sheep, and Fanny Cornforth (Pat Ashton) against a musical background of "There's No Business Like Show Business", although at first startling, seems appropriate for Ruskin's remark that Rossetti "will never be happy nor truly powerful till he gets over the habit of doing nothing but what pleases him". This anachronistic song is a representation of the spontaneous, loony, over-sexed side of the protagonist, and Russell succeeds in disorienting the audience with music. In turn, this feeling of disoriention and/or comic relief tends to reduce the probability of any heavy-handed moral censure or massive lack of sympathy for the protagonist at this point in the film.

The editing in the film also supports the idea of development through parallelism, since the women in Rossetti's life are often pictured in similar fashion. For instance, Annie Miller on the see-saw should come to mind when much later in the film we see Janey Morris (Gala Mitchell) on the swing just before her husband departs for Iceland. The situations are nearly identical. Hunt had left Annie in Rossetti's care while on a journey, and Morris is about to do the same. More often than not, however, the women are juxtaposed in some fashion to Lizzie Siddal. Fanny Cornforth, "the faithful elephant", offers Dante Gabriel the sexual release that Lizzie denies him before marriage and is presented as an "image of savage, active health" in contrast to pale Lizzie, "the sick elephant". The crosscutting of fun-loving Annie Miller with long-suffering Lizzie enduring "the cure" on the coast of France is even more direct, but this technique also prepares for one of the most extravagant sequences in the film—a moment of pure fabrication. Lizzie's return from France is similar to the famous Inn at Upton sequence from Tony Richardson's *Tom Jones*: Lizzie, Fanny, Annie, Ruskin, and Dante Gabriel's family converge on the studio at the same time with wildly comic results, but Russell again underscores the comedy with music rather than with visual gimmicks.

Visual parallelism for other purposes also reverberates throughout the film. Close-up shots of Rossetti looking through the branches of a tree at Morris and Janey together at Red House are repeated later at Kelmscott Manor, but the roles of the men have reversed. Also, there is the moment when Rossetti leaves his wife on the night that she takes her own life. As he rushes down the stairs, the distraught Lizzie extends her arms and pleads, "Don't leave me." Later, he will scream these same words as Janey (in a fantasy sequence) sails away from him in a boat with her arms outstretched in a manner similar to Lizzie.

The use of historically exact settings is also notable throughout the film, but when desirable, Russell foregoes this accuracy for thematic and/or structural concerns. Thus the fortunes of Rossetti are revealed against an exquisite lake shore scene which serves as a basis for contrast. Early in the film, the initial charm of the chaste young lovers is suggested through the lyrical music of John Ireland, the lush photography, and Dante Gabriel's composition of poetry for Miss Siddal.

I looked and saw your eyes
In the shadow of your hair,
As the traveller sees the stream
In the shadow of the wood;
And I said, "My faint heart sighs,
Ah me! to linger there,
To drink deep and to dream
In that sweet solitude."[15]

Finally, he spontaneously tosses Lizzie's bonnet from the hilltop as a symbolic gesture of freeing her from Madame Tozer's dress shop.

Later, after the marriage, they stand before the sea. The music on the sound track, a dirge-like rendering of the wedding march, provides an appropriate background for Dante Gabriel's internal recitation of "Even So", a poem which clearly shows that the joys of their past can never be recaptured.

So it is, my dear.
All such things touch secret strings
For heavy hearts to hear.
So it is, my dear

Very like indeed:
Sea and sky, afar, on high
Sand and strewn seaweed,
Very like indeed.

But the sea stands spread
As one wall with the flat skies,
Where the lean black craft like flies
Seem well-nigh stagnated,
Soon to drop off dead.

Seemed it so to us
When I was thine and thou wast mine,
And all these things were thus,
But all our world in us?

Could we be so now?
Not if all beneath heaven's pall
Lay dead but I and thou,
Could we be so now![16]

This belief is further emphasized visually through the limited and controlled use of slow motion and through a lingering long shot of the newly-married couple standing side by side not looking at each other but at the vast sea stretching before them.

In the last sequence, Dante Gabriel returns to the lake scene where he first courted Lizzie, only now he is accompanied by Fanny.[17] The background music, "Neptune, The Mystic" from *The Planets*, with its quiet, ethereal mood and drifting voices which seem lost somewhere in the distance, is especially appropriate here, as the aging Rossetti, desperate and drugged from chloral, leans against the stump of a dead tree, reaches out to the "ghost" of the long departed Lizzie and mumbles the lines of "Alas, So Long", a poem probably inspired by her idealized youth.

Ah! dear one, we were young so long,
It seemed that youth would never go,
For skies and trees were ever in song
And water in singing flow
In the days we never again shall know.
Alas, so long!
Ah! then was it all Spring weather?
Nay, but we were young and together.

Ah! dear one, I've been old so long,
It seems that age is loth to part,
Though days and years have never a song,
And oh! have they still the art
That warmed the pulses of heart to heart?
Alas, so long!
Ah! then was it all Spring weather?
Nay, but we were young and together.

Ah! dear one, you've been dead so long,—
How long until we meet again,
Where hours may never lose their song
Nor flowers forget the rain
In glad moonlight that never shall wane?
Alas, so long!
Ah, shall it be then Spring weather,
And ah! shall we be young together?[18]

The only response to the sentiments of the poem, however, is the narrator's ironic "too late, old man", and Rossetti, before he leaves, flings his bottle off the hilltop. This act, in contrast to the earlier tossing of the bonnet, brings the film full cycle. Finally, the music over the end credits, a calliope version of "I Want to Be Happy", contrasts with the Neptune piece we have just heard and provides additional ironic commentary on the man whose life we have just seen.

Rossetti, although both poet and painter, is the only literary figure whose life Russell has committed to celluloid, and this is understandable given Russell's preoccupation with music and images at the expense of words. His use of Rossetti's poetry in *Dante's Inferno*, however, is not all that different from his approach to the artistic output of composers and painters—that is, what the artist produces reveals the man and can provide a sub-structure to the film. This method is especially appropriate for the life of a poet whose works contain such biographical significance. From "Beauty and the Bird", to "Valentine to Lizzie Siddal", to the sonnets from "The House of Life", these poems define the man and his emotions, and the additional poems of Christina, Topsy, and Lizzie present further perspectives on their characters. More than this, however, the poems become yet another means whereby Russell reveals his ironic response to these figures. For instance, Rossetti's humorous tipping of his hat to the refrain of Morris's "Beata Mea Domina", which is chanted with mock reverence by Swinburne and Burne-Jones, punctures the seriousness of the pursuit of ideal love which infuses so much of Morris's and Rossetti's poetry.

The counterpointing and parallelism which are so important in the musical and visual patterning of the film are also reflected in the choice of poems and how they are used. Certainly, the three poems already cited must be seen as a progression in which the conclusion of "Even So" reinforces the narrator's comment after "Alas, So Long", but there are, of course, a number of other examples as well. Excerpts from Lizzie's "final piece" written on her death bed

I am gazing upwards to the sun,
Lord, Lord, remembering my lost one.
O Lord, remember me!

How is it in the unknown land?
Do the dead wander hand in hand?
Do we clasp dead hands, and quiver
With an endless joy for ever?
Is the air filled with the sound
Of spirits circling round and round?
Are there lakes, of endless song,
To rest our tired eyes upon?
Do tall white angels gaze and wend
Along the banks where lilies bend?
Lord we know not how this may be;
Good Lord, we put our faith in Thee—
O God, remember me.[19]

contrast with Rossetti's own meditations on death in "Lost Days".

The lost days of my life until to-day,
What were they, could I see them on the street
Lie as they fall? Would they be ears of wheat
Sown once for food but trodden into clay?
Or golden coins squandered and still to pay?
Or drops of blood dabbling the guilty feet?
Or such spilt water as in dreams must cheat
The undying throats of Hell, athirst alway?

I do not see them here; but after death
God knows I know the faces I shall see
Each one a murdered self, with low last breath
'I am thyself,—what hast thou done to me?'
'And I—and I—thyself," (lo! each one saith,)
"And thou thyself to all eternity!"[20]

This poem,[21] in turn, is juxtaposed with his vain desire in the last stanza of "Alas, So Long" to find fulfillment beyond the confines of a world limited by time.

These levels of visual, musical, and poetic patterning along with the film's tripartite perspective give some indication of the complexity of Russell's method of adapting Rossetti's life to film form. Of course, the ambiguities in the poet-painter's life lend themselves to this kind of complicated portrait, and Russell's freedom to draw upon material from various sources (even though Doughty's book is crucial to the film) allows him to devise a cinematic shape without the slightest concern for a pre-existing literary structure. These conditions, however, are not always to be found in the material which serves as the basis for film adaptations.

Not only were the source materials for Russell's next BBC film *Song of Summer* (1968) of a different nature than those used in *Dante's Inferno*, but Frederick Delius, the subject of the film, was temperamentally different from Debussy, Isadora Duncan, and Rossetti. Although as excessive as any of these figures, Delius never fell victim to the constant conflict between the quest for the ideal or mythic dream and an ultimate subjection of the harshness of reality. True, there is the discrepancy between the beauty and lyricism of his artistic achievements and his contempt and indifference for humanity, and this may link him to Debussy and Rossetti, but this "hard, stern, proud, cynical, godless, completely self-absorbed"[22] man valued strength and refinement in a way that the above mentioned artists, with their penchant for vulgarity, couldn't begin to understand. His isolated world revolved around his own rather limited, but strikingly beautiful music. The concerns of the romantic artist composing from the subjective "burning flame" of his emotions or the "objective view" of the classicist meant nothing to him. "He was concerned in his own personal way with the 'eternal present', and the particular way he had not found by study, but by doing."[23]

Just as he had been contemplating a film on the Pre-Raphaelites before the opportunity arose to do *Dante's Inferno*, Russell had a serious interest in doing a film on Delius long before he began work on *Song of Summer*. Only with Delius, he had actually attempted to write a script dealing with the composer's younger days. He soon discarded it because it seemed boring. Indeed, Russell's own brief description of the composer's wanderings from Bradford to Florida to Leipzig edited to his music and following much the same outline as Sir Thomas Beecham's adulatory biography *Frederick Delius* makes this treatment seem a bit too much like another *Elgar*.[24] *Song of Summer*, however, has little in common with the romanticism of *Elgar*.

Even though Russell attempted this early script on Delius, curiously enough he has indicated that he "had little sympathy" for the composer,[25] and one must imagine that Fenby's story of Delius (*Delius as I Knew Him*) became attractive to him because of the interplay between Fenby and the composer.

> But Fenby and Delius together . . . it's one personality feeding on another; a person saving another and being destroyed for his trouble. It's the most Catholic film I've ever done. Fenby was a newly-converted Catholic when he volunteered to help Delius and he sacrificed himself, his life and his future for an ideal and a talent he thought greater than his own.[26]

Certainly spurred on by what he could now see as the center of his film, Russell sought the best way to formulate his material for a screen adaptation. The task, however, was further complicated by his feelings that he "didn't know enough about Delius and his milieu"[27] and probably by the fact that he was making a dramatized film about two central figures, one of whom was still alive.

Fenby in his lectures frequently described the manner in which he and Delius worked, and he even acted out his discussions with the composer. This "performance", in turn, gave Russell the idea of presenting the film through Fenby taking his own son to the Delius house at Grez.

> I'll have the house as a museum, and there'll even be Delius, stuffed, sitting in the corner with his old Gramophone, his piano and his pictures on the walls. Fenby remembers the lot. His son would ask him questions and they would talk, going deeper and deeper into it. Fenby would say, "I would sit in this chair at night and put records on this gramophone."[28]

Russell, however, decided that Fenby's son was not a good enough actor and abandoned the idea.

Soon after, Russell and Fenby went to Grez for a visit, and during that time Fenby revealed a number of facts not mentioned in his written account, the most notable of which was that Delius had actually died of syphilis.

> So I took all these things, plus the backbone of his book, plus his remarkable ability to dramatize vividly his life with Delius, and based the film on these. I'd ask Fenby about a particular event and he'd just tell me the dialogue for it. It was the most immediate impression I've ever had of any person I've filmed. We changed a few lines but most of the script was taken from his recollections of their own words.[29]

Although Russell's film was the first biography in which it was revealed that Delius died of syphilis, and although Fenby coached Christopher Gable (Fenby in the film), taught Max Adrian to speak like Delius, and added appropriate dialogue, especially in the sequences dealing with the method of composition, the film depends first and foremost on Fenby's memoir, and one must begin any analysis of the film with a consideration of this book.

In 1928, Eric Fenby, a young man from Scarborough who was deeply interested in music as "the one and only art that can give expression to the mystery of heavenly things",[30] read about the plight of Frederick Delius, the English composer of *Mass of Life*, who was now blind, paralyzed, and unable to work. Touched by Delius's condition and moved by much of his music, Fenby wrote a letter to the composer offering his assistance for a period of three to four years so that Delius could complete his life's work. So until the middle of 1933, aside from a few short trips back to England, Fenby spent all of his time with Frederick and Jelka Delius at their house in Grez-sur-Loing. Finally, a few months after his departure from Grez, he was called back to his ailing friends and was present when Frederick died on June 10, 1934.

Delius as I Knew Him, published in 1936, is the account of Fenby's five years with Delius, and perhaps since it was written so soon after the composer's death, it manages to achieve a degree of truth which might not have emerged had a number of years intervened before the memoir was written. In any event, the book is a sympathetic but not uncritical portrait of the composer which aside from displaying Delius's working methods also reveals the extreme differences in temperament and philosophy which governed these two men who worked so closely together. The memoir is broken down into four sections, but only the first, "An Interlude in the Life of Frederick Delius", and the last, "The Sundown", retain a narrative framework. The others are devoted to specific considerations of working methods and character analysis. The second section, "How He Worked", is a rather technical account with reprints from the scores to demonstrate the results of their efforts, but the text also illustrates the difficulties that Fenby had to overcome to be of any assistance in this enterprise. The third section, "Some Aspects of the Composer as I Knew Him", is probably the most intriguing section of the book for someone who is not intimately concerned with the technical aspects of composition. It is a character study of the composer which begins with the author's own reflections on the nature of biography.

> There are some who say that knowledge of the man behind the work of art is unnecessary, and they are probably right, for few of us improve in closer acquaintanceship. Yet there are others who, the more they hear or see a work of art, the more keenly are they interested in the conditions and circumstances under which it was created. This, I think, is a natural and healthy curiosity so long as a true sense of values is maintained. That is not easy in this godless age; it is well-nigh impossible. A constant, almost superhuman effort is required if one would detach oneself yet mingle freely with the throng and preserve intact one's innocency of vision.[31]

Fenby's "innocency of vision" is that man by himself can create nothing: the impetus of all creation comes from God, and thus he describes Delius as spiritually blind to what he was doing. That a man could keep his vision intact after working with such a cynical atheist as Delius so closely and for such an extended period of time seems almost beyond belief, and the constant philosophical clashes detailed in this section of the book do much to explain why Fenby suffered a nervous breakdown when he returned to England in 1933.

The chapter is a revelation in itself of its author's personality. Unable to exert his presence before the overpowering will and self-obsession of Delius when living with the composer, Fenby now builds his case to counter the cynical arguments of this strange father figure. As such, the chapter recounts the discussions of religion which occurred at Grez, but now Fenby marshals a defense of sorts. Delius had given Fenby a copy of *Thus Spake Zarathustra* with the hope that it would influence the young man in the same way that it had him in his youth. Here, Fenby quotes lengthy sections of the work so that he can counter with the words of John of Ruysbroech, a mystic whom Delius would have refused to read. In fact, throughout his memoir, Fenby uses literary allusions to Keats, Goethe, Johnson and Whitman in order to clarify further his philosophical clash with Delius.

The structure of *Delius as I Knew Him* appears to have more to do with Fenby's psychological state than with aesthetic patterning. A psychiatrist might look at the book as part of Fenby's effort to regain his own personality, but in any event, the book had to be altered in some fashion in order to be presented in the dramatic form of a biographical film, and Russell's simple solution did not radically wrench the form of the work as it presently existed. Fenby (Christopher Gable) would narrate his own story, and the development of the film would follow what was presented in parts I and IV of the book. Parts II and III would be incorporated into the narrative at appropriate junctures and in such a way as to reinforce the visual/aural patterns already established through the action of the narrative. The numerous literary allusions, as expected, would be replaced by a subtle pattern of visual motifs which served the same purpose. Finally, the dialogue would consist almost entirely of words found in the text supplemented by suggestions from Fenby himself. This is important in that it established a pattern that Russell was to use in all of his future films taken from a single source and scripted primarily by himself: *Women in Love, The Devils, The Boy Friend* and *Tommy*.

The weakest aspect of Russell's creative genius is his use of words,[32] and thus he depends on much of his dialogue being taken directly from the original source. His greatness as an adaptor-creator, however, rests with his ability to find the visual essence of literary conception—that is to transform the original verbal description which accompanies the dialogue into appropriate and, more often than not, striking visuals which in turn give the dialogue additional meaning and impact. Frequently, much of this visual impact is achieved through shock cutting, but Russell is also a master of subtle patterning and *mise-en-scène*.

After seeing the film and reading Fenby's memoir, one can readily understand how Fenby could say that the film was exactly as he remembered Delius in his last years. Although not determined by a pedestrian "this happened and then this happened" pattern, the 75-minute film succeeds remarkably in capturing little details exactly as they are recorded in Fenby's account: the music room itself, Percy Grainger's little warm-up exercise, the playing of the Revellers' recording of "Ol' Man River", the serving of spinach with nearly every meal, the nature of the daily routine—the list could go on for pages.

Russell's tripartite structure as manifested in *The Debussy Film, Isadora Duncan,* and *Dante's Inferno* is altered considerably in *Song of Summer*. The historical perspective is reduced to a minimum: in this case a brief radio broadcast at the end; and instead we see Delius as Fenby saw him. Russell's own vision of the artist is also present, but it is ever so subtly hidden in the structure and patterning of the film and manifests itself only occasionally as a counter argument to Delius's position in much the same way as literary allusions and the words of John Ruysbroech are used by Fenby in the book.

First of all, the nature of Fenby's sacrifice and the unnerving effect of the entire experience on the nearly egoless amanuensis are underscored through subtle visual motifs. It is significant that the film opens with Fenby improvising on a theatre organ to the images of Laurel and Hardy dancing in a graceful ballet sequence from one of their comedies. These images associate humor and physical mobility, especially dancing, with the "normal" world—the world of Fenby before his journey to France. Life at Grez, on the other hand, is isolated and somber, and the physical paralysis of Delius becomes the appropriate metaphor to suggest the effect of the Grez experience on Fenby's psychological condition. Early in the film, when things become too much for the sensitive Fenby, he can find release only by running down the road toward the railway station. As the length of his stay increases, however, Fenby's mobility decreases. This condition becomes especially evident during the visit of Percy Grainger —"That's Percy Grainger. . . . Sometimes he composes". All of the visits of Delius's few friends are condensed into this one by Grainger, and the choice is an apt one, aside from the fact that the Australian-born composer had been a special favorite of Delius from the day they met. All of the events, even Percy's throwing of the tennis ball over the roof and running through the house to catch it before it hit the ground in the yard on the other side, can be documented from Fenby's account, but the sequence with Grainger stands out so dramatically because of his unfailing vitality and energy in contrast to the stasis at Grez. Before Grainger leaves, he and Fenby run along the road playing catch with a tennis ball, but the awkward Eric can only fall by the wayside in a feeble attempt to catch the ball. Grainger "runs" on—away from Grez and into the outside world, but more and more, Fenby is unable to function in this outside world. When he does return to England, his sister throws a party in his honor, but Eric can only stand meekly in a corner as other young people dance madly about him. After the party, he suffers a nervous breakdown and for a brief period of time is unable to walk.

The recurring images of dancing and running and the effects they have in revealing Fenby's internal condition are also supported by the use of music. It is only in these sequences (aside from the moments when Delius requests to hear the Revellers sing "Ol' Man River" or briefly listens to the radio) that music not composed by Delius is used. The music for the silent movie, Grainger's *very* English "Country Gardens",[33] and the jazzy popular music of the period are all part of the outside world which contrasts with the self-centered enclosed world of Delius.

The effect of Fenby's encounter with Delius is further delineated through the use of paintings. Early in the film shortly after a sequence which establishes the potential talent of Fenby and his link with nature, we see him playing chess with his father and listening to "On Hearing the First Cuckoo in Spring". In the background there are paintings of a landscape and a seascape. Delius, however, whose music moved Fenby because it evoked the pleasures and beauties of nature, wrote his music not in a summer garden, but in a "sinister" room surrounded by Munch's paintings and lithographs, a portrait of Nietzsche, and Gauguin's "Nevermore". Again, all of this is an accurate representation, but Russell uses these works, especially "Nevermore" and Munch's "Madonna" and "Puberty", to suggest Fenby's anxieties and perhaps to foreshadow in a subtle fashion the hidden cause of Delius's death. On a number of occasions, for instance, Delius is lying on a couch with Gauguin's painting of a sensuous South Sea native girl stretched out above him, and this particular painting even plays a role in the *mise-en-scène* of the final sequence when the corpse of the composer is laid out in the music room. The anxiety-ridden portraits by Munch also function in the *mise-en-scène* of the film to reveal the hidden sexual tensions within Fenby when Delius tells him that an "artist should never marry", and later when the doctor tells him that Delius is dying of syphilis.

More than any other Russell biopic this is a stark, economical film, and thus those few moments of escape from the confines of Delius's world seem so extreme. In fact, the entire film hinges on obvious contrasts.

> By then I'd learned that each film should have its own style, a style demanded by the subject. Sometimes it worked, sometimes it didn't, but that was always the intention. On *Song of Summer,* for instance, we shot the film with very high contrast. Delius was a hard character who talked in very black and white terms. Everything was good or everything was bad, so the environment had to be very contrasty.[34]

John Baxter has suggested that such comments belie the complexity of Russell's images, and, of course, there is much more involved than the fact that Delius spoke in "black and white terms". The high contrast black and white photography establishes the formality of

Delius's house which, like its owner, lacks any sense of warmth. It also helps to play up the conflicts between Delius and the man who was willing to sacrifice so much for him.

The sequences in which Fenby attempts to write out the "ter-te-ter-ter-te-te-ter" melodies of Delius are nearly direct transcriptions from Fenby's book,[35] but the contrasts in lighting and costumes, the effective use of close-ups, and the superb performance of Max Adrian in what has been considered his greatest role increase the dramatic impact of these scenes. Russell manipulates the circumstances of Delius's illness to describe the nature of the creative act, and these sequences, along with the Torso sequence from *Savage Messiah*, illustrate, more than anything else in Russell's canon, that art is basically hard work with only about five per cent inspiration.

Song of Summer also contains one of those impressive mountain sequences which are so much a part of Russell's style and vision; only here the ambivalence is greater than in any other comparable sequence. The incident depicted on the screen, however, actually happened and is vividly described in Fenby's account.

> Latterly Grainger had visited Delius at his tiny house up in the wilds of Norway, and to the Herculean efforts of his young friend he owed one of the sights of his lifetime, and this just before it was too late. Delius, with something of the same restlessness that had animated his youth . . . had insisted on being carried up a high mountain close by, to watch the marvellous sunset on the great hills in the distance. Grainger at one end, and Mrs. Delius and two servants at the other, had borne the brunt of that seven hours' ascent, lugging him up the mountain track in an improvised chair on poles. As they had neared the summit all had seemed in vain, for enormous clouds now piled themselves up as if to spite the very mountains their grandeur, so jealously did they hide the sun from view. But at the great moment, "knowing that Nature never did betray the heart that loved her", not even so far as deny this singer a last sight of the high hills whose song he had sung, the clouds dispersed at her bidding, and the dreamer revelled in his sunset. Within a few minutes a dense mist had settled over the scene, and the party began the perilous descent.[36]

In the film this episode is a flashback told to Eric by the laughing Jelka (Maureen Pryor) and Percy (David Collings). There is only one servant who has a sprained wrist, so the burden of the seven-hour climb falls on Jelka and Percy, who, sweating and obviously in pain, struggle to bring Delius to the top of the mountain for that moment of pure beauty as he sees the sun for the last time. The sequence is, on one level, a glowing and moving tribute to the triumph of a man in transcending his limitations, but Russell does not let us forget Delius's lack of concern for those who suffer on his behalf.

This callousness, which is obvious throughout the film, reflects one of Russell's major themes, but again the basis for the presentation is found in Fenby's book, and the dialogue is frequently taken almost verbatim.

> "Well, you must never marry," he [Delius] continued severely. "No artist should ever marry. He should be as free as the winds. Amuse yourself with as many women as you like, but for the sake of your art never marry one. It's fatal. And listen; if you ever do have to marry, marry a girl who is more in love with your art than with you. It's from your art only that you will get lasting happiness in life, not from love. Love is a madness. . . . You are a fool if you ever marry."[37]

In the film, after Eric endures these remarks and listens to Jelka's account of Delius's nearly inhuman heartlessness even before his illness, he retreats to the village church for comfort—only to find the priest embracing one of the village girls. Cut to Delius and Fenby in a rowboat with the composer openly attacking his amanuensis's religious beliefs. "Eric, I've been thinking. The sooner you throw away those great Christian blinkers and get rid of all this religious humbug the better. Tell me, what Catholic ever wrote a piece of music worth hearing?" Again, the mood, however, abruptly changes as Delius begins to work once more on the opening of *A Song of Summer*. "I want you to imagine that we are sitting on the cliffs in the heather looking out over the sea. The sustained chords in the high strings suggest the clear sky, and the stillness and calmness of the scene."

This kind of juxtaposition exists throughout the film, and clearly Russell has structured some of the incidents in such a way that he forces the audience to recognize the discrepancies between the life of the artist and his creative accomplishments. As such then, the film might even be described as a visual delineation of Fenby's verbal analysis of his mentor.

> The musician Delius was greater than the man Delius. He lives for us now in his music, and not by reason of his outstanding qualities as a man. I doubt whether we should ever have heard of him apart from it.[38]

The ending of the film is especially effective in conveying that Delius the artist transcends the severe limitations of the man. The BBC announcement of Delius's death in which he is linked to Wordsworth in that "he learned to hear in . . . [nature] the still, sad music of humanity" is a facile generalization given what we have just seen. Delius probably found inspiration in nature as a defense against humanity rather than as a means of finding man through nature. The broadcast ends, however, with a moment from *A Song of Summer* as Fenby and Jelka strew roses over the corpse. It is one of those secular sacramental moments which punctuate Russell's films and reveals art as perhaps the greatest means through which man can transcend himself, but placed here at the very end of the film its optimistic impact is even greater. It is a remarkable moment in what Richard Schickel claims to be "the best biographical film" he's ever seen.[39]

Possibly no film could be further in attitude or approach from *Song of Summer* than *The Dance of the Seven Veils: A Comic Strip in Seven Episodes on the Life of Richard Strauss* (1970), Russell's last BBC film. If Eric Fenby had said that the portrait of Delius was exactly as he remembered him, Richard Strauss's son threatened to sue Russell and the BBC because of the "slanderous" portrait of his father.

The genesis of *The Dance of the Seven Veils* can be traced back to a request from John Culshaw, head of the BBC Music Department. For some time Culshaw had invited Russell to do something for his department, and the possibility of doing a satirical film on Strauss arose after Russell read a book "on Strauss by an American—I forget his name—in which he mentioned Strauss's involvement with the Nazis".[40] Such a film, because of the problem of submitting a script to the Strauss family and possible difficulties with Boosey and Hawkes, the composer's publishers, could not readily be done as a feature; but the BBC framework allowed Russell to make the film and to show it before anyone could complain. The rumpus which took place after its initial telecast, however, prevented the film from being shown publicly again.

The Dance of the Seven Veils clearly derives from George Marek's *Richard Strauss: The Life of a Non-Hero.*[41] Marek is an American, and his biography of Strauss is the only one to deal in depth with the composer's activities during the reign of the Nazis. The book, however, can only be said to stand behind the film in a manner similar to Doughty's book for *Dante's Inferno*. The Doughty book provides two distinctive attitudes toward Rossetti which Russell employs in the film; Marek's book reveals the morally bankrupt response of the composer to the Nazis and presents numerous examples from Strauss's letters which Russell uses in the dialogue of the film—in translations which aside from minor changes are the same as Marek's.

In *Richard Strauss: The Life of a Non-Hero*, Marek attempts to elucidate the man by considering him and his music in terms of the changing events of the times in which he lived, and contrary to the more sympathetic German biographies, he suggests that a glaring contradiction exists between the conventional, temperate, calculating, and dignified persona of Strauss and the bombastic, often banal, egocentrism of the music. Marek's method is to begin each of the major chapters with a series of generalizations about attitudes of the period or about the relationship between the artists and society, and then to place Strauss within the context of these statements. As a result, he examines compositions not only as they relate to Strauss's own development but also how they reflect the ideals of the period in which they were composed. For instance, Marek's analysis of the "bombastiloquent" *Ein Heldenleben* depends on his description of the "heroic pomposity" of the Wilhelmian era and the way in which Strauss was infected by "the spirit of the times".

Marek is especially concerned with the central enigma of "the decline in quality in his musical output"[42] and with the composer's behavior during the Nazi period. To his credit, Marek refuses to accept Strauss's supposed political naïveté as a justification for his totally self-serving conduct.

> In short, Strauss's attitude to and relationship with National Socialism were as contradictory as Strauss's whole character. He swerved from pro to con; both the pro and con were prompted by what he thought was better for him, not what was better for the world, for his country—or for music.[43]

In fact, Marek shows that Strauss's wavering anti-semitism, his conscious courting of the Kaiser's favor, and his alternating responses of narrow-minded patriotism and an incipient belief that World War I "was conceived as a private plot against him, robbing him of access to his librettist and of performances of his works outside Germany"[44] form a pattern of behavior which reflects his indifference to the world outside of him and his guiding sense of opportunism.

Marek claims that the aims, methods, teachings, and blatant inhumanity of the Nazis could not have been unknown to Strauss, and he refuses to "whitewash" the composer. His moral censure of Strauss, however, is dispersed by his approach. Strauss the man and his music reflect the general debasement of German culture and the "tottering of the European foundation".

> He [Strauss] gave us much. He might have given us more.
>
> He might have given us more, had not his judgments become warped by a degrading environment, had his character been immune to the dry rot that beset his country and his nation.[45]

Russell in his portrait of the composer, however, gives no quarter. There is no backdrop of history to elucidate the character of the man, no academic presentation of facts, no ambiguities or feelings of ambivalence, and finally no restraint.

> It was meant to be an upsetting film, insofar as it's an upsetting subject. It's the artist just throwing his responsibility to the winds, and going along with the establishment. If he's in the communication business and isn't totally on the side of commerce—and I think Strauss would

> have thought he was the last person to be so—then he's got a duty to his fellows, and Strauss sold everyone down the river very fast. He was *a Fascist composer*. Everything he did, I think, was a glorification of the Master Race. But no one's ever stood up and said it, of if they have its been in very half-hearted or pedantic or academic terms. He had the possibility of affecting the lives of the nation. I don't think it's putting it too strongly to say that. He could have done a lot, and prevented a lot of suffering.[46]

The Dance of the Seven Veils is Russell's most scathing denunciation of the artist as self-server, and it reflects, of course, Russell's growing preoccupation with the artist's responsibility to himself and to the world around him; but the film is also an outrageous attack on those imitations of his own early biopics which began to emerge with astonishing regularity from British TV studios.

> I was cocking a snook at the whole dramatised documentary idea, this mess which in a way I had left behind me at the BBC, the assumption that you could just dress people up in old clothes and it would suddenly be "real". The whole deal had degenerated into a series of third-rate clichés, I wanted to dress people in old clothes and do it in a totally *un*real way, and thus make it more real than ever, and in the process send up this new civil service/academic way of doing things which *Monitor* had instigated.[47]

Perhaps Russell is correct when he suggests that it was this change in method which upset so many people.[48] The tripartite structure previously discussed in connection with Russell's films is here wrenched so far that what emerges has little to do with fact or legend. What we have is Russell's vision of the man—a vision which uses many of Strauss's own words as found in his letters and the man's music to shape a "metaphorically true" portrait of the composer. There is no attempt to explain anything about Strauss's behavior; he is reduced to a one-dimensional comic strip figure—as the subtitle to the film suggests. The subject matter, the role and responsibilities of the artist, is deadly serious, but the treatment is devastatingly comic. Finally, on top of everything else, the film emerges as probably Russell's most experimental in matching image to music.

The fact that the BBC realized that Russell's new methods might cause difficulties is indicated by the disclaimer presented by the announcer just before the film begins.

> *Omnibus* now presents a new film by Ken Russell, *The Dance of the Seven Veils*. It has been described as a harsh and at times violent caricature of the life of the composer Richard Strauss. This is a personal interpretation by Ken Russell of certain real and many imaginary events in the composer's life. Among them are dramatised sequences about the war and the Nazi persecutions of the Jews, which include scenes of considerable violence and horror.

This disclaimer, however, did little to assuage the "tidal wave" of complaints which followed the telecast. Phone calls flooded the BBC lines, and the clamor even reached the Houses of Parliament, where six Conservative M.P.s submitted a motion that the BBC should be denounced for showing the film. Even Mrs. Mary Whitehouse, "Britain's tireless watchdog over media morality", tried unsuccessfully to sue the Post Office for transmitting the film over their lines.[49] Finally, the BBC broadcast a program on Strauss in which critics, conductors, and musicians praised the composer, and now with "equal time", things quieted down. Russell, however, has never made another film for the BBC.

The key to *The Dance of the Seven Veils* is that everything in the film is presented on a metaphorical level, and this is what Russell means by doing it in an "*un*real way" to make it more real than ever. In this sense, *The Dance of the Seven Veils* is essentially a camp ballet in which Strauss's own absurd language serves as a bridge for the seven episodes in which outlandish visuals complement the most bombastic excerpts from the composer's music. Together the music and images delineate the megalomania and foolish pomposity of the man rather than depicting the events of his life or times.[50]

The structure of the film revolves around a stylized sequence (imitating the opening of Disney's *Fantasia*) in which Strauss conducts *Thus Spake Zarathustra*. The sequence reappears throughout the film with slight but significant changes and, as such, underscores the view that the composer had always reflected fascist ideals in his music and life. They existed in his youth ("I will reveal the Superman") and survive even after the war when Strauss, the aged and officially de-nazified composer, journeys to London to conduct some of his music in a special Strauss festival. In actuality, he did not conduct *Thus Spake Zarathustra* there, but for the purposes of this film it is the only piece that could be used. As he raises his infirm arms to lead the orchestra, strength and vigor flow back into him until he rips off the mask of subservient old age to reveal his old fascist self, with his Superman fantasy still intact. Perhaps, given the importance of this tone poem in the film, Russell would have done better to call his biopic *Thus Spake Strauss*.

The "real" Strauss subscribed to Nietzsche's belief that hope for mankind would come "when Christianity had perished from the earth",[51] and Russell establishes this attitude through the use of visual images throughout the film. Strauss as Zarathustra is tied down at the cave of Mary with rosaries before being sexually assaulted by the nuns he is supposed to be liberating. Later, as Don Quixote, he is not carried high aloft by the arms of a windmill but is crushed to the ground by a large crucifix. However, in the second half of the film, which opens with Strauss now dressed as a Nazi conducting *Thus Spake Zarathustra*, the conquest of Christianity is finally achieved. Zarathustra becomes Hitler who destroys the statue of Mary, and after the nuns throw their crucifixes to the ground, the crosses are transformed into swastikas.[52]

Russell sees all of Strauss's music as developing from *Thus Spake Zarathustra* and a preoccupation with the idea of the Superman. In the film, Strauss claims that he "was the real Superman . . . but one cannot be a Superman the whole of the time. Sometimes it's a relief, a relaxation, as it were, to be a mere hero." Thus super-Strauss fantasizes his greatness through the programmatic content of his music. He becomes "a dashing war-like hero, a hero the fatherland could be proud of—a Don Juan, of course". The hilarious visuals to accompany excerpts from the tone poem *Don Juan* include Strauss acting out the role of a Von Stroheim/Don Juan figure drinking champagne from the ridiculously oversized boot of his female conquest.

> Scenes like the opera house extract from *Don Juan* which is a bit reminiscent of Von Stroheim weren't just done for kicks. A lot of his music seems to me to be on the level of the entertainment film. When Strauss was in Berlin as a young boy he was turned on by that Prussian military business. He thought it was great, and they were his heroes, so it's quite feasible that he saw Don Juan in those days as the super-duper Prussian/Hungarian Von Stroheim character.[53]

After Don Juan come heroic Macbeth and Don Quixote, yet another hero "plagued by the religious mania", but these are just a prologue to *Ein Heldenleben* with super-Richard himself as hero.

> I was even attacked about writing a symphony about myself. I can't see why. I am just as important as Alexander the Great or Napoleon, and so, when I composed my *Hero's Life*, I not only paid homage to my own crowning achievements but absolutely demolished the critics as well.[54]

Excerpts from "The Hero's Battlefield" section are accompanied by shots of Strauss and members of the orchestra attacking the hostile critics with musical instruments. The humor of the sequence, however, is laced with serious implications, especially in the series of shots where Strauss conducts the hero's theme as he emerges triumphant over his adversaries. Previously, he had associated unfavorable criticism of his music with "the voice of the Hebrew", and now when we see him leading the orchestra from high atop the piles of bodies of dead critics, the allusion is only too clear.[55]

"No hero would be complete without his heroine", so we now see Strauss's music fulfilling his fantasies of the ideal heroines: Clytemnestra, whose humor captivates him; Salome, whose obese decadence overwhelms him and provides him with enough funds to construct his "magnificent villa at Garmisch", and Potiphar's wife who seduces him with gold coins which are ultimately lost to him because "the damn allies declared war". Foremost of these heroines is Pauline, the composer's wife, and Russell's visuals for extracts from *The Domestic Symphony* are probably among the most controversial in the film. Richard and Pauline copulate on a bed in front of the orchestra, with Strauss signalling "Now" to the conductor (Russell himself) for simultaneous climaxes in bed and in the music. Of course, the sequence is outrageous and very funny, but it is also what Russell intended it to be, a metaphorical representation of the composer's egotism.

World War I brought no change in Strauss's work habits,[56] and the visuals to accompany the *Alpine Symphony* again metaphorically delineate the composer's attitude. In a dream sequence, he is forced to watch the rape of his wife (who appears to enjoy it) and the death of his child at the hands of soldiers who also hold a gun to his head, but

> the image dissolves into that of his son with a toy gun and then the camera pulls back to show the Strauss family in a kind of *Sound of Music* Tyrolean setting completely removed from the realities of the war. This is the insulated atmosphere in which Strauss wrote his *Alpine Symphony*: as if the war didn't exist.[57]

After the war and the Depression, Hitler came to power, and almost from the beginning, Strauss accepted him as the "supreme architect who would sweep all the rubble away and redeem our shattered German nation. We needed a Superman." Russell depicts this response through a comic ballet to "The Dance of the Tailors" from *Bourgeois Gentilhomme* in which the obsequious composer entertains high Nazi officials, including a Chaplinesque Hitler (Kenneth Colley) who carries Strauss piggy-back style on his back while both play violins. Later, after their elegant dinner, the Führer exchanges medals and awards with Strauss for recordings on the Swastika label.[58]

A counterpart to the *Alpine Symphony* sequence follows in which Strauss conducts the music score composed for the *Rosenkavalier* film (a strictly commercial venture undertaken for the money). The sparkling melodies of the Viennese waltzes distract the composer from the realities of life in Nazi Germany—here represented by SS men torturing a Jew in the audience by carving a hexagonal star on his chest, and when the screams begin to impinge on his fantasy world, Strauss simply urges the orchestra to play louder.

Finally, near the end of the film Russell shifts perspective slightly and for the first time allows another figure aside from Strauss to speak. It is Goebbels (Vladek Sheybal) who has intercepted Strauss's letter to Stefan Zweig and who provides the necessary background for the composer's letter of abject apology to Hitler, a section of which is used in the film.

> Mein Führer! My whole life belongs to German music and to an indefatigable effort to elevate German culture. I have never been active politically nor even expressed political views. Therefore, I believe that I will find understanding from you, the great architect of German social life, even after my dismissal as president of the Reichsmusikkammer.
>
> Confident of your high sense of justice, I beg you, my Führer, most humbly to receive me for a personal discussion, to enable me to justify myself in person.
>
> I remain, most honored Herr Reichskanzler, with the expression of my esteem,
>
> Yours, forever devotedly,
>
> Richard Strauss

After the war, during his visit to England, Strauss attempts to justify his actions, and Russell has him speak lines taken from the letter which he sent to Zweig in 1935. This anachronism and Gable's enunciation and speech rhythms (which now sound very much like Vladek Sheybal's as Goebbels) suggest that Strauss's views never really change throughout his life and thus prepare for the removal of the mask of subjection and the return of his old Superman self at the end of the film.

These last films for the BBC reveal three of the major variations possible within Russell's tripartite structure. *Dante's Inferno* balances history, legend, and Russell's own interpretation of the poet-painter; *Song of Summer* focuses on the facts and presents a picture of Delius as Fenby knew him; and *The Dance of the Seven Veils* concentrates almost exclusively on the filmmaker's own view of the composer. All of Russell's feature films develop from these three approaches, although the specific method for each depends on the nature of the subject matter. More and more, however, especially in his films on composers, Russell emphasizes his own personal response and defines the central figure through a metaphorical presentation.

NOTES

[1]Cited in Oswald Doughty, "Preface", *Dante Gabriel Rossetti: A Victorian Romantic* (New Haven: Yale University Press, 1949, London: O.U.P., 1960), p. 5.

[2]Eric Fenby, *Delius as I Knew Him* (London: Icon Books Ltd., 1966), p. 162.

[3]Cited in Lee Langley, "Ken Russell: A Director Who Demands the Right to be Outrageous", *Show*, October 1971, p. 37.

[4]John Baxter, *An Appalling Talent/Ken Russell* (London: Michael Joseph, 1973), p. 132.

[5]Cited in David Bruxner, "Russell's Rossetti", *Manchester Guardian*, 26 November 1966, p. 7.

[6]Cited in Doughty, p. 5.

[7]Evelyn Waugh, *Rossetti: His Life and Works* (New York: Dodd, Mead, & Co., 1928), pp. 13–14.

[8]Doughty, pp. 8–9.

[9]Private conversation with Russell on June 19, 1974.

[10]Cited in William Gaunt, *The Pre-Raphaelite Tragedy* (New York: Harcourt, Brace, and Co., 1942), p. 65.

[11]Doughty, p. 475.

[12]*Ibid.*, pp. 225–30 and 248.

[13]Some of her contemporaries claimed that Janey Morris was an admirable talker; others including George Bernard Shaw found her shy, retiring, and, at times, rather silly. Watts-Dunton, a friend of Rossetti, claimed that she was intellectually superior to her husband. See Doughty, pp. 370–1.

[14]See Philip Henderson, *William Morris: His Life, Work, and Friends* (New York: McGraw Hill, 1967), p. 44. "The subject he [Morris] chose for his wall painting was 'How Sir Palomydes Loved La Belle Iseult with exceeding great love out of measure, and how she loved not him but rather Sir Tristram', a subject curiously prophetic of the future emotional pattern of his own life. It was, however, one that he had already treated in his story 'Frank's Sealed Letter', and was to return to again and again and again, not only in his uncompleted novel, but in many of his poems."

[15]Dante Gabriel Rossetti, "Three Shadows", *The Complete Poetical Works of Dante Gabriel Rossetti,* ed. William M. Rossetti (Boston: Little, Brown and Co., 1898), p. 245.

[16]D. Rossetti, "Even So", *The Complete Poetical Works,* p. 178.

[17]In 1881, Rossetti did set out for the lake country with Fanny and Hall Caine, and even climbed Great How which is some 1200 feet high. See Doughty, p. 636.

[18]D. Rossetti, "Alas, So Long", *The Complete Poetical Works,* pp. 248–9.

[19]Cited in Doughty, p. 298.

[20]D. Rossetti, "Lost Days", *The Complete Poetical Works,* p. 204.

[21]The entire "Lost Days" sequence harkens back to the end of *The Debussy Film* where Debussy, alone in a castle working on his unfinished opera version of Poe's "The Fall of the House of Usher", is confronted by the ghosts of his former mistresses who had attempted suicide. "The end of the film . . . was an analogy of the lost romantic ideal he had destroyed by his disregard for people. You can be an egomaniac up to a point but in the end it can destroy you, or your work, or both." Russell, cited in Baxter, *An Appalling Talent,* p. 129.

[22] Fenby, *Delius,* p. 191.

[23]*Ibid.,* p. 192.

[24]See Baxter's original draft of *An Appalling Talent,* TS, p. 173.

[25]Richard Schickel, "Great Lives on TV", *Harper's,* January 1971, p. 30.

[26]Baxter, *An Appalling Talent,* p. 136.

[27]Gene Phillips, "An Interview with Ken Russell", *Film Comment,* 6. No. 3 (Fall 1970), p. 12.

[28]Baxter's original draft of *An Appalling Talent,* TS, p. 173.

[29]Baxter, *An Appalling Talent,* p. 137.

[30]Fenby, p. 173.

[31]Fenby, p. 161.

[32]Huw Wheldon underscores this point in his analysis of Russell.

> The reason why words were tricky for Ken is that words on the whole carry rationality. They define. Words are my friend in that sense. They are not Ken's. When he did come finally to use them it's indicative of Ken that he used them rhetorically and abrasively, irrationally. He's learned his way about even with these suspicious instruments of logic and analysis, of course. He's a very intelligent man. But left to himself, he uses them now-days in this irrational way, apparently; and he may be right. Certainly that is where his strength lies, in the imagination, in the leap of the mind's eye.

See Baxter, *An Appalling Talent,* pp. 123–4.

[33]It is noteworthy to mention that Delius refused to acknowledge the existence of English music. "English music? (pause) Did you say English music? What's that? I've never heard of any."

[34]Cited in Baxter's original draft of *An Appalling Talent,* TS.

[35]Fenby, pp. 30–3 and 131–56.

[36]*Ibid.,* pp. 74–5.

[37]*Ibid.,* p. 185.

[38]*Ibid.,* p. 162.

[39]Schickel, p. 28.

[40]Cited in Baxter's original draft of *An Appalling Talent,* TS, p. 177.

[41]George R. Marek, *Richard Strauss: The Life of a Non-Hero* (New York: Simon and Schuster, 1967, London: Gollanz, 1967).

[42]*Ibid.,* p. 15.

[43]*Ibid.*, p. 287.

[44]*Ibid.*, p. 230.

[45]*Ibid.*, p. 331.

[46]Baxter's original draft of *An Appalling Talent*, TS, p. 178.

[47]Baxter, *An Appalling Talent*, p. 138.

[48]The following extract is again taken from Baxter's original draft of *An Appalling Talent*, TS, p. 178.

> What upset people was not so much the film—because I could have put those facts in a straightforward documentary and hardly caused any stir at all—but the terms in which I did the film. It was a comic strip (and would have been a lot more like a comic strip if I'd had a better art director and more money) because Strauss's music to me is like a comic strip. . . . There couldn't be music (*Ein Heldenleben*) as bad and banal. It's painted colours, bold colours, and it's superman comics.

[49]Peter Mezan, "Relax, It's Only a Ken Russell Movie", *Esquire*, May 1973, p. 168.

[50]Even the color helps here. It is Russell's only TV film in color, and everything is done in the blatant colors of comic book illustration.

[51]Marek, p. 230.

[52]The extreme overacting of everyone, especially Christopher Gable as Strauss, is perfectly in keeping with Russell's approach, and the numerous borrowings and references from past films is also especially appropriate to the "comic strip" technique. Two of the most notable borrowings are the presentation of Strauss-Zarathustra as a type of Buster Keaton cave man (*The Three Ages*, 1923) and the gathering of Nymphs at "Lifes" Waterfall done as a parody of Busby Berkeley's "By a Waterfall" (*Footlight Parade*, 1933).

[53]Cited in Baxter's original draft of *An Appalling Talent*, TS, pp. 178–9.

[54]These words are spoken by Strauss in the film, but the "real" Strauss wrote a letter to Romain Rolland in which he said "that he did not see any reason why he should not write a work about himself; he found himself quite as interesting as Napoleon or Alexander the Great". See Marek, p. 132.

[55]Again, the "real" Strauss found occasion to attack the Jews when his work received adverse criticism. After a specially bad performance of *Don Juan* by Hans von Bülow, Strauss blamed the Jews. "Bülow had become friendly with an 'ugly Jewish circle'. They made him vain, spoiled his artistic probity and tempted him toward affectation and exaggeration." See Marek, p. 91.

[56]In a letter to Stefan Zweig, Strauss noted that all was well. "I am at work, just as I was eight days after the outbreak of the famous World War." See Marek, p. 275.

[57]Cited in Phillips, *Film Comment*, p. 13. Marek also confirms this attitude in his biography of the composer.

> Strauss did not actually suffer from the war. He was rich enough to get food, though that was particularly difficult in Berlin. In Garmisch he could get it from the farms all around him. He saw, he must have seen, the suffering as he walked the streets of Berlin or looked out of the windows of his villa. He withdrew himself from the life around him. He withdrew not only into the world of music but into a kind of music particularly removed, so to speak, a landscape and a philosophical fairy tale. See Marek, p. 234.

[58]Marek again supports the idea that Strauss welcomed Hitler from the very beginning. "He swallowed the fable that the new regime would 'uplift German art' and expunge 'the decadent'." He met a number of times with Hitler, Göring, and Goebbels and in 1933 was elected president of the Reichsmusikkammer.

> He willingly accepted honors tendered to him. On his seventieth birthday, in June 1934, he was presented with two silver-framed photographs, one of Hitler, inscribed "To the great German composer, with sincere homage", and one of Goebbels, "To the great tonal master, in grateful homage".

Strauss, in turn, composed an Olympic Hymn for the opening of the 1936 Olympics in Berlin and *Japanische Festmusik* to honor the royal family of Japan. See Marek, pp. 271–2.

4

Women In Love

Novel into Film

> Here at last was a chance to do a feature film about real people, just like the *Monitor* films; after the double disaster of *French Dressing* and *Billion Dollar Brain,* I'd come to believe my films would only be good if they were about real people or characters I believe to be real.
>
> Ken Russell[1]

After making *Dante's Inferno*, Russell began his third venture as a feature film director, but if his sensibilities were alien to the comedy of his first effort, *French Dressing* (1963), his interests and particular genius were even further removed from the world of secret agent Harry Palmer, the protagonist of *Billion Dollar Brain* (1967). Russell and John McGrath wrote the screenplay, but only after sorting out the collection of plot twists, meaningless patterns of movements, and unexplained actions of improperly motivated characters in Len Deighton's novel. The humor of Harry's one-liners and the word play of the Pike brothers, perhaps the only redeeming aspects of Deighton's dull novel, were dismissed by McGrath and Russell along with much of the sagging plot. Even so, the film remains faithful to many of the conventions of the spy-thriller genre, and the script is even more successful than the book in establishing Palmer as a hero caught between insane conflicts—here represented by the fascist General Midwinter and Colonel Stok, the Russian chief who emerges as the real hero of the film.

The film flaunts an anti-American, pro-Russian tone, but one senses that since Russell couldn't become involved with the material, he concentrated on creating sequences which he enjoyed or which were cinematic jokes—even though they had little to do with the overall tone or style of the film. There are a number of humorous references to other films. When Harry first arrives in Finland and calls his contact, he is told to wait by "the Big Wheel" as in Carol Reed's *The Third Man*, but here it turns out to be only a small children's playground ferris wheel. The major joke, however, is the cinematic homage to Eisenstein's "Battle on the Ice" from *Alexander Nevsky*. Russell had already used footage from this sequence in his film on Prokofiev, and now he filmed corresponding shots in *Billion Dollar Brain* and choreographed the entire sequence to Dimitri Shostakovitch's *Leningrad Symphony*. This ending bears no resemblance to the denouement of Deighton's novel, but the idea possibly sprang from suggestions actually found in the novel. At one point, for instance, Harry, while flying from Leningrad to Riga, looks out at Lake Peipus, "scene of Alexander Nevsky's great battle when the Knights of the Teutonic Order probed too far eastward and went, complete with horses and heavy armor, through ice-crust and into the deep black water".[2] Later near the end of the novel, Stok drives Harry to the airport after Harvey Newbegin's death and discusses the day he was wounded in World War II and how the tanks went through the ice on Lake Ilmen.[3]

In addition to these allusions, there are the expected scenes of intrigue often punctuated with Russell's typical figures in the landscape shots and superbly executed sequences using camera movement to define character. These sequences, however, although often exciting in themselves, have little relation to the style of the rest of the film. The most notable example is the cross-cutting of the rally at the Midwinter ranch in Texas with General Midwinter, in his computer complex, spouting about the dangers of communism until drowned out by a soundtrack of distorted Charles Ives-like reworkings of patriotic songs. Russell's constantly swirling and careening camera and the intense close-ups also complement the madness of the atmosphere. It is an impressive but wasted sequence, perhaps even wrongheadedly inappropriate in this particular film.

United Artists, however, liked the film, and the opportunity to direct *Women in Love* (1969) came about, according to Russell, because they thought *Billion Dollar Brain* deserved much better than its critical and box-office receptions. The film rights to Lawrence's novel had been purchased by an American, Larry Kramer, who had pushed the project for some time and had even worked out a script with Silvio Narrizano (director of *Georgy Girl* and *Blue*). Narrizano was unsuitable to U.A., which seemed to be the only company at all interested in the project;[4] and David Chasman and David

Picker, two of the company's executives, suggested that Russell was the right person for the job. As a result, Kramer brought his script to Russell, who read it and then read Lawrence's novel.

> It [the novel] made the script look the tawdry piece of sensationalism it was. To alter the story so much that it ended with Gudrun on Gerald's horse galloping off into the sunset was so laughable it doesn't bear laughing about. Great, wonderful, magnificent scenes had been totally missed out. The picnic at the Crich's wasn't there and neither was the crucial scene of Gudrun and the cattle. Not much of the Swiss stuff was in evidence either, but there was a lot in the script that wasn't in the book—where, for instance, Gudrun and Gerald have it off in the mine, which when I read the script *had* struck me as a little odd.[5]

Russell expressed interest in the project but wanted to revise the script, so he and Kramer met to piece together a new screenplay. According to Russell,

> I would go around to Larry's flat in the afternoon and say, "These are the bits I like in the book. I've underlined them. I've also written a bit of dialogue to link these scenes together." He'd say, "Well, just read it out." I read it out and he typed it. Some things he agreed with, others he didn't, but he went along with most of it, and suggested one or two things himself. We only kept in two or three sequences from the first script. One was the party at Hermione's (though the Greek ballet send-up wasn't in it, nor the fig scene. I found this in a book of Lawrence's poems. Like all good poems it was about twenty different things at once and seemed to sum up in a few verses what Lawrence had taken thousands of words to encompass in the book. It was a gift from heaven.) The business about Gudrun being a woman who had murdered her husband, and the Greek mythology bit concerning Ursula was all Kramer's, as was the market scene at night, which was only alluded to in the book. He wrote some good dialogue for this scene and helped build up the atmosphere of the town a bit. This was all good stuff and the only things I can recall that remained from his original version, apart from the classroom scene.[6]

Russell then was the person "responsible . . . for the film's fidelity to Lawrence",[7] and an inspection of the novel confirms that most of the dialogue in the new script was taken directly from the novel.

This method, of course, is basic to Russell's entire approach to the task of adaptation. He uses words from the original to form a new structure appropriate to the film medium, and to create a series of often overpowering visual images which become the major means of transmitting themes. With *Women in Love*, however, the images are mostly literal rather than metaphorical delineations of the dialogue, and perhaps because of this conservative approach, the film remains one of Russell's most successful features, for both critics and the public.

For some film critics like Pauline Kael, and literary figures like F. R. Leavis, Lawrence's novel was best left alone because it in no way lent itself to adaptation from prose to film. Yet it is interesting to note that in the mid-twenties, when it was first suggested that *Women in Love* could be made into a film, Lawrence did not vigorously object to the idea.[8] Moreover, a noted Laurentian like Harry T. Moore has observed that "*Women in Love* is somewhat cinematic, at least in the way in which events whirl away and come back as other events".[9]

Women in Love is Lawrence's most elaborate and complexly organized novel, and as such demands to be examined from other, more significant, vantage points. The unconventionality of the structure, the methods of characterization, and the stylistic techniques employed by Lawrence have been subject to various explanations. In an often cited letter to Edward Garnett concerning *The Rainbow* (and thus by extension *Women in Love*), Lawrence cautioned his friend and mentor not to "look for the development of the novel to follow the lines of certain characters: the characters fall into the form of some other rhythmic form".[10] Also, in the "Foreword" to *Women in Love*, he justified the rhythmic repetition of his style by saying "that it is natural to the author; and that every natural crisis in emotion or passion or understanding comes from this pulsing, frictional to-and-fro which works up to culmination".[11]

At present, *Women in Love* is hailed as Lawrence's crowning achievement and as one of the five or six important novels of the century.[12] Through creating a series of tensions, variations, repetitions and richly symbolic set scenes delineating two contrasting love affairs, Lawrence weaves together material into a complex fabric in which every conversation, slight detail of description, and minor character assist the development of the major themes. A detailed examination of this dialectic would necessitate a volume by itself, and some of the better commentaries on the novel have offered various insights into the form and structure of the work.[13] For the purpose of this study, some general remarks on its organization may prove helpful.

It is a novel obviously built on counterpointing. Each chapter with its focus on two or more interrelating characters is offset by another chapter concerning other characters or other aspects of the initial relationship. It follows the typical pattern found in most Laurentian works of fiction. The central characters find themselves trapped in a kind of symbolic limbo, in which they must choose between a death-in-life submission to a machine-like existence in modern society, or a radical, new kind of resurrected life of reintegration into "being". In *Women in Love*, however, the "waters are muddied" in that the fates of Gerald and Gudrun seem fixed from the beginning.

> Gerald as a boy had accidentally killed his brother. What then? Why seek to draw a brand and a curse across the life that had caused the accident? A man can live by accident, and die by accident. Or can he not? Is every man's life subject to pure accident, is it only the race, the genus, the species, that has a universal reference? Has *Everything* that happens a universal significance? Has it? Birkin, pondering as he stood there, had forgotten Mrs. Crich, as she had forgotten him.
>
> He did not believe that there was any such thing as accident. It all hung together, in the deepest sense.[14]

Clearly, no such sense of fate or destiny is attached to the Birkin–Ursula relationship, and perhaps this contrast is yet another part of the dialectic movement of the novel.

In any event, George Ford pushes beyond this characterization of the thematic interplay of the novel, citing an especially intriguing observation by Angus Wilson that the work has a form as strict as a court dance. He uses this as a point of departure for his own analysis.

> Subtle counterpointing, or whatever is its choreographic equivalent, *Women in Love* has in abundance. The intricate linking of scene to scene, the pairings, variations, crossings, repetitions, as the four lovers live their parts, reinforced from time to time by further variations introduced by other characters, by Hermione and Loerke in particular, surely justify the analogy to an artfully designed and patterned dance. Yes, a court dance.[15]

Although unfamiliar with Ford's book, Russell also sensed the dance-like variations which served as the backbone of Lawrence's novel, and he created a film patterned after the structure of dance rhythms. In fact, in a jocular comment about his method of adaptation, he indicated that he "should have turned the whole thing into a musical; it wasn't far off in some ways".[16] Indeed, even on the most literal level Russell uses dance as a means of character development, as a counterpointing device, and as a dominant image which assists in providing a pattern of unification. Background music also functions in this way, as well as providing Russell with yet another way of commenting on the characters, and on Lawrence's particular vision.

Perhaps another reason for the extensive use of dance in *Women in Love* stems from the fact that the ghost of Russell's biopic of Isadora Duncan haunts this particular film. The sequence depicting a Greek ballet performed by Hermione (Eleanor Bron), Ursula (Jennie Linden), and Gudrun (Glenda Jackson) is clearly a satirical thrust at both Hermione and the particular kind of dance style made popular by Isadora, and even some of Hermione's phrasing owes more to Isadora Duncan than to D. H. Lawrence. John Weightman, for instance, rightly sees Russell's conception of Hermione as that of an insufferable, Pre-Raphaelite lady, but strenuously objects to her retort, "My ass!" to Birkin's half-hearted apology for destroying the effect of her dance.

> Hermione may be erotically complex, but there is no excuse for making her speak like this. In any case, is it remotely conceivable that a pre-1914 society lady would use the expression?[17]

Perhaps not, but in all probability Russell inserted this response into the script because it echoes a similar reaction ("Communists, my sweet ass!") made by Isadora in an equally "proper" situation. For Russell, Hermione's sense of decorum is only a thin veneer covering the vulgarity and decadence which linger just below the surface—the "My ass!" remark is comparable to her licking of spilled champagne from Birkin's (Alan Bates) chest. As such, she may not appear exactly in the same light that Lawrence presented her (although, it should be remembered that Lawrence portrays her with both satire and cruelty), but she makes an even greater visual counterpart to Loerke (Vladek Sheybal), who appears in the last quarter of the film to catalyze the destruction of the relationship between Gudrun and Gerald (Oliver Reed).

For Russell, the parallels to Isadora go beyond verbal and visual links:

> Gudrun would have liked to be Isadora, but a bit more intellectual with it. I see them as rather similar characters, whether Lawrence meant it or not. The only comparable thing to a woman dancing to cattle in Lawrence's experience would have been Isadora dancing to the waves on the beach. She was the first woman to be aware of the elemental sense around her and respond to it in dance. Lawrence must have been conscious of this.[18]

Perhaps as a result of this dubious interpretation, Russell has Gudrun dance throughout the film to express her emotions; but more than just functioning as a unifying device, these moments of dance underscore theme and delineate character.

Most of Lawrence's novels revolve around the conflict between what might simplistically be described as life forces and a death-in-life quest for dominance and possession, and the use of dance in Russell's film reflects this dichotomy. Hermione's "Greek ballet" concerns women who have become widows, and almost all of Gudrun's dances reveal a quest for domination. The most obvious example, of course, is Gudrun's dance before the herd of Highland cattle, which finally succeeds in putting them to flight. Lawrence's prose makes it clear that this act symbolizes Gudrun's reaction to

Gerald, but Russell achieves this same feeling in visual terms through the choreography of this sequence. It begins simply enough with Gudrun's spontaneous dance improvisations, as the lake and trees provide a natural backdrop proscenium. With the appearance of the cattle, both the music and nature of the dance become sinister. Finally with the arrival of Gerald and Birkin, the nature of the relationships between the men and the women are revealed through dance, gesture, music, and cross-cutting. Birkin dances up to Ursula as he sings "Oh, You Beautiful Doll" and exclaims, "It's a pity that the world isn't madder." Russell then cuts to dissonant music accompanying Gudrun's pursuit of the cattle, and to Gerald's response. The masterful dissolves and moving camera shots, taken by Russell himself, capture the feeling conveyed by Lawrence's prose description of the scene. Gudrun's gestures to Gerald as she "dances" before him parallel her movements when teasing the cattle. Russell returns to Ursula and Birkin walking along the lake shore in much the same playful fashion that Dante and Lizzie did in the opening of *Dante's Inferno*.

Gerald declares his love for Gudrun at the end of this dancing episode, and the beginnings of Loerke's affair with Gudrun occur during a dance at the mountain lodge. The perverseness of the relationship between Gudrun and Loerke is also underscored by their pantomime-dance of Nina and Peter Tchaikovsky's honeymoon journey to a recording of the homosexual composer's *Pathetique Symphony*. This sequence is one of the most criticized in the film, possibly because it was seen as self-advertisement for *The Music Lovers*, but the episode has its basis in Lawrence's novel.

> They played with the past, and with the great figures of the past, a sort of little game of chess, or marionettes, all to please themselves. They had all the great men for their marionettes, and they two were the God of the show working it all.[19]

This sequence, as well as the one depicting Herr Leitner in Loerke's bed, helps through contrast, to dispell any label of homosexuality which some viewers might attach to Gerald's relationship to Rupert. Loerke is the bisexual to whom Gudrun finally abandons herself when, dancing before the highest mountain and humming "I'm Forever Blowing Bubbles", she decides to follow her "rat-like" mentor to Dresden. Finally, in contrast to these dances of domination are the spontaneous Charlestons and roughhouse, comical polkas which usually involve Birkin and Ursula.

John Weightman objects to Russell's use of ragtime and popular commercial songs on the grounds that Lawrence would have looked upon them "as part of the decadent sophistication of modern society",[20] and again this is probably true. The counterpointing of the songs in the film, however, works on a variety of levels aside from providing a contrast to Gudrun's dances. They become one of the means through which Russell presents his own responses to Lawrence's characters and philosophy. Although written in its first form in 1913 and rewritten and finished in 1917, *Women in Love* was published in the United States only in 1920 and in England in May 1921. Given this lapse of time between completion and publication, Russell may be justified in setting the film in 1920. However, by presenting ex-soldiers begging in the streets and a funeral sequence in which a memorial statue is commemorated, Russell reminds his audience of the war. This is especially appropriate, since Lawrence indicated that he wished "the time to remain unfixed, so that the bitterness of the war may be taken for granted in the characters".[21] Russell claims that in his research, he uncovered the fact that the major popular song of 1920 was "I'm Forever Blowing Bubbles".[22] The song suggests period verisimilitude, but even more, its frequent repetition throughout the film acts as a comment on the dreams and false hopes of the protagonists.

The dance-like rhythms of *Women in Love* are also suggested in a number of other ways, including vivid visual counterpointing, parallel sequences, and parallel shots with slight but meaningful variations. Part of this method is simply exhibited in the editing, as in the combination of close-ups and close middle shots during the wedding sequence which, like Lawrence's opening chapter, clearly links Ursula with Birkin and Gudrun with Gerald. Other examples are more subtle and include the now famous cut from the nude bodies of the drowned Laura and Tibby to the entangled bodies of Birkin and Ursula immediately after making love. Such parallels abound throughout the film. The discussion of catkins, for instance, should come to mind when Rupert lectures on the ways in which to eat a fig, and both of these incidents provide the backdrop for the scene in which Rupert and Ursula argue in the corn field and finally achieve harmony through Ursula's gift of the wild flowers. Gudrun sees a miner with his woman embracing in an underground passageway early in the film, and later returns to the same location to act out the scene with Gerald.

The rhythmic structure is also evident in the complex use of mirrors and reflections throughout the film, and in the frequent repetition of objects such as fire places, statues, and cups in the *mise-en-scène* of the shots depicting the discussions between Gerald and Birkin. The use of parallelism and variations also extends to Shirley Russell's costuming for the film. In many sequences, for instance, Gerald wears dark trousers and a striped sports jacket, while Birkin wears his straw hat and white suit; yet his tie is almost the same color and pattern as Gerald's jacket.

These patterns of parallels, variations, contrasts and counterpointing in *Women in Love* work on a number of levels, much as they did in *Dante's Inferno*. In fact, this film, although considerably more literal, is also close to the film on Rossetti in reflecting a balanced manipulation of the tripartite structure. In both films, Russell successfully fuses biographical facts, the characters as they see themselves—or, in this case, as Lawrence conceives them—and his own interpretation of and attitude towards these figures.

Russell was conscious of the fact that many of the characters in Lawrence's novel were drawn from some of Lawrence's friends and acquaintances. Once he began working on the film, he refrained from reading other novels by Lawrence and critical studies of *Women in Love*. Instead, he read biographies of the author.

> I knew, for instance, that in *Women in Love* Birkin was based on some things Lawrence saw in himself, and that Gerald was in fact someone he knew who owned the local mine, and that he knew two school teachers in Nottingham on whom he based Gudrun and Ursula, and Hermoine [*sic*] was Lady Ottoline Morrell. This gave me a sort of factual foundation on which I could build the script. Of course Lawrence falsified some of these people. I read a little about Lady Ottoline Morrell and her parties, and though they sounded ridiculous —Lloyd George was always being pushed into a lily pond—I knew Lawrence satirised her because he disliked her. She *may* have been one of the greatest minds of the century and I know she was a catalyst and brought a lot of brilliant people together, but so far as Lawrence was concerned she was just a pretentious, selfish woman. And finally, whether the book was fact or not, it *was* the book I was interpreting. I put in the things Lawrence saw in her, and the fact that I knew she was a real person was a real bonus.[23]

This statement, however, does not suggest that Middleton Murry, and perhaps Richard Aldington and David Garnett may have served as models for Gerald. Nor does it mention that Ursula and Gudrun were partly taken from Frieda Lawrence and Katherine Mansfield. The women in the film are perhaps almost entirely realized from the novel and Russell's interpretation, rather than from biographical references. Oliver Reed, on the other hand, although not physically ideal for Gerald, sports a mustache just as did Sir Thomas Philip Barber, the Eastwood mine owner whose experience contributed to the characterization of Gerald. The most obvious of the biographical references relate to Birkin, who as played by Alan Bates is given a beard and made not merely Lawrence's spokesman but, on occasion, almost Lawrence himself. Perhaps because of this emphasis, Russell is even more at ease in giving this character dialogue drawn from some of Lawrence's other works. The settings of Shortlands and Breadalby in the film are overly exaggerated in elegance beyond what is found in the novel, but even here there is evident concern for biographical authenticity. Harry T. Moore, for instance, notes that Russell "mischievously included a quick glimpse of the 1915 Bertrand Russell in the Breadalby sequence".[24]

It is the manner in which Russell visually captures Lawrence's characters and themes while also reflecting his own responses, however, that makes the film a significant adaptation. For a number of critics, even some who basically like the film, Russell's additions were seen as impertinent liberties which kept a good film from being a much better one.[25] Thus even though the film was generally well reviewed, only a few individuals, like Ana Laura Zambrano, realized that

> Russell's *Women in Love* is not a pure translation from the novel, nor is his treatment of the characters completely unaltered; but the film provides masterful and penetrating insight into Lawrence's themes, and it enriches our appreciation of the beauty and complexity of the style of both artists.[26]

Russell's approach to his material is obvious even in the prologue to the film which appears before the titles. The emotional coldness of Mr. and Mrs. Brangwen is visually manifest through the economical use of two medium close shots, while the more or less unconventional attitudes of the sisters are made known by their clothing, which sets them off from the townspeople. The visuals which accompany their discussion also exemplify Russell's approach. As Ursula suggests, for instance, that marriage might very well be the end of experience, Russell presents a shot of a couple pushing a baby carriage. The musical background of "I'm Forever Blowing Bubbles", as mentioned earlier, also comments ironically on the major characters' idealistic hopes for love, since so much of the film, as Russell presents it, concerns illusion.

In the novel, Lawrence simply has Ursula and Gudrun watch the Crich wedding from the low stone wall of the grammar school just outside the churchyard, whereas Russell places the girls in the church graveyard. Thus as Gudrun complains that "*Nothing materializes!* Everything withers in the bud," she falls back on a tomb and folds herself up in the position of a corpse. The image at this point in the film is not obvious because as yet we know so little about the characters, but like the terrifying cuttle-fish image in Gudrun's Chinese lantern (described by Lawrence in the "Water-Party" chapter), it suggests that Gudrun is a doomed character long before the journey to the continent.

The movement from sequence to sequence in the film frequently involves paralleling of events and consistency of imagery: for example, the transition from the wedding to Gerald's diving into a lake. This sequence parallels Ursula's flashback of her encounter with Rupert, but perhaps the incident was included because it is yet another example of the water imagery which runs throughout the film. There is, of course, the water-party episode and a later series of shots of Rupert fishing from the bank of a stream near his mill house. Before he was convinced by Oliver Reed to film the nude wrestling exactly as Lawrence depicted it, Russell had intended to film this sequence in the moonlight by the mill house stream.[27] In any event, as it now stands, the water from the "Diver" sequence becomes the visual link to Hermione's swimming pool at Breadalby and the luncheon party in which the four major characters confront each other face to face for the first time.

The next few sequences, like so many of the early chapters in the novel, juxtapose character against character. But more than that, Russell seems to have pitted moments of vitality and spontaneity against episodes depicting death, both in literal and symbolic manifestations. Rupert's suggestive discourse on the various ways to eat a fig (which like Hermione's affected response to the catkins is punctuated with a bell) contrasts with Hermione's "trooping off in a group", while Gerald and Rupert remain behind to discuss the meaning of love in their lives, and eventually, their reasons for living. Hermione's pretentious dance depicting the women's responses to the deaths of their men follows immediately thereafter, only to be interrupted by the pianist's shift to ragtime music and couples dancing the Charleston. Even visually, the composition of the barely glimpsed shots of the spontaneous "necking" of Tibby and Laura is contrasted with the rigid, symmetrical shots of Hermione and the other dancers in the ballet. Of course, none of this dance episode is taken from Lawrence, but the themes as delineated by Russell are consistent with other episodes presented in the prose account.

This juxtaposition of "life" and "death" forces continues through the next few sequences. The discussion of sensuality and spontaneity between Rupert and the frigid Hermione takes place in her dimly lit sitting room, with both seated at the ends of a long divan which is placed directly below the painting of a nude woman. After Hermione attempts to smash his skull with a lapis lazuli paper weight, Rupert flees to the freedom of the blue and green natural world outside, where he removes his clothes and attempts to purify himself in a ritual communion with nature. This solitary true "communion", however, is immediately juxtaposed with the false religious "communion" of the memorial ceremony for the dead war veteran, to which Birkin reacts with words borrowed from a discussion with Ursula in the chapter entitled "An Island". Again the visuals fit the meaning of the words although the episode was not taken from Lawrence, and as such, the sequence delineates the theme in a way appropriate to the medium of film, in keeping with the film's structure.

Russell notes that one of his major difficulties in writing the script was to condense and cut out much of what seemed to be needless repetition; as a result, he was severely criticized for castrating Lawrence's novel.[28] Such, however, was not the intention nor the result.

> A lot of the book seemed pretentious and repetitive, and I left a lot of it out because films lasting twenty-four hours are frowned on by distributors and partly, as I say, because Lawrence simply repeated his theme about the separate-yet-united philosophy of love eight times over in different disguises. I thought twice would be enough in the film for most people to get it. When you read a book you put it down and pick it up again, so I guess Lawrence just had to keep reminding his readers of his point, but if you have to condense it into two hours it's just not on. It's the same with some of his other themes. The chapter called "Rabbit", for instance. Some people criticised us for leaving that out, but in essence it says the same thing as the sequence concerning the train and the horse. We did shoot the rabbit scene, in fact, but in the final cut it was obviously superfluous and ended up on the cutting room floor.[29]

One suspects that the choice of the horse sequence over the rabbit episode again derives from the effort to unify visual and verbal imagery. This encounter aside from further defining the attitudes of Ursula and Gudrun and establishing Gerald's need for dominance, links up with the sequence in which Loerke shows the Brangwen sisters the photo of his sculpture piece of the young girl on the massive horse and discusses his control over the model.

The episode of Gerald holding the white mare (changed from Lawrence's account in which the horse is red) at the crossing gate near the loud but slowly moving locomotive is followed by scenes of Gerald at the mines, and the ride with his father in the spotless white car through the throng of coal-dust-covered men establishes a visual link between the two areas (sexual and economic) of Gerald's dominance. Also, Gerald's remark that the miners' hatred for him is better than his father's so-called love for them recalls Rupert, who in a previous sequence attacked the minister's sermon on brotherhood by claiming that one might as well say that hate is the greatest thing the world has ever known. "In the name of righteousness and love, you shall have hate."

These patterns and textures exist throughout the film, but like Lawrence's novel, they demand a different means of approach from the usual event-oriented structure that too many readers and film-goers expect. For instance, just as "Water-Party" (Chapter XIV) is the center of the symbolic structure of the novel,[30] the party sequence at Shortlands in the film ends the delineation of the early relationship between the sisters and their respective lovers. It also looks back to the death-in-life relationship of Hermione and Birkin in the beginning of the film and ahead to the will to power, destructive relationship of Gerald and Gudrun. More than anything else, however, the sequence allows Russell to express his own attitudes towards the views of the characters, especially Birkin and Ursula, through the editing and the shifting of events. The conversation between Birkin and Ursula after the thematically appropriate drowning of Laura and Tibby (rather than Diana and a local doctor) is drawn directly from the novel (though there the couple do not make love). In the film, the seduction is both erotic and comic, but through the intercutting shots of Birkin and Ursula in the same position as the drowned victims, Russell successfully punctures Birkin's philosophical attempt to transcend himself through a kind of selfless love.[31]

Again, for the event-oriented viewer or for the critic who sees the adaptor as a mere translater rather than as an active creator, such liberties must be condemned; but for one who understands and accepts Russell's methods, such a transformation becomes especially effective. What is awry in this sequence is Hermione's line that it's "better to die than live mechanically a life that is a repetition of repetitions". In the novel, this line is part of Ursula's thoughts only a few hours after the unhappy events at Shortlands, and reflects the momentary depths of her despair. In the film, the line is uttered by Hermione during what will be her last appearance, and in no way have we seen her depressed to a degree justifying such an observation. This example seems to be one of the very few cases where Russell has switched around the dialogue without first considering the effect on characterization.

The movement from the literal deaths of Tibby and Laura to the physical confrontation between Gerald and Birkin is signalled by a transition from water to fire, which also becomes another key visual image in the film. The movement from death to life, or at least vitality and the potential for a unique physical (not necessarily sexual) relationship, should be obvious in this especially striking visual sequence, in which the lighting, music and high angle shots suggest a sensuality and ritualistic secular communion. Indeed, the two men stand before the fireplace with the symbolic chalice placed on the ledge between them.

The following sequence, in which Mrs. Crich lets loose the watch dogs on the miners who come to see her husband, is taken directly from the novel; but there the incident exists only in Mrs. Crich's fantasy. Russell, in the film, raises the incident to the level of reality because he vastly increases the significance of this character, so she can become an effective visual comment on the nature of Gerald's relationship with Gudrun. Also, her additional dialogue in this scene (especially such lines as, "Ah yes, I know. Love thy neighbor. And you love your neighbor—more than your own family.") harkens back to the theme of the limitation or even uselessness of the conventional rhetoric of love which society accepts and even advocates.

If conventional approaches to love are dead ends, the unconventional "self-transcending" love of Birkin and Ursula, as posed by Lawrence, is in no way accepted by Russell as his own love ethic. Certainly, the love affair between Birkin and Ursula is meant to contrast sharply with the sinister, dark, and morbid relationship of Gerald and Gudrun. But Russell still mocks the pretensions of Birkin and Ursula by picturing them making love in slow motion in a wheat field, and filming them with a swirling, tilted camera amidst an overly lush, conventionally lyrical music score. The difficulty here is that too many critics and film viewers have accepted conventional advertising's vision of lyricism, and therefore they miss the irony in this sequence.

In contrast to the pseudo-lyricism of Birkin and Ursula, however, stands the dark, subdued atmosphere of the Crich games room as Gerald talks to Gudrun and waits for his father to die. The confrontation with his half-crazed mother illustrates the degree to which antagonism and isolation now exist between husband and wife and mother and son; it also foreshadows the kind of relationship which will emerge with Gudrun and Gerald. In fact, Russell further underscores the link at this point in the film by having both Gudrun and Mrs. Crich answer Gerald's remarks by saying "Yes" with exactly the same intonation.

Gerald tries to flee from his past—the dominance of his father and the growing inability of his mother to be involved or to share in the world around her—by journeying to Gudrun's house to make love with her for the first time. In the novel, Lawrence underscores the failure of their relationship by showing that it grows directly from death and involves no real give and take. In fact, it is described as basically a perverse encounter between child and mother rather than lovers.

> Like a child at the breast, he cleaved intensely to her, and she could not put him away. And his seared, ruined membrane relaxed, softened, that which was seared and stiff and blasted yielded again became soft and flexible, palpitating with new life. He was infinitely grateful, as to God, or as an infant is at its mother's breast. He was glad and grateful like a delirium, as he felt his own wholeness come over him again, as he felt the full, unutterable sleep coming over him, the sleep of complete exhaustion and restoration.[32]

Russell's visuals for this sequence communicate this idea, but again in a manner appropriate to the film medium. Shots of Mrs. Crich laughing uncontrollably at her husband's funeral are intercut with shots of Gudrun and Gerald making love.

Russell does comment on Lawrence's ideas as well as the characters' illusions. The failure of Gerald and Birkin to establish the kind of relationship Birkin so ardently seeks is visually underscored by Russell, who thinks that what Lawrence desires through Birkin is impossible. When Birkin discusses "the additional perfect relationship between man and man", the *mise-en-scène* of the shots undercuts his entire argument. A statue of two dancing women which separates the men looms forward in the frame. In the background the chalice and fireplace are replaced by mirrors, reflections of a woman's portrait, and a sculpture of a woman's head.

> Continually counterpointed with Birkin's philosophy is the feminine ideal of the statues, the bust, and a woman's portrait—all reflected in mirrors about Birkin and silently repudiating his philosophy until at last Rupert's own mirrored reflection epitomizes the futility of his search.[33]

With the shift of the scene to the Swiss Alps, the film "opens up" visually, but while light and whiteness seem ever present, there is no heat—no fireplaces, for example, which are Russell's most obvious and significant symbol of communion. This last section of the film is also a final working out of parallels found in the first section. The relationship between Loerke and Gudrun is established through close-ups, in much the same way they were used initially to link the sisters with Gerald and Birkin, and just as Birkin and Ursula argued over Hermione, Gerald and Gudrun discuss Gudrun's attraction to the German sculptor who believes that art should interpret industry. Also, just as Hermione revealed her limited nature through her lifeless dance, Loerke presents his true depths through his little esoteric games of sensual reduction. Finally, just as Hermione's quest for dominance resulted in the attempted murder of Birkin, Gerald's inability to construct a meaningful union with the willful, emasculating Gudrun results in his attempt to kill her. Unlike Birkin, who found communion with nature, Gerald's excursion into nature ends in his death in the snow-covered mountains.

Like Lawrence's novel, Russell ends his film with Birkin and Ursula back in the warmth and comfort of the mill house, seated in front of the fireplace. Russell satirizes Ursula to a much greater degree than found in Lawrence's account, and at no point does he suggest that she has freely grown to accept Birkin's Laurentian attitudes. Instead, with Jennie Linden's unfortunate resemblance to Debbie Reynolds, she emerges as a somewhat conventional figure who ultimately accepts conventional ideals. It is Ursula, however, who receives the final emphasis, unlike Lawrence's ending. In the novel, the discussion ends in the following manner:

> "You can't have two kinds of love. Why should you?"
> "It seems as if I can't," he said. "Yet I wanted it."
> "You can't have it, because it's false, impossible," she said.
> "I don't believe that," he answered.[34]

The film ends with this same exchange, but the final shot returns to a close-up of Ursula, held as the cast credits appear over her face. The effect is to reinforce Ursula's position rather than Birkin's.

Ken Russell's *Women in Love* clearly follows the tripartite approach to biographical films that he evolved with *The Debussy Film* and brought to fruition in *Isadora Duncan*, but it in no way pushes beyond the achievements and experimentations in *Dante's Inferno*. In *Song of Summer*, Russell rightly emphasized the literal in order to present Delius exactly as Fenby remembered him. In *Women in Love*, Russell balanced biographical facts, Lawrence's attitudes, and his own response to the characters; but perhaps the film is too literal to utilize fully the advantages of this particular method. As a result, montages such as the shots of the drowned lovers intercut with Birkin and Ursula emerge so strongly as to mislead the viewer to expect a literal working out of the suggested consequences. By any standard the film is a good one, but given the entire Russell canon, its importance as a motion picture is not as great as is casually supposed.

NOTES

[1]John Baxter, *An Appalling Talent/Ken Russell* (London: Michael Joseph, 1973), p. 169.

[2]Len Deighton, *The Billion Dollar Brain* (New York: Berkley Medallion–G. P. Putnam, 1973: London, Jonathan Cape, 1966), p. 105.

[3]*Ibid.*, p. 237.

[4]Baxter, *An Appalling Talent,* p. 167.

[5]*Ibid.*, pp. 168–9.

[6]*Ibid.*, pp. 169–70.

[7]Gene Phillips, "An Interview with Ken Russell", *Film Comment,* 6 (Fall 1970), p. 12.

[8]Harry T. Moore, "D. H. Lawrence and the Flicks", *Literature/Film Quarterly*, 1 (January 1973), p. 3.

[9]*Ibid.*

[10]Cited in David J. Gordon, "*Women in Love* and the Lawrencean Aesthetic" in *Twentieth Century Interpretations of Women in Love*, ed. Stephen J. Miko (Englewood Cliffs, N. J.: Prentice-Hall, 1969), p. 50.

[11]D. H. Lawrence, "Foreword", *Women in Love* (New York: The Viking Press, 1961. London: Heinemann, 1954), p. viii.

[12]This claim was especially popular with a number of film critics who reviewed the film in mixed or unfavorable terms.

[13]See George Ford, *Double Measure: A Study of the Novels and Stories of D. H. Lawrence* (New York: Holt, Rinehart and Winston, Inc., 1965); Julian Moynahan, *The Deed of Life: The Novels and Tales of D. H. Lawrence* (Princeton, N.J.: Princeton Univ. Press, 1963); Mark Spilka, *The Love Ethic of D. H. Lawrence* (Bloomington, Indiana: Indiana Univ. Press, 1955); and Eliseo Vivas, *D. H. Lawrence: The Failure and Triumph of Art* (Evanston, Ill.: Northwestern Univ. Press, 1960).

[14]Lawrence, *Women in Love*, p. 20.

[15]Ford, *Double Measure*, pp. 208–9.

[16]Baxter, *An Appalling Talent*, p. 176.

[17]John Weightman, "Trifling With the Dead", *Encounter*, January 1970, p. 52.

[18]Baxter, *An Appalling Talent*, pp. 174–5.

[19]Lawrence, *Women in Love*, p. 444.

[20]Weightman, p. 52.

[21]Lawrence, "Foreword", *Women in Love*, p. vii.

[22]Baxter, *An Appalling Talent*, p. 176.

[23]*Ibid.*, p. 169.

[24]Moore, p. 10.

[25]See Richard Combs, "*Women in Love*", *Monthly Film Bulletin*, 36, No. 431 (1969), pp. 263–4; Stanley Kauffmann, "Stanley Kauffmann on Films", *New Republic*, 19 April 1970, p. 20; and Pauline Kael, "Lust for 'Art' ", *New Yorker*, 28 March 1970.

[26]Ana Laura Zambrano, "*Women in Love:* Counterpoint on Film", *Literature/Film Quarterly*, 1 (January 1973), p. 54.

[27]Baxter, *An Appalling Talent*, pp. 177–8.

[28]Elliott Sirkin, "*Women in Love*", *Film Quarterly*, 24 (Fall 1970), p. 45.

[29]Baxter, *An Appalling Talent*, pp. 175–6.

[30]See Angelo P. Bertocci, "Symbolism in *Women in Love*", in *A D. H. Lawrence Miscellany*, ed. Harry T. Moore (Carbondale: Southern Illinois Univ. Press, 1959), pp. 83–102.

[31]Ana Laura Zambrano makes a similar observation in "*Women in Love:* Counterpoint on Film", p. 51.

[32]Lawrence, *Women in Love,* p. 338.

[33]Zambrano, p. 47.

[34]Lawrence, *Women in Love,* p. 473.

5

The Music Lovers

The Importance of Metaphor

> Most of my films on composers evolve through a stream of consciousness in which the man and the myth, the music and its meaning, time, place, dream and fact all flow and blend into the mainstream of the film itself.
>
> Ken Russell[1]

> A man takes wine to delude himself, to give himself an illusion of contentment and pleasure. And a heavy price he pays for that fraud! The reaction is terrible. It is true that wine gives forgetfulness of bitterness and anguish for a moment—only. Is this the same with music? It is not illusion, it is revelation. And the reason for its victorious strength is that it reveals to us different spheres of elements of beauty, to experience which is not transitory but is for ever a reconciliation to life.
>
> Tchaikovsky[2]

Although some American critics paid lip service to Russell's previous TV biographies in their reviews of *The Music Lovers* (1970), few of them actually saw any of these films,[3] and thus the majority responded to this new film by suggesting that the director's budding genius as evidenced by *Women in Love* had already over-ripened into bad taste and garish vulgarity. Russell's more or less straightforward transformation of *Women in Love* from a novel into a film could be understood by most of the critics; probably because of this fact the film has received the most favorable critical reception of any Russell features to date. But the mixture of the literal and metaphorical in *The Music Lovers,* Russell's screen life of Tchaikovsky, was altogether misunderstood, and as a result the film was unfairly dismissed.[4]

In the United States, since it was expected that the film would be a visually exciting documentation of the "facts" of the composer's life, the numerous and often savage attacks on the film focused on its historical inaccuracies. As a result, the film was linked to the "Hollywood biography tradition"—the very tradition *The Music Lovers* so mercilessly parodies.

Judith Crist, for instance, claimed that the film is "shockingly bad because it reduces the art of biography to a semi-porno film in Victorian-meller terms";[5] and William Wolf of *Cue* argued that "the mixture of heavy drama and soaring music is as old-fashioned as bygone movie biographies".[6] Pauline Kael makes this type of comparison even more explicit in her comment that "Russell's hyper-Hollywood vision of life" should not be imposed on Tchaikovsky or any other historical figure.

> Ken Russell is establishing a reputation based on a profusion of bad ideas, a richer mix of the same ideas that used to make Hollywood biographies of artists such campy drivel. . . . *The Music Lovers* has about as much to do with Tchaikovsky's actual life as *A Song to Remember,* starring Cornel Wilde, had to do with Chopin's.[7]

Finally, Gary Arnold of the *Washington Post* loses control of his own rhetoric in his denunciation of the film's excesses.

> *The Music Lovers* . . . is such a monstrosity of a motion picture that, like the abominable snowman or the Loch Ness monster, it probably has to be seen to be believed. . . . *The Music Lovers* is right up there among the worst movies I've ever laid eyes on. . . . Russell doesn't merely uncover scandalous material . . . he revels in it. Moreover, Russell is such an enthusiastic and unscrupulous reveller that he fabricates scandals and traumas and neuroses and psychoses on the flimsiest of historical rumors in order to keep the cinematic orgy rolling.[8]

Russell's defense of his film against attacks of this nature began even before any of these reviews appeared. Dimitri Tiomkin, supervisor of a Russian film version of Tchaikovsky's life which had its Moscow premiere in September 1970, suggested that Russell's film was a sensationalized account of the composer's life, undertaken to exploit the publicity already given to his film. Russell responded by claiming that "we did vast research and screened the truth. The Russians have made a film on the same subject, but because Tchaikovsky is a national hero, they have whitewashed him."[9]

Truth, however, has a slightly different meaning in each of Russell's films. Those seeking the "realistic" truth of *Song of Summer* could only respond with bafflement to the method of *The Music Lovers*, which presents "psychological" truth through the manipulation of both history and metaphor, and which seeks to reveal the essence of the man through his music.

> To me, Tchaikovsky personifies 19th century romanticism, which is based on a death wish. People call *me* self-indulgent but he was the most self-indulgent man who ever lived, insofar as all his problems and hang-ups are stated in his music. Some might say overstated but then they never experienced what he went through and wouldn't have the guts to put it down on paper even if they had. An enormous amount of his music is about frustrated love or the frustrated artist. You've got *Hamlet, Romeo and Juliet, Francesca da Rimini, Swan Lake* with the hero unable to distinguish between true and false love, *Eugen* [sic] *Onegin*. You've even got *Manfred*, where the poet's in love with his sister. Nobody seems to have seen these themes as a parallel between his music and his life, but that's the concept on which I based my film; the notion that these themes and his treatment of them would illuminate his problem and his obsession.[10]

The Music Lovers owes much to the experiments of *The Dance of the Seven Veils*, and the above quotation echoes some of Russell's comments about the Strauss film, but one must not link these films too closely together. The Superman comic book style of *The Dance of the Seven Veils* is evident from the very opening of the film, and the viewer is never tempted to accept the protagonist on any level beyond the one-dimensional portrait which emerges. Tchaikovsky, however, as a character in this film, exists on a variety of levels. As Russell himself has noted, his feature films on composers merge history, myth, facts, dreams, and his own interpretations of the music into a complexly patterned work of art in which the structure and the exact proportion of these ingredients depend on the nature of the subject himself, and on the director's personal response to him.

In a sense, this method represents a further ramification of the tripartite structure used in a number of Russell's films; the viewer is now no longer readily able to discern the specific components—self-image, the perspective of history, or Russell's own personal vision—and how they function. The demands on an audience of a film such as *The Music Lovers* are astonishing; and if an individual is unwilling to unravel its complexities, the result, as so many reviews illustrate, may be a complete misunderstanding of the film.

Tchaikovsky in Russell's eyes is something of a comic, even ridiculous figure. Although still captivated by some of his music, Russell structures the film as a bitter, satirical rebuttal of the romanticism of the Elgar film. But instead of satirizing a single figure (Strauss), the film debunks a particular attitude towards life.

> *The Music Lovers* was not so much the story of Tchaikovsky as it was a black comedy about the decadence of romanticism. That scene in the country—the scene with everybody running about in the lush green grass—that was made up of images from cigarette commercials. It was meant to be a huge send-up. The core of the film is the destructive force of dreams, particularly on reality. The television ad-man's trick of passing off his dream world as an attainable and desirable reality is to my mind the great tragedy of our age.[11]

Given this purpose behind the film, one can readily see why Tchaikovsky could not be approached in any traditional biopic fashion, and why the emphasis could not be on the composer as a real character in the same sense that Delius and Fenby were "real". In some ways the impact of Russell's method is lost on people who are caught up in the very kind of responses to life that Russell is attacking. That is, commercials have already brainwashed some of us into associating soft-focus, slow-motion cigarette fantasies of eternal Springtime (or even Russell's early Black Magic Chocolates TV commercial, with its image of a woman running free and wild along the edge of a sunlit lake) with that which *is* lyrical, beautiful, and real. Clichés, after all, are presently accepted by many in our culture as accurate delineations of the so-called "good life". For these people, there is little humor or irony in this film.

Russell argues that if even these people pay the slightest attention to the "shape" of the film, they will see that its very structure supports its ironic vision.[12] The dream world of Tchaikovsky may have saved him from responsibility for his actions; he could escape into a world of music and purge his obsessions there. His false dreams and fantasies, however, helped to destroy people around him, most notably his wife. Everything that happens to Nina in the last half of the film, especially the harsh, violent, *Marat/Sade*-influenced sequences of life in a mental institution, undercuts the pseudo-lyricism of images accompanied by the *B Flat Minor Piano Concerto*. In a section of John Baxter's original draft of *An Appalling Talent/Ken Russell* which Russell altered before publication, Russell admits that his intense preoccupation with commercials as harmful "fantasies on modern life" may have been "to the detriment of the film". It distracted him from concern with Tchaikovsky as a real person, and it meant his giving less attention to Nina.

> If the film has any failure I think it's that I didn't show Nina's background enough, what she'd sprung from, what she was escaping from; I think I got what she aspired to, but there wasn't enough of the fact that this was a desperate attempt to find a place, and that Tchaikovsky destroyed her with his self-indulgence.[13]

Much, especially the embellishment of Nina's character as it exists in the film, the use of her mother to show "what she was escaping from", and the use of her mother to parallel Modeste's exploitation of his brother, comes from Russell's imagination. As in all the biopics, he draws his inferences from research, but he then depends specifically on one particular source. In this case, the script, written by Russell and Melvyn Bragg,[14] was adapted from the somewhat suspect biography *Beloved Friend: The Story of Tchaikovsky and Nadejda von Meck* by Catherine Drinker Bowen and Barbara von Meck. The reasons for his choosing this particular book as a major source are not difficult to find. First of all, although constructed in narrative rather than epistolary form, the basis for the biography is the collection of letters between Tchaikovsky and Madame von Meck, here published in English for the first time. More often than not, Russell likes to use the exact words of the actual personages even if the context may be totally different from its original use.[15] Secondly, the biography recognizes the existence of Tchaikovsky's homosexuality and even attempts to suggest how this trait influenced the composer's life and music.

The biography itself is considered spurious by many music scholars because of its supposed overemphasis on so-called lurid details of Tchaikovsky's life, and because of Ms. Bowen's use of novelistic devices to reveal what she imagines to have transpired in the minds of her protagonists.[16] It is not these characteristics, however, but her ill-conceived addresses to the reader—the sentimental purple-prosed asides—which injure the credibility of the book. Witness the following example.

> Oh, do not worry, the reader wants to cry. Peter Ilyich, do not feel this guilt! In all justice, you should be exempt; you of all people need not wander footsore past the Trojans. Heaven made you, Peter Ilyich, a museum piece yourself. Go home and write your music.[17]

This kind of prose places Ms. Bowen within the ranks of "the Music Lovers" in the film who manipulate the composer's music for their own emotional purposes. Even so, for the kind of film that Russell has in mind, the Bowen–von Meck book is ideal.

Of course, other books must have been involved[18] in the actual writing of the script, but the essence of the film, as of the Bowen–von Meck book, stems from the letters between Madame von Meck and the composer. Also, many of the incidents Bowen imagines happening to the major characters are taken over in a variety of ways by Bragg and Russell in the film.

What emerges from the weaving together of all this material is a cinematic statement which, although dense and complex, may not impress the casual viewer on first screening. It is only with repeated viewings that one sees the subtle visual patterns which are so often ignored because of the startling effects of Russell's shock cutting. Indeed, contrary to the prevailing critical pronouncement that the film is pure gallimaufry, *The Music Lovers* contains nothing gratuitous.

The prologue to the film offers a rousing visual accompaniment to the exuberance of Tchaikovsky's music as Count Chiluvsky and the composer ride down the fairground sled-run; and the opening titles "Ken Russell's Film on Tchaikovsky and *The Music Lovers*" reveal that the film will focus on the complex relationships between the composer and those around him. The action of this opening is carefully choreographed to the "Dance of the Clowns" from *The Nutcracker*, and the entire sequence with its Shrovetide carnival setting—its gliding, dollying, and careening camera movement, its quick cuts to marching soldiers, dancing gypsy girls, and performing acrobats, and its atmospheric shots of troikas, torches, and celebrating peasants—captures the feeling of a rich, sensuous, over-blown romanticism. This section, however, provides much more than thrilling visuals to illustrate program music. Russell claims that "nothing in the film is meant as pure description. There is a meaning behind all the music."[19] This opening is no exception. Tchaikovsky, Chiluvsky, Nina Milyukova, Madame von Meck, Modeste, Sasha, Davidov, and the young lieutenant are all thrust together here at this one moment, and Russell attempts a subtle visual delineation of their relationships to each other. Nina is linked to the soldiers' sexual preoccupations exhibited by their carrying off of the gypsy girl. Madame von Meck and Modeste withdraw and distance themselves from such activities. Even Tchaikovsky's crucial conflict between his love for his idealized sister and his attraction to Chiluvsky, his homosexual partner, is suggested in these opening minutes. The basic substance is all here, but perhaps can only be seen after repeated viewings of the entire film.

The meaning of the similar kind of encounter at the private premiere of the *B Flat Minor Piano Concerto*, however, is more obvious. This concert as presented by Russell is not historically accurate, but the lengthy sequence is required for delineation of the film's major theme, and so literal representation has little place or purpose. The *B Flat Minor Piano Concerto* was composed in 1874, and the piano part was played by Tchaikovsky for Nicholas Rubenstein on Christmas Eve of the same year, two years before Madame von Meck had even heard of Tchaikovsky's music. However, she did frequent the Moscow Conservatory to listen to concerts, and she was seated in the balcony to listen to the premiere of the *Violin Concerto in D* some four years later.[20] Nina, of course, could not have been present for the first performance of the piano concerto; but Ms. Bowen notes that although we don't know where Nina first saw Tchaikovsky, "perhaps she saw him at the Conservatory, perhaps at the concert—by this time Tchaikovsky was one of the prides of Moscow".[21]

Finally, the folk melodies of this particular concerto, one of the composer's most popular works, are especially appropriate for Russell's desire to link the music to banal, pseudo-lyrical images. The medium and full unmasked shots of Richard Chamberlain as Tchaikovsky playing the piano, and the dizzying tilted shots up and down the keyboard to complement cadenzas would surely have been the envy of Hollywood's Charles Vidor. Of course, these shots are cross-cut with shots of the audience response, including some reaction shots used for ironic effect—Modeste's deaf and dumb protégé tickling his mentor with a peacock feather and Rubenstein yawning and shaking his head. The second movement of the concerto provides an opportunity for the composer to reflect on the memories supposedly transmitted into his composition. These images of an ideal life create a strictly canned lyricism, presented in a slick style with slow motion, rear lighting, dissolves, and soft focus. The images themselves are a virtual catalogue of clichés: bouquets of daisies, pastoral romps through forests of birch trees, children blowing bubbles in rowboats while their father lazily fishes from the shore, men smoking pipes and relaxing in hammocks, and swans swimming in the lake while the family dances a ballet on shore. Clichéd daydreams, however, are not limited merely to the composer. Nina also uses the music as a means to fantasize—in her case, a Romberg-style dream courtship which ends in marriage—but upon opening her eyes, she finds that the object of her affection, the same young lieutenant from the opening, has already departed from his seat in front of her.

The images of Tchaikovsky's second fantasy to his own music do more than present the sources of his inspiration; they define in metaphorical terms his most deep-seated conflict. They show him caught between his love for his idealized sister and his passion for Chiluvsky, a symbolic representation of all his homosexual lovers, and he fears losing both. These images make obvious the conflict already subtly suggested in the opening sequence.

Finally, in the closing of the concerto, the camera, in a series of parallel shots, zooms past the head of Tchaikovsky to close-ups of Chiluvsky, Sasha, Nina, and Madame von Meck, in an effort to register the effect of the music and its composer on them. Chiluvsky[22] grins in his characteristically Mephistophelian manner, Nina sensuously parts her lips, Sasha smiles lovingly, and Madame von Meck simply seems overwhelmed by music which reminds her "that life can be rich and full of meaning".

The dominant narrative technique throughout the remainder of the film is this cross-cutting between these figures and their relationships to Tchaikovsky, the single person who links them all together.

The following sequence begins this task by tracing the reactions of all these figures after the concert. Tchaikovsky, who had transformed his fantasies into his music, must now face the reality of Rubenstein's damning criticism.[23] To Sasha, the music captures "all of last summer", but she is quickly whisked away by her brother Modeste into the cold winter snow. Nina, still caught up in her courtship-marriage fantasy, bumps her head on the portal of a doorway as she returns to her disheveled room in order to write a letter to her young lieutenant. Madame von Meck also wishes to put her dreams into reality by making contact with the Conservatory so that she can learn more about the composer of this magnificent music, but she is met at home by the mundane reality of a family gathering for a Christmas celebration.

This is a film in which the romantic fantasies of the protagonists are undercut, until a state of recognition or a final destruction is achieved. For most of the characters, this lesson takes a dreadfully long period of time. The effect of Nina's letter to the army officer, for instance, is a brutal rape, but she only changes the male object of her fantasies to Tchaikovsky. Even Tchaikovsky himself can't escape entirely from life into music. While at Rubinstein's, he hears Mozart's "Porgi Amor", his mother's favorite song, being sung by a young woman in a bathtub, and this sound linked with this image forces him to relive the horror of the infamous cholera remedy which killed his mother. This graphic sequence depicting Alexandra Tchaikovsky being immersed in a bath of boiling water has been criticized as a needless fabrication, but echoes of images from this sequence reappear throughout the film and help to explain Tchaikovsky's later behavior. They are found, for instance, in the famous railway carriage sequence, later when Nina is subdued after her "fit" of recognition in the madhouse, and finally when Tchaikovsky himself dies in the same manner as his mother.

Tchaikovsky did not see his mother die; in fact, he was not even in the same city when she died. But this sequence contains meaningful visual images to delineate the impact of this event on him. As a child, he had been especially close to his mother, and every biographer emphasizes this relationship when discussing his character. When his mother brought him to the School of Jurisprudence in St. Petersburg in 1850, "he broke away from those holding him and tried to cling to the turning wheels" of her carriage as she left.[24] The effect of his mother's death was even more traumatic. For two and a half years, he was unable to write to his former governess, Fanny Durback, about his mother's death, and for the remainder of his life he remembered the day his mother died by noting sorrowful comments in his diary.[25] For most biographers, this attachment was not the ordinary love of a son for his mother.

> Whether Piotr Ilych's frantic and undiminishing love for his mother was the result of congenital abnormality, or whether abnormality developed out of that love, it is impossible to read his childish letters to her, feel his crushed and despairing reaction to her death, or even look at his remarks about that death decades later, without becoming certain that there was a casual connection between his emotional relationship to Alexandra Andreyevna and his homosexuality.[26]

Russell's sequence then, although not literally true, is psychologically accurate. For the purposes of the film, it forcefully contrasts with the banal fantasies we have just seen at the concert and also provides a key visual motif in the organization of the film.

The major characters in *The Music Lovers* all attempt to transform fantasy into reality, but Tchaikovsky even goes further. In other Russell films, we see artists who transcend the limitations of their lives through their art, but woe to those who, like Debussy and Rossetti, attempt to merge life and art. It is Tchaikovsky, however, who is the worst offender, and who provides Russell with the opportunity, through "The Letter Song" from *Eugene Onegin*, to evolve his most successful working out of this theme.

While working on the opera *Eugene Onegin*, Tchaikovsky received a love letter from Nina Milyukova, a young woman whom he had never met, and the situation he found himself in directly paralleled the plot of the opera. In the opera, Tatyana, the heroine, declared her love for Onegin in a letter, but he claimed that he was unsuited to marriage. His refusal, in turn, led to Tatyana's loveless marriage and Onegin's realization, years later, that this act of rejection had ruined his life. "To a man lost in an imaginary world in which a young girl declares herself passionately to a man who has showed no interest in her, a similar declaration addressed to himself by a real girl would not seem extraordinary."[27] Coincidence, then, was never considered a sufficient explanation. For Tchaikovsky it was fate, and he was being warned not to play the role of Onegin and destroy his own life.

In the film, the narrative of Tchaikovsky's life is furthered through his music, and the reality of Nina writing her fateful letter is intercut with Olga Bredska singing "The Letter Song" from the opera. Even before this sequence, however, there is a transition in which Madame von Meck's letter to Tchaikovsky is paralleled to Nina's, and as Tchaikovsky drinks to Madame von Meck, "the woman who'll change my life", the camera ironically cuts to Nina's daydream in which the composer kills the lieutenant in a duel. The words of "The Letter Song" express Tatyana's misery and her desire for love, but they also serve as a commentary on the emotional responses of Sasha, Nina, and Madame von Meck towards Tchaikovsky; and this link among the women is revealed through intercutting and complementary visual motifs. Nina, in her fantasy, blows Tchaikovsky a kiss just before he shoots the lieutenant, and then dance-embraces with him. Later, when Tchaikovsky tells Sasha that he thinks of her when he writes the music for his woman in love, she blows him a kiss, and at the climactic moment of the song, dance-embraces with him. Her lying on the couch just before this scene is not, as Michael Dempsey suggests, exhaustion from "all this intensely cultivated emotionalism",[28] but rather a moment of conscious recognition of her feelings for her brother. The words of the song ("No, I could not endure it./I could not love another man. My fate is yours to leave or share it. . . .") expose her plight, and Russell humorously compares her romantic agony with Madame von Meck, who stands emotionally transfixed by the music to the song. "You see, he sends me the music the moment he writes it. . . . This is love, my sons. This is *real* love!" Finally, Russell cuts back to Nina walking in the rain to deliver the fateful letter. Art and reality then come together when Tchaikovsky picks up the letter and walks out with Sasha into the rain, as Olga Bredska sings the last verse of the song in the voice-over sound track.

In one sense, this sequence, although a working out of the art-life theme, is yet another variation of the methods and concerns manifested in the carnival and concert sequences. It also serves as a touchstone of Russell's genius as an adaptor. Russell, the detective, reconstructs certain episodes from Tchaikovsky's life and attempts to fill in the gaps. One such gap is the composer's possible response to Nina's letter in terms of the opera that he is writing. Weinstock's biography, one of the most reputable, proposes that the composer saw Nina through the romantic fog of his own wish fulfillment as his own real-life Tatyana and acted accordingly.[29] Russell takes over this theory and creates a sequence presenting it in a way appropriate to his medium, and in a style consistent with his own personal vision of the characters.

When Tchaikovsky meets Nina for the first time, he imagines her dressed in the same white gown she wore in her courtship fantasy during the concert. Like that daydream, this one ends in marriage. The reality of wedded life, however, soon replaces the dream, and Tchaikovsky's realization of his tragic error becomes readily apparent during an outdoor performance of *Swan Lake*. The couple is joined by Chiluvsky, who explains the story line of the ballet to Nina as Russell's camera, in a fashion similar to the Oxford mural sequence in *Dante's Inferno*, shows the parallel relationships between Tchaikovsky, Nina, and Chiluvsky (who like Birkin and Gerald in *Women in Love*, wear color-complementary clothes), and the ballet's Prince Siegfried, Odile, and Rotbart, "the wicked uncle". Here is yet another example in which Tchaikovsky sees life imitating art. For he, like Prince Siegfried, has also lost his true love through an unfortunate marriage based on deception, and for a brief moment, Tchaikovsky in his mind sees his beloved Sasha dancing the role of Odette, the beautiful swan woman.

This realization and the following humorous episode with the camera obscura (yet another example of Nina failing to distinguish illusion from reality) prepare for the train carriage sequence, in which Tchaikovsky's psychological state is depicted through a series of graphic expressionistic images. This sequence when seen in context again reflects the dominant pattern of organization used throughout the film. All incidents further the narrative development of the film, but all the events are selected and structured to underscore the major concept behind the film—dream fantasies without foundation lead only to destruction.

The basis for the train episode is Tchaikovsky's letter to his brother, Anatol, shortly after his marriage to Nina.

> I should lie to you if I said I was already quite happy, quite accustomed to my new position. After such a terrible day as the eighteenth of July, after that ghastly spiritual torture, one cannot recover quickly. I suffered intensely to see how you were afflicted for me, yet you were responsible for the fact that I fought so bravely with my agony. When the train started I was ready to scream; sobs choked me. But I had to entertain my wife with conversation as far as Klin to earn the right to lie in the dark in my own armchair, alone with myself.[30]

And the emphasis for Russell is obviously on the sexual horrors imagined by Tchaikovsky.

> We use the Sixth Symphony, the most tortured music he wrote, in this nightmare honeymoon experience he has. And we base it on a letter of his—there is no dialogue in the sequence. He said in the letter he felt he was going mad at the realization of what he had let himself in for, when he found himself locked in a sleeping compartment with Nina on a train, hurtling through snow at sixty miles an hour, rocking violently. It's like hell. Almost like *Huis Clos.* It's a little box six feet square. And he gets her drunk in it—as he did: he said himself he got her drunk. We show her taking off her things, and suddenly he's with a piece of meat. . . . She's a naked drunk. She passes out cold. And she just rocks about on the floor, and he is trapped with this . . . piece of meat![31]

Russell's own words, however, fail to do justice to this sequence and its effect in forcing the viewer to understand Tchaikovsky's despair and horror of the female form. *Everything* in the sequence contributes to the creation of this sexual nightmare. The tight framing is surprisingly successful, considering that the film was made in cinemascope; and the wide angle lens effectively distorts

Nina's body and face in close-ups. The constant rocking of the coach and the swinging lamp—the single source of illumination for the entire sequence—suggest an hypnotic, almost sexual rhythm; and even the objects found in the coach assume sexual associations. The champagne is never gently poured: the necks of the bottles are plunged into glasses, and a phallic bottle swirls about in its ice bucket receptacle. Even Nina's hooped bustle cage becomes a giant vagina which seems to engulf Tchaikovsky. Finally, her nude body slips to the floor and slams from side to side against the furniture. As Michael Dempsey notes,

> Nina's writhing body becomes for him a disgusting carcass; to his eyes she presents an overwhelming image of decay and insanity, one that links up with both his memory of his cholera-scarred mother and our later sight of Nina confined in a filthy bedlam.[32]

The excessive drinking, the position of the characters, and the high angle shots near the end of the sequence also link it to the scene depicting the lieutenant's sadistic sexual assault on Nina. This, in turn, should suggest to the audience that although both men have entirely different motives and goals, they both treat Nina in a similar fashion.

Before returning to Moscow, Tchaikovsky and Nina had visited her mother, but Russell reverses this and brings her mother to stay with the newly married couple. Nina's mercenary mother is Russell's own invention, and as such, is meant to parallel Modeste, Peter's own mercenary brother.[33] For a brief time, she acts as a buffer between Nina and Peter, but the relationship between husband and wife deteriorates further, and Tchaikovsky finally writes to Madame von Meck that his marriage has become "a dreary, unbearable comedy".

One possible solution to complex emotional problems is suicide, and some time between September 29 and October 5, 1877, Tchaikovsky made a half-hearted attempt to end his life. He walked into the Moscow River until the icy water reached his waist, and emerged a short time later hoping that he would soon die of pneumonia.[34] Russell's version of this suicide attempt, however, is yet another satire on the romantic agony of his protagonist. It is a beautiful, warm fall evening, and Tchaikovsky, accompanied by the mournful sounds of his *String Quartet No. 3*, plunges into the water to sink only up to his knees. The comedy of this sequence is further underscored by the appearance of a fashionable society woman walking her dog; she can only respond to the ridiculous state of the composer with a fixed, ambiguous Mona Lisa smile. Tchaikovsky ignominiously climbs out of the river and makes his way home.

Unable to kill himself, Tchaikovsky attempts to strangle Nina when he returns home. There is no historical basis for this incident, but it appears that Russell and Bragg derived it from Catherine Drinker Bowen's speculations about what happened during that night.

> Tonight, for instance, when he came in she had run to him; exclaiming over his wet clothes. She had knelt to help him off with his boots and the most horrible, ghastly impulse had come over him. He wanted to lift his foot and smash the girl in the face; he wanted to reach down and take that white neck in his hands and twist it until the breath was gone from it.[35]

After his near breakdown, Tchaikovsky recuperates at the smaller house on Madame von Meck's Brailov estate, and although he never comes face to face with his wife again, his actions are constantly cross-cut with hers to remind the viewer of his influence on her life. In a misguided attempt to make her husband jealous, she resumes her writing of love letters, but when Rimsky-Korsakov and Borodin fail to respond, her unscrupulous mother foists their identities onto the clients she procures to feed Nina's fantasies and her own pocket. The results of these continuing fantasies are nymphomania and an increased inability to function in the everyday world—both of which finally lead to her being committed to a madhouse. Thus the grotesque, physical horror of Nina which had existed only in Tchaikovsky's mind during the first half of the film becomes actuality in the second half. The fantasy generates its own hideous reality.

All of this, of course, contrasts with the lush beauty of Madame von Meck's estate, and the ideal relationship in which the composer expresses his love for a woman through his music rather than through physical contact. Under these circumstances, the ideal visions of Tchaikovsky and Madame von Meck remain untarnished by reality. Their occasional chance meetings only serve to heighten their emotions. To the historical Tchaikovsky, however, the close proximity of Madame von Meck caused some moments of uneasiness, and she was quick to reassure him that their relationship would not change merely because they met while she was riding in a carriage and he was walking in the nearby woods.

> You apologize, dear friend, because you met me, while I am delighted to have met you! I cannot tell you how comforting it was to meet like that. It convinced me of the reality of your presence at Brailov. I don't seek any close personal relationship with you, but I love to be near you passively, tacitly—to be under the same roof with you, as in the theatre in Florence, and to meet you on the road. To feel you, not as a myth but as a living man whom I love sincerely and from whom I receive so much—this gives me greatest delight. To me these occasions are extraordinary good fortune.[36]

Russell, however, depicts the repressed sexual longings of Nadejda von Meck in a memorable sequence in which the composer visits the main house at Brailov while Madame von Meck is away. This incident is based on fact,[37] but in the film, it is heightened and exaggerated until it assumes a dream-like aura. The music on the sound track is from *Romeo and Juliet*, and while Tchaikovsky wanders through the house, Madame von Meck speaks the words of the impassioned letter that brought him there.

> In your music, I hear myself: my notes that echo my feelings, my thoughts, my grief. We are apart only in distance. But for that we should be nearly one person. I respect your wish for privacy, seclusion, but I want to share more with you. . . . Come to my house while I'm away and by the spirit of your presence envelop me. The love that is in your music is already in my veins; it has become part of my flesh and blood, part of my being. Your music is mysterious, inexplicable, marvellous, intoxicating. One would like to die experiencing it. How I love you!

Madame von Meck's illusions about the composer of this overwhelming music will be destroyed in the next sequence when Chiluvsky informs her of Tchaikovsky's homosexuality, but even here during the moment of her richest fulfillment, Russell reminds us that it is illusory by cutting from a shot of the estate to a painting of the same scene and from a painting of Madame von Meck's summer lake house to the reality of the scene of her writing to the composer. There are also humorous, almost satirical, shots of the rococo paintings of angels playing various instruments to accompany the music.

When Madame von Meck returns to the Brailov house, she perversely fondles the objects that Peter has touched, and even sensuously caresses his half-eaten peach, but her state of ecstasy culminates in her discovery of the composer himself asleep in one of the beds. Without touching her "love", she places herself next to him on the bed, and as the strains of *Romeo and Juliet* reach their climax, a crane shot reveals these two dreamers posed much like Gothic *gisant* sculptures. The irony is further enforced by a cross-cut to Nina's hyper-active sexual activity—with yet another shot reminiscent of the aftermath of the "rape" by the army officer, the train carriage sequence, and the horrible sight of her spread-eagled over the grate in the madhouse.

Russell's solution to the perplexing question of why Madame von Meck withdraws her support is thematically appropriate (the destruction of an illusionary vision with the unpleasant facts of reality), but it is also credible. Both Weinstock and Bowen lean towards the idea that she began suffering from a guilt complex as the result of the sickness of her eldest son, Vladimir, but John Briggs considers the possibility that she learned about "The" (as Tchaikovsky referred to his homosexuality in letters to his brothers):

> Had the discovery come suddenly and unexpectedly, making clear in a flash the reason for Tchaikovsky's keeping her at a distance and for the failure of his marriage, the shock might have prompted her farewell letter.[38]

The abandonment by Madame von Meck is compensated by extensive conducting tours, and Russell condenses the next four years of Tchaikovsky's life with wild metaphorical visuals set to the *1812 Overture* and executed in a style derived from the comic book methods of the Strauss film. Tchaikovsky, like Strauss, is another artist who "sold out" to the establishment for popular success and, as such, is turned into a stone statue at the end of the sequence. Before that, however, he is pursued by all the "music lovers" of his past life, until they are relegated to a Cocteauesque wind-blown "zone".[39] Popular triumph saves Peter, and the personal manager of the tour, Modeste, then sets off cannons which decapitate all those who "haunted" Peter's life—all those except Nina, who survives in a madhouse.

Russell's treatment of the last days of Tchaikovsky's life is reasonably accurate in terms of the events and the actual language spoken. Modeste did convince his brother to change the title of the Sixth Symphony from "The Tragic" to "The Pathetique", and Tchaikovsky did drink unboiled water in Petersburg during the cholera season. But unlike Russell, no biographer suggests that this act was suicidal. For Russell, this interpretation is perfectly in keeping with the theme of self-destruction through the pursuit of dream fantasies.

Throughout this last section of the film, Tchaikovsky makes a number of vague references to "her", and at times, these references seem to include his mother, Sasha, Madame von Meck, and Nina. When Nina is suggested, however, Russell forces us to see Nina's pathetic condition matched to excerpts from the Sixth Symphony, and he further links the fates of Peter and Nina through the editing and repetition of visual forms. Peter's realization that his mother was the only woman he ever remembers loving is followed by his fateful drinking of the water. Cut to Nina and the moment of realization that Peter hated her. Her response only causes her to be subdued by guards, dragged away (emphasis on the limp legs), and strapped to her bed, which resembles the shape of the bathtub to be seen in the next sequence. Cut to Peter in bed as Modeste and the doctor discuss the boiling water remedy. Finally, the assistants drag Tchaikovsky (emphasis on the limp legs) into the bathroom and place him in the tub of water. After his dead body is taken from the tub, Russell cuts back to the nearly motionless face of Nina staring out from the bars of her cell, and the credits are placed over this shot. This ending seems excessive only to those who have failed to see that *The Music Lovers* is a radical critique of romantic self-indulgence and romantic evasions.

NOTES

[1]Ken Russell, "Mahler the Man", *Mahler Brochure* (London: Sackville Publishing, 1974).

[2]Cited in John Warrack, *Tchaikovsky* (New York: Charles Scribner's Sons, 1973, London: Hamish Hamilton, 1973), p. 125.

[3]Only *Isadora Duncan, Dante's Inferno,* and *Song of Summer* have been screened on U.S. television.

[4]Alexander Walker, the most vociferous of Russell's critics in England, fits into the pattern described above even though he has seen a number of the Russell TV films. He did give *Women in Love* a favorable review, but since then, he has attacked each new Russell feature with increasing hostility. When asked on the BBC "Film Night—Confrontation" program of February 28, 1971 why he disliked *The Music Lovers,* he replied as follows:

> Well in one word, rape. I don't really like to see a composer raped for the delectation of a director's sense of what is theatrical. It seems to me it's a film that has developed out of an increasingly hysterical line of television programmes in which the more grotesque elements of the composer are the things that are highlighted. Yes, I liked the quieter ones of the Elgar and the Delius at the beginning. This coupled with the *1812 Overture* style which is a kind of advertisement is great; it almost conceals the fact that you've got nothing to sell except your own sense of fantasy and theatricality.

This statement illustrates that Walker, like most of the American critics, responds favorably only to Russell's literal films. He can't or won't accept the validity of Russell's metaphorically true portraits. This refusal to do so is further revealed through the way in which he links the Elgar and Delius films chronologically, when, although similar in terms of presenting *real* characters in a *realistic* framework, they are separated in time by over six years.

[5]Cited in "*The Music Lovers*", *Filmfacts* 14 (1971), p. 147.

[6]*Ibid.*

[7]Pauline Kael, "Genius", *New Yorker,* 30 January 1971, p. 76.

[8]Gary Arnold, "Music Lovers", *Washington Post,* February 25, 1971, Section C, p. 14, cols. 1–2. It should also be noted at this point, however, that there were some notable exceptions to these generally hostile responses. Michael Dempsey's analysis of the film, for instance, is probably the best single critical appreciation of Russell's vision, and as such, part of his article stands behind my own analysis in this chapter. See Michael Dempsey, "The World of Ken Russell", *Film Quarterly,* 25 (Spring 1972), pp. 13–25.

[9]Ken Russell, cited in "*The Music Lovers*", *Filmfacts*, p. 147.

[10]John Baxter, *An Appalling Talent/Ken Russell* (London: Michael Joseph, 1973), p. 183.

[11]Cited in Guy Flatley, "I'm Surprised My Films Shock People", *New York Times*, Arts and Leisure Section, October 15, 1972, p. 15, cols. 4–7.

[12]Private discussion between Russell and the author on June 19, 1974.

[13]Baxter original draft of *An Appalling Talent*, TS, p. 245.

[14]Melvyn Bragg had already collaborated with Russell on *The Debussy Film, Always on Sunday*, and the unfilmed Nijinksy script, and all three works reflect themes that are also found in the Tchaikovsky film. For instance, Bragg and Russell had constructed sequences in these other works (the very structure of *The Debussy Film*, the Jarre play in *Always on Sunday*, and the Petrushka ballet performance in the Nijinksy film) in which art and life merged together. Now they collaborated on a film in which the protagonist, as they saw it, destroyed himself because of this fixation of making life imitate art. In a letter dated December 2, 1973, Bragg informed the writer of this study that both he and Russell were working on a screen adaptation of *Rogue Herries*, but this novel by Hugh Walpole is clearly something which holds more interest for him than for Russell, who at no time acknowledged this as a future project.

[15]In another deleted unnumbered section of the original draft of *An Appalling Talent*, Russell discusses his use of quotations in his films.

> There are more quotes than most people think in my films, words that the people actually said themselves. Whole scenes are often made up from things the people said at various times. . . . I know words don't necessarily mean the same thing when they're taken out of context and used in a film—there's a difference in degree if not in meaning—but I think that's an irrelevance. I don't take the degree into consideration because the original circumstances may have been *more* fantastic than anything I can invent. The meaning a phrase had when it was said can depend on what the weather was like on that day, whether the sun was shining, whether he was sitting or standing up—but at least *he* said it, and that's the best you can do. I believe you've always got to be accurate to the spirit or the word all the time when you're doing a biography or an adaptation; otherwise you might as well do something else. Even in the Strauss film, though I took the ridiculous liberty of making his music into a comic strip, I used his words. And the fact that everybody was very cross with me may have been because they *were* his words. I've always found that imaginary dialogue can be beautiful or meaningful or sympathetic or pathetic or whatever you like, but it doesn't annoy people, or make them sit up, whereas if you throw in a few real statements that may be totally out of context to when an event actually happened, they've got some curious resonance.

[16]See Herbert Weinstock, *Tchaikovsky* (New York: Alfred A. Knopf, 1966), p. x.

[17]Catherine Drinker Bowen and Barbara von Meck, *Beloved Friend: The Story of Tchaikovsky and Nadejda von Meck* (New York: Random House, 1937), p. 356.

[18]It seems likely that Bragg and Russell at least read the following works: John Briggs, *The Collector's Tchaikovsky and the Five*; Edwin Evans, *Tchaikovsky*; Rosa Newmarch, *Tchaikovsky: His Life and Works*; Modeste Tchaikovsky, *The Life and Letters of Peter Ilyich Tchaikovsky*, and Herbert Weinstock, *Tchaikovsky*.

[19]Terry Curtis Fox, "Conversations with Ken Russell", *Oui*, June 1973, p. 104.

[20]Bowen and von Meck, *Beloved Friend,* pp. 58 and 220.

[21]*Ibid.,* p. 92.

[22]Like Max in *Mahler,* Count Chiluvsky is a symbolic figure into which a number of Tchaikovsky's male lovers have been distilled. Vladimir Shilovsky was for a time a favorite pupil and travelling companion, and it is likely that he was one of the composer's homosexual partners. Perhaps Russell and Bragg used this name because of the existence of Shilovsky, but his role in reality was much closer to that suggested by Alexei in the film. See Weinstock, *Tchaikovsky,* p. 47.

[23]Rubenstein's response in the film is taken directly from an account of the event written in a letter to Madame von Meck dated January 21, 1878. See Bowen and von Meck, *Beloved Friend,* pp. 57–9.

[24]John Briggs, *The Collector's Tchaikovsky and the Five* (New York: J. B. Lippincott Co., 1959), p. 20.

[25]John Warrack, *Tchaikovsky,* p. 29.

[26]Weinstock, *Tchaikovsky,* p. 22.

[27]Weinstock, *Tchaikovsky,* p. 139. Weinstock's theory about Tchaikovsky's response to *Eugene Onegin* is, of course, quite similar to the interpretation that Russell puts forth in his film.

[28]Michael Dempsey, *Film Quarterly,* p. 18.

[29]Weinstock, *Tchaikovsky,* p. 138.

[30]Bowen and von Meck, *Beloved Friend,* pp. 106–7.

[31]Cited in Gordon Gow, "Shock Treatment", *Films and Filming,* July 1970, p. 10. In no letter does Tchaikovsky mention that he got his wife drunk on this train trip, but in a letter to Madame von Meck, dated August 9, 1877, he mentions that his wife became more abhorrent to him with each passing hour and that wine was one of his only consolations.

[32]Michael Dempsey, *Film Quarterly,* p. 19.

[33]Modeste exploits his brother for profit late in the film when he convinces him to undertake a series of conducting tours solely for money and popular success (figurative prostitution), while Nina's mother acts as procurer for her daughter's literal prostitution.

[34]See Weinstock, *Tchaikovsky,* p. 149 and Bowen and von Meck, *Beloved Friend,* p. 132.

[35]See Bowen and von Meck, *Beloved Friend,* p. 132.

[36]*Ibid.,* p. 332.

[37]*Ibid.,* p. 330.

[38]Briggs, *The Collector's Tchaikovsky,* p. 82.

[39]Jean Cocteau, "*Orphée*", *Three Screenplays* (New York: Grossman, 1972), pp. 180–1.

6

The Devils—Russell's Major Achievement

Sources

> And the subject [for *The Devils of Loudun*] leads naturally into all kinds of problems, historical, philosophical and psychological which call for treatment on the way.
>
> Aldous Huxley[1]

As with most of his earlier films, Ken Russell's *The Devils* (1971) was not highly regarded by the majority of European and American film critics. In fact, only the Italian critics praised Russell and his film ("one of the outstanding stylistic talents in the contemporary cinema . . . a great film about which it is possible to speak well and also ill").[2] In England and America, the film generated the most scathing, abusive attacks that Russell's work has received to date. George Melly in *The Observer* argued that "instead of contrasting the use of political power with the hideous pantomime it promotes to gain its ends, the whole film is a hymn to sado-masochism. It is vulgar, camp and hysterical."[3] Charles Champlin in the *Los Angeles Times* called the film "a degenerate and despicable piece of art", and Judith Crist in *New York* claimed "we can't recall in our relatively broad experience (400 movies a year for perhaps too many years) a fouler film".[4] Some of the criticism sounded remarkably similar to that which appeared when Huxley first published his account of the incidents at Loudun. For instance, Ann Guarino of the *Daily News* raised questions about the motivations for making such a film. "Even if the characters did exist and the behavior and times depicted are true, to what purpose does one exploit a couple of rotten pages in history?—It's like opening up a can of worms."[5] As usual, much of the attack also focused on the director himself.

Newsweek critic Paul D. Zimmerman claimed that the film proved that "Russell has gone beyond extravagance to insanity", and "Verr" of *Variety* concurred that Russell had "gone berserk".[6]

Only a few of the adverse criticisms considered the film in relationship to its sources, and, all too often, simply for the sake of a cutting gibe. The British Film Institute's *Monthly Film Bulletin* saw hysterical overstatement and concerns with sex and sadism replacing "John Whiting's cool and lucid analysis",[7] and Vincent Canby of the *New York Times* compared Russell to "a hobbyist determined to reproduce 'The Last Supper' in bottle tops".[8] Two defenders of the film, Roger Manvell and Michael Dempsey,[9] also mentioned the film's original sources while discussing its remarkable achievements, but their discussions were too brief to be useful.

In the final analysis, if one is to understand why *The Devils* should be considered as Russell's major achievement, it is necessary to study the film's relationship to its sources *in depth*—in order to see a rationale for method and style and in order to appreciate the genius of Russell's creation through adaptation.

About a year and a half before his death in 1963, Aldous Huxley wrote to his son, Matthew, about a proposed film version of *The Devils of Loudun*.[10] "Meanwhile there is to be a film of the *Devils of Loudun*. What on earth will they make out of it? I feel a great deal of curiosity—and some apprehension."[11] Huxley's concern should not be interpreted as hostility to the idea of adapting this particular work. As early as 1953, he had considered collaborating on a dramatic version, but in a letter to Ned Rorem he expressed only a mild interest in Rorem's suggestion that it be made into an opera. The difficulties of the libretto form simply seemed too great and the possibility of success too remote.[12] Huxley the prophet and teacher wished to expose his ideas to new and larger audiences, and theatre and motion pictures offered more potential than opera. In fact, one of his reasons for settling in Southern California was his desire to establish significant connections with the American film industry.[13]

Huxley's own unfortunate Hollywood experiences probably caused some misgivings about a projected film version of *The Devils of Loudun*, but in the ten years following the publication of the book in 1952, Huxley also became more and more fearful that the material contained in his strange biography might prove too powerful for many audiences when transformed into the more direct experience of a film or theatrical performance. After all, many reviewers had initially condemned the book as an offensive work which purposely raked up old corruptions.[14] "Not since Swift has anyone so resented the fact of bathrooms; not since Donne, our decomposition."[15] And when the book was published in a British edition, the account of

Grandier's torture was considerably moderated (though with the permission of the author).[16] Finally, in 1960, when John Whiting sent him an early draft of the play version, Huxley again noted his concern for its impact on an audience:

> I have just finished your script of the *Devils*, and find most of it poetical and powerfully dramatic. Indeed, I wonder if some of the scenes in the last two acts may not prove almost too powerful. The possession, exorcism and torture episodes were hair-raising enough in the narrative (incidentally, I exaggerated nothing; everything in the book is drawn from original sources). Dramatized and well-directed and acted, they may be almost more than many people can take. In any case, it will be very interesting to see how an audience reacts to the horror and strangeness of the story. You have done a great deal to make it acceptable by presenting the horrors within a framework of poetical reflection.[17]

Later, in the same letter, Huxley further claimed that the real problem was "to prevent the piece from becoming too frightful or too extravagantly indecent and blasphemous".

These terms, interestingly enough, have been used by various critics to describe Russell's film version. Huxley himself might have been dismayed by some of the extremism that Russell employs in bringing the story of Grandier and Sister Jeanne to the screen, but it is doubtful he could condemn this screen adaptation on the grounds of gross distortion. Russell remains faithful to the tone and the dominant themes of the original, and to a great extent even to Huxley's basic methods. Both works are "founded on fact, but considerably beholden to imagination and art".[18]

Aldous Huxley's chameleon-like career as a writer spans over four decades and reflects a number of shifting concerns: social satire, Laurentian vitalism, anti-utopian prophecy, and finally a mystical quest for union with the Divine Ground. For many critics, this evolution killed Huxley's sensibility as an artist and created the prophetic, didactic persona of Huxley the guru. "The austerity of the aspiring mystic had destroyed the austerity of the novelist. . . . To gain one kind of vision often means to lose another."[19] Still, Huxley's later struggle for self-transcendence was not entirely catastrophic for his experimentation with aesthetic forms. In fact, his pedagogical concern created the need for him to experiment. He practiced a remarkable fusion of biography, fiction, memoir, speculative essay, and social and philosophical history: *Grey Eminence*, "Variations on a Philosopher", and *The Devils of Loudun* are major examples of this medley in the Huxley canon. Its artistic success, however, was of minor importance to Huxley; he saw it more simply as a method for presenting his particular vision to the general reading public. The new form allowed him to push beyond the confines of a purely fictional approach, of a dry, didactic essay, or of an "accurate" biographical rendering. He could freely structure a work to include various digressions on a variety of subjects, as well as use his fictive imagination to allow the reader to get into the minds of his central characters.

That Huxley clearly recognized the functional aspects of this form is again indicated in his letters. In a letter to Hubert Benoit, he suggests that certain subjects must be treated in a manner

> which would more forcibly attract the attention of the critics and the public. . . . I myself, during these last months, have had an experience which—though not completely successful—has convinced me of the methodological value of a philosophical exposition in the framework of a life; for I have just brought to conclusion a long essay, not in, but *around* Maine de Biran—an essay in which political, metaphysical and mystical problems are dealt with in the light of a particular life and teaching.[20]

Thirteen years later in a letter to Humphrey Osmond, the doctor who supervised his experiments with mescalin, he is even more specific about his method of biography, citing *Grey Eminence* and *The Devils of Loudun* as examples.

> I am for the Eileen biography. But it must be more than a straight biography. You can use it (as I used Father Joseph and Grandier-Surin stories) as a device for expounding, in concrete terms and therefore all the more penetratingly, a great variety of general ideas. My own feeling is that philosophy is best expounded through a biography, real or fictional, or a historical narrative. The narrative doesn't suffer from being made the centre, it is actually enriched by its association with general ideas. And the general ideas take on greater force through being concretized in, and illustrated by, a particular case history.[21]

Huxley first became interested in a biographical-historical study of the strange events which took place in seventeenth-century Loudun while researching material for *Grey Eminence*,[22] but he was unable to get the necessary documents and books, until after the end of World War II. Even after the war, when he did not immediately begin research for this work, he remained haunted by the themes of damnation and demonic possession. As a result, in 1947 he wrote *Ape and Essence*,[23] a short, rather awkwardly conceived, anti-utopian novel written in the guise of a screenplay. The action of the script section of the novel takes place in 2108 in post-World War III America, which has regressed to a condition of barbarism because of the victory of the diabolic principle in human history.

Just before beginning *The Devils of Loudun*, Huxley gathered together a number of essays that he had written since 1946 and published them in a volume entitled *Themes and Variations*. The last essay, written in 1950, dominated the volume and clearly influenced his method in the Loudun project. "Variations on a Philosopher" is a study of the French philosopher, Maine de Biran (1766–1824), and although it remains within the essay genre, it employs most of the methods basic to the longer biographical studies. For instance, like Father Joseph in *Grey Eminence,* Biran is introduced through an imaginary episode, and from this portrait, the reader encounters his essential character. "Next", as George Woodcock notes, "we are given enough biography to set him in time and place; then Huxley proceeds to consider his pattern of behavior, his role in the world, and the inner man whom the behavior and the role so deceptively present."[24]

This kind of progression is crucial to understanding the structure of *The Devils of Loudun*, but Huxley begins this particular work not with a sketch of Grandier, but with a description of the Jesuit world which created him. A quotation from Joseph Hall notes that while a number of churches on the continent had been destroyed by the religious wars, the number of Jesuit colleges grew rapidly. The schools expanded because eminent and respectable citizens wanted their children to obtain the best possible educations, and the Jesuits were only too willing to fulfill this need. Like many other children from middle class families, Huxley notes that Urbain Grandier entered the Jesuit college in his area, but unlike most of his peers, he emerged ten years later as a brilliant secular priest ready to embark on a career which promised to fulfill his grandest expectations.

Huxley is not a biographer who meticulously subjects himself to the limitations of specific sources, nor does he clutter his narrative with excessive footnotes. Rather, he submerges himself in the culture and history of an age, and uses his encyclopaedic mind to create a controlling vision which shapes his work. Although, for instance, no material exists documenting the childhood and youth of Grandier, Huxley takes great pains to suggest that Grandier had much in common with contemporaries such as Jean-Jacques Bouchard, who did leave behind autobiographical records of early sexual exploits, so that this material can serve as a base from which one can project an image of the young Grandier. Also, Huxley suggests that the moral atmosphere which formed Bouchard and Grandier was not radically dissimilar from that which shaped Louis XIII, except that Louis in later life exhibited a noted aversion to women and a decided inclination for men. This seventeenth century world of lax sexual restrictions made it possible then for Grandier, who had no aversion to women, to make the best of the secular and religious worlds. Thus, as Huxley describes Grandier entering the gates of Loudun, with a "corpse or two hung, moldering, from the municipal gallows",[25] his character is established, and since Huxley seems at times to agree with Hardy's dictum that "character is fate", his fate seems set as well.

Initially, Grandier's "superiority" captivated the inhabitants of Loudun. The young women were charmed by this handsome priest; the aristocrats welcomed him into their social world because of his cleverness and intelligence, and even his enemies were forced to concede that he possessed a remarkable number of talents, not the least of which was his amazing eloquence. Still, the less satisfactory aspects of Grandier's character, namely pride and vanity, manifested themselves in such a way as to forge links in a "chain that would draw him to his doom".[26] For the mere pleasure of asserting his own ego, he rudely and unwisely claimed precedence in a procession over the Prior of Coussay, who was later to become the King's first minister, Cardinal Richelieu. Grandier also relished verbal combat with his detractors and even found delight in creating new enemies. Still, it is Huxley's claim that sensuality sealed his fate.

Grandier's visits to Ninon, the receptive widow, provided for possible moments of self-transcendence—"to annihilate the persona and transcend the ego in an obscure rapture of sensuality, a frenzy of romantic passion, or, more creditably, in the mutual charity of the perfect marriage".[27] The seduction of Philippe Trincant, on the other hand, is presented as a ruthless, ego-intensifying act of self-affirmation made all the more enticing because it becomes one of the blackest of crimes—a betrayal of friendship as well as a corruption of innocence.

At this point, Huxley writes by the requirements of structure, a dramatic impact, character revelation and, perhaps, even philosophy, rather than historical accuracy. Clearly, the following passage displays the novelist's imagination at work.

> Then one day, in the middle of his story about King Francis's drinking cups for debutantes—those flagons engraved on the inside with amorous postures, which revealed themselves a little more completely with every sip of the concealing wine—she interrupted him with the curt announcement that she was to have a baby, and immediately burst into a paroxysm of uncontrollable sobbing.
>
> Shifting his hand from the bosom to the bowed head and changing his tone, without any transition, from the bawdy to the clerical, the parson told her that she must learn to bear her cross with Christian resignation. Then, remembering the visit he had promised to pay to poor Mme. de Brou, who had a cancer of the womb and needed all the spiritual consolation he could give her, he took his leave.[28]

Grandier's transition from lover to priest is amazingly simple. His act is not hypocritical; he simply sees no contradiction in combining the fruits of two worlds. The passing reference to Mme. de Brou is the device of an imaginative writer establishing a suggestive link which leads the reader directly to the rather different involvement in the next chapter, when Grandier falls in love with Mlle. de Brou, "a woman recognized as a person and loved for what she actually was".[29]

Huxley's second chapter catalogues Grandier's secret marriage, further scandals resulting from vanity and pride, and efforts by his enemies, now led by M. Trincant, to discredit him. There are also digressions into areas of social history and the practice of seventeenth century medicine, and finally an account of Grandier's last major victory, when acting as Loudun's vice-governor, he forced Baron de Laubardemont's wrecking crew to desist from destroying the inner walls of the city.

Up to this point in the book, it is difficult to tell exactly where Huxley intends to take his reader. Chapter Three, however, suspends the narrative development and makes part of his purpose clear. He introduces Joseph Surin, another Jesuit, who came to Loudun only after Grandier's charred remains had been scattered to the winds. Grandier, the man of this world, stands in marked contrast to Surin, a man of the other world, the mystical world of the Kingdom of God within, and this contrast creates the opportunity for Huxley to reflect on the nature of transcendence of the self.

For Huxley, man's need for self-transcendence is as powerful as his need for self-assertion, and this necessary urge to pass beyond the confines of the sweating, limited self in some strange way reveals that something unconscious within us seeks union with the Ground of all being.

> When the phenomenal ego transcends itself, the essential self is free to realize, in terms of a finite consciousness, the fact of its own eternity, together with the correlative fact that every particular in the world of experience partakes of the timeless and infinite.[30]

Without such an understanding of the needs and methods of self-transcendence, man cannot understand past history, or for that matter, even his own times.

Not all methods of self-transcendence, however, are liberating. Downward movement into the subhuman, or horizontal movement into merely something wider than the ego, are not adequate substitutes, but even within the area of upward transcendence there are numerous possible setbacks. For instance, even after Surin's achievement of "extraordinary graces" through ascetic austerities, there remains a hostility to external nature which must be overcome in order to gain total Awareness. If the often foolish and silly (by worldly standards) Surin takes the long arduous road to upward transcendence, Grandier, more often than not, settles for fulfillment on the horizontal level, and Sister Jeanne flees from the self by descending into the realm of the sub-human.

Huxley's introduction of Jeanne in Chapter Four is contrived to force the reader to contrast her with Grandier. Unlike the physically attractive and intelligent priest, Jeanne is a limited creature, hunch-backed, and given to the deriding abuse of others in order to shield her own inadequacies. Whereas Grandier unconsciously rationalizes discrepancies between his roles as lover and priest, Jeanne consciously dissembles; she is a hypocrite, the ultimate actress, who is also affected with "bovarism", a tendency to imagine herself to be a kind of person that she is not.

At age 25, Jeanne des Anges became Prioress of the Ursuline Convent at Loudun, a mini-empress with seventeen followers bound to her by vows of strict obedience, and although some outsiders believed her to be a model of Christian devotion and holiness, Huxley presents her as a victim of what D. H. Lawrence called "sex in the head". Gradually, after she learned the gossip about the sexual exploits of Grandier, this priest of St. Peter's whom she had never met became the object of her obscene fascination. A few years later, Canon Moussaut, the Ursuline spiritual director, died, and Jeanne quickly wrote to Grandier requesting that he become the new Ursuline confessor. With his refusal, Jeanne's last hope for a face to face meeting disappeared, and the fact that her desire soon turned to bitterness was reflected by her next selection, Canon Mignon, a cousin to Philippe Trincant and noted Grandier detractor. According to Huxley, this new confessor soon learned the innermost secret fantasies of the nuns and their Prioress, and plotted with his fellow conspirators to bring shame and ruin to Grandier by charging that he was responsible for the demonic possession of these good sisters.

Huxley's account of the public exorcisms of the nuns is punctuated by biting sarcasm, but his graphic, convincing descriptions of these proceedings reveal his power as a writer and his intent as a teacher. The depictions of the horrors of the "miraculous enema" and the giant clyster for forced "colonic irrigation" are especially vivid, and the metaphors quite appropriate. "Barré had treated her [Jeanne] to an experience that was the equivalent, more or less, of a rape in a public lavatory."[31] Throughout this section, Huxley alludes to our own times, for just as *Ape and Essence* is as much about present trends in society as about a dreaded future, *The Devils of Loudun* is about the horrors of our times as well as about those of our ancestors.

This intention is made perfectly obvious at the beginning of Chapter Five. Under the pretext of discussing the legal aspects of a sorcery trial, Huxley reminds his readers how all the evils associated with the beliefs of organized religion flourish today without any necessary beliefs in the supernatural.

> In medieval and modern Christendom the situation of sorcerers and their clients was almost precisely analogous to that of Jews under Hitler, capitalists under Stalin, Communists and fellow travellers in the United States. They were regarded as the agents of a Foreign Power, unpatriotic at the best and, at the worst, traitors, heretics, enemies of the people. Death was the penalty meted out to these metaphysical Quislings of the past, and in most parts of the contemporary world, death is the penalty which awaits the political and secular devil-worshippers known here as Reds, there as Reactionaries. . . . And when the current beliefs come, in their turn, to look silly, a new set will be invented, so that the immemorial madness may continue to wear its customary mark of legality, idealism, and true religion.[32]

Huxley's method should now be obvious. By suspending the narrative line, he reduces any kind of sustained dramatic impact, but through numerous allusions and lengthy discussions, he forces the reader to see the implications for his own time and place. Grandier's tragedy functions as something unique and individual, but his case also serves as a microcosm offering a potent warning to all of us. The major difference then between *Ape and Essence* and *The Devils of Loudun* is not that one deals with the diabolic in prophetic terms and the other in historical terms; the difference stems from the subtlety and effectiveness of the rendering of Huxley's vision.

Chapter Six returns to the narrative with a detailed account of the see-saw legal battles between De Cerisay, who was convinced there was no genuine possession, and the exorcists, who finally took their case to Richelieu and succeeded in having the case placed above the law. Finally on December 7, 1633, Urbain Grandier was arrested and then subjected to "tests" in an attempt to prove that he was in league with the devil. Through fraud (probing with both sharp and blunt instruments to show that marks of the devil—pain free spots—existed), "scientific" truth joined forces with legal and theological truth, and as a result, the outcome of Grandier's trial was never in question.

Chapter Seven again suspends the narrative development; this time in order to present the particular "frame of reference within which the men of the early seventeenth century did their thinking about human nature".[33] Grandier's contemporaries believed that the soul, infused into the foetus six months after conception, was indivisible, although composed of the unity of vegetal, sensitive, and rational functions. Thus, the notion of a so-called split personality and the realm of the subconscious were impossible, and if a person's behavior exhibited two or more "selves" in evidence, it was assumed that the evil spirits, attested by theology, were responsible.

Huxley, after suggesting the limitations of such a view of human nature, does not entirely dismiss the possibility of demonic possession. Instead, he shows how vicious the proceedings at Loudun actually were because of the examples of obvious fraud and the fact that Barré's premise that "duly constrained, the devil is bound to tell the truth" and his insistence on public exorcism were in direct conflict with the teachings of the Church.

Finally, Huxley uses all of this detail again to force the reader to relate the issues to his own age.

> Though frequently Manichaean in practice, Christianity was never Manichaean in its dogmas. In this respect it differs from our modern idolatries of communism and nationalism, which are Manichaean not only in action, but also in creed and theory. Today it is everywhere self evident that *we* are on the side of Light, *they* on the side of Darkness, *they* deserve to be punished and must be liquidated (since *our* divinity justifies everything) by the most fiendish means at our disposal. By idolatrously worshipping ourselves as Ormuzd, and by regarding the other fellow as Ahriman, the Principle of Evil, we of the twentieth century are doing our best to guarantee the triumph of diabolism in our time. And on a very small stage, this precisely was what the exorcists were doing at Loudun.[34]

Near the end of the chapter, Huxley returns to the narrative line: Sister Jeanne's attempted suicide, her retraction of the accusations against Grandier (which was not believed), and finally her further plunge downward into a sub-human freedom from the self. The next chapter continues the narrative account with an intricately detailed, graphic description of the torture and painful death of Grandier, but these actions are also presented in such a manner, mainly through authorial commentary, that the twentieth century man can in no way feel superior to his barbarous ancestor. True, Grandier's legs were horribly crushed to splinters and his mangled body was burned alive, but for Huxley, this is minor compared to the diabolic accomplishments of modern society.

> Our ancestors invented the rack and the iron maiden, the boot and the water torture; but in the subtler arts of breaking the will and reducing the human being to subhumanity, they still had much to learn. . . .
>
> For the totalitarians of our more enlightened century, there is no soul and no Creator; there is merely a lump of physiological raw material molded by conditioned reflexes and social pressures into what, by courtesy, is still called a human being. . . . Physical extermination by shooting (or, more profitably, by overwork in a slave labor camp) is not enough. It is a matter of observable fact that men and women are not the mere creatures of Society. But official theory proclaims that they are. Therefore it becomes necessary to depersonalize the "enemies of Society" in order to transform the official lie into truth.[35]

With Grandier dead, Huxley now concentrates on a more psychologically oriented study of transcendence—in this case, a struggle between the hopelessly downward plunge of Jeanne and the incessant upward push of Surin. Grandier was a clever but understandable product of his environment with an above-average capacity through which he attempted to transcend the normal self. Unjustly punished for crimes he did not commit, he managed finally to achieve a meaningful relationship with the God whom he believed would judge him in eternity. Sister Jeanne never came to any recognition or salvation, but Jean-Joseph Surin achieved an experience of eternity here on earth, and this clearly intensified Huxley's interest in him, and in his relationship with Sister Jeanne. Although often imprudent and silly, Surin believed firmly in Jeanne's possession and desperately attempted to free her. By involving himself so much in speculation about supernatural evil, "Surin drove himself to a pitch of madness uncommon among secular demoniacs. But his idea of good was also supernatural and metaphysical, and in the end, it saved him."[36]

Sister Jeanne, the bovarist, was inspired by the pious example of Surin to envision herself as a saint, and although this conversion was not instantaneous, finally even Behemoth, the last of her seven devils, agreed to disappear after she made a pilgrimage to the tomb of St. Francis. The journey was triumphant and included audiences with Richelieu, Queen Anne, and Louis XIII, but soon Jeanne was forced to return to the humdrum existence of convent life.

Although Huxley resists a purely comic treatment of Jeanne's later years, he fully recognizes her as a foolish figure with whom we cannot identify but only judge from the outside. Grandier and Surin, on the other hand, are tragic figures in whose lives we can participate; and just as he attempted, through graphic description, to make his readers respond to the torment of Grandier, Huxley strives for similar results in the presentation of Surin's torments and release.

Besieged at intervals by an inability to speak or to walk and by an extreme weakness that made the simple removal of a shirt excruciatingly painful, Surin waged a war of union with God through the eradication of nature. Slowly, he sank further and further into a belief that he was irrevocably damned. Tempted by suicide and harassed by those around him, Surin resigned himself to further humiliation until finally, in 1648, a Father Bastide rescued him through simple kindness and charity. Slowly, he recovered from his physical and mental ills and even managed, shortly before his death, to respond to the external world which he had denied for so long. He even recorded in his journal that

> on a number of occasions my soul was invested with these states of glory, and the sunlight seemed to grow incomparably brighter than

usual, and yet was so soft and bearable that it seemed to be of another kind than natural sunlight. Once when I was in this state, I went out into the garden of our college at Bordeaux; and so great was this light that I seemed myself to be walking in paradise.[37]

Thus, in his last years, Surin achieved the kind of peace that Huxley so earnestly sought for himself and his fellow man.

The "Appendix" contains further amplification of the concepts of transcendence originally presented in Chapter Three and, as such, stands between Huxley's vision in *The Perennial Philosophy* (1945) and his attitude in *The Doors of Perception* (1954).[38] The major emphasis here is on the failure of those "grace substitutes", alcohol, excessive sexuality, drugs, and crowd delirium, through which men constantly try to escape the pain of being merely themselves, and of these, it is crowd delirium which commands most of his attention. If there had been no exorcists to incite the demonic orgies of Sister Jeanne and the Ursulines, then Grandier would not have been executed, but the superstitions which created crowd hysteria in this particular instance are insignificant compared to the methods of the present age.

Everyone now knows how to read and everyone consequently is at the mercy of the propagandists, governmental or commercial, who own the pulp factories, the linotype machines and the rotary presses. Assemble a mob of men and women previously conditioned by a daily reading of newspapers; treat them to amplified band music, bright lights and the oratory of a demagogue who (as demagogues always are) is simultaneously the exploiter and the victim of herd-intoxication, and in next to no time you can reduce them to a state of almost mindless subhumanity. Never before have so few been in a position to make fools, maniacs or criminals of so many.[39]

The Devils of Loudun, in the final analysis, is not merely an embellished biography or a chronicle of certain aspects of seventeenth century life; it is an apocalyptic statement which fuses biography, fiction, and essay to warn about present trends that can lead to world destruction, and to instruct people in the quest for the alternative "divine peace" which comes from upward self-transcendence.

John Whiting's *The Devils* opened at the Aldwych Theatre in London, on February 20, 1961, and the British critics, many of whom had been grossly unfair to Whiting's previous work, hailed his last major effort as a near masterpiece.[40] Although commissioned by the Royal Shakespeare Company and based on Huxley's book, the play reflects the playwright's continuing concern with the theme of self-destruction, and with the solving of problems of dramatic structure. In fact, in an interview with Tom Milne and Clive Goodwin,

Whiting himself chose this particular play on which to focus while discussing the difficulties in writing plays.

> The story is elementarily simple. A rakish and libertine priest of great charm, high intelligence—well, he wasn't but I've made him so—has his women, has power. He is handsome, reasonably rich, and up at the convent there is this lunatic, this crazy mother, who suddenly begins to have terrible ideas that Beelzebub is lodged in her stomach, or in her lower bowel, or something like that and is speaking with the voice of the priest. The situation is simply that local superstition—politics, fear, revenge—all subscribe to the fact that people come to believe it, and he is arrested, tried and burned. Now, that's all it is. Well, I mean this could all be put down on half a page. But the thing is a play, somebody's got to say something and therefore one has got to find the significant points in it, and a shape. Where do you start? Well, I have started in the gutter, I mean literally in the gutter, and the play gets up out of it. That's the overall shape, but how do you do it? You have to do it by a series of steps. Now these steps again are not important, except to the very few people who want to know how these things are written. The public is not concerned with the finesse of making a play or a chair or anything else. It merely wants a serviceable article which will do a certain thing—and that can be anything, it can frighten them, or stimulate them or work them into a frenzy of rage: all these things are perfectly permissible.[41]

The shape that Whiting imposes on his material then evolves from the role of the Sewerman, who of course is not found in Huxley's account (since drains did not exist in Loudun) but who is clearly drawn from the realm of theatrical conventions. His most common function is to listen to Grandier and thus remove any awkward dependence on monologues, but he is also a probing character who harkens back to the grave digger in *Hamlet*, or even to the stock figure of the court jester who can question and mock with impunity. He is also a symbolic character who establishes the central metaphor of the world as a sewer—a world from which Grandier attempts to raise himself. Finally, this character, the wise and witty everyman of the city, helps to unify this episodic play by commenting on the action—the hanging of the young man, Grandier's marriage, Grandier's moment of mystical ecstasy, and the execution—and by frequently shifting the play's mood between comedy and seriousness.

If the Sewerman and the metaphor of the gutter shaped the overall structure of the play, Whiting, after a few early drafts, was still rather ill at ease with some of the so-called "steps", and his agent, A. D. Peters, sent an early draft to Huxley for advice and reactions. Huxley wrote back a number of suggestions, and it appears from later letters and the final version of the play that Whiting made use of many of them, including one for the first scene.

> An idea for the actual opening has occurred to me. It is this. Cut out the first speech by Grandier altogether. Open with the scene at the city gate. Have the Sewerman (who is a fine Shakespearean character) doing his work. . . . I think you could make a very interesting opening with the aid of corpses hanging from the municipal gibbet. Have Adam and Mannoury casting greedy eyes on the corpses, which they hope to dissect. (This fits in with the later scene, where they have the head of one of the criminals.) Have Philippe Trincant asking her father what they were hanged for, and Trincant telling her that they (or he—for it will be best to have only *one* malefactor) was hanged for debauching a young girl and stealing her jewels. Then have Grandier come in, get into conversation with the Sewerman and begin by informing him that he officiated at the criminal's execution and gave the man absolution and a benediction as he was turned off. He should speak of this in a humane and forgiving way and should comment on the monstrous injustice of hanging a man for an offence motivated by irresistible sexual desire and irresistible hunger. (Perhaps the criminal did not take the girl's jewels—merely stole half a crown after sleeping with her, to buy himself a good meal at a local inn.) This opening will give a certain symmetry to the play—an execution with Grandier at the forgiving end in the first scene and an execution with Grandier as the victim of unforgiving friends at the end—and can be made to enrich the conversation with Sewerman, emphasize Philippe's innocence and purity, and provide a good introduction to two minor, but important characters, Adam and Mannoury.[42]

Huxley's sense of dramatic parallelism may not be strikingly original, but his suggestions supply a sense of structure which Whiting himself knew was lacking. Even these parallel scenes and significant metaphors, however, do not entirely rescue the play from the verge of chaos. The texture, density and scope of the material, the 50 scenes in a three-act play, the cast of 23 characters (excluding townspeople, people from the country, priests, nuns, and soldiers), and the loose, episodic presentation created problems Whiting had not encountered in his previous plays.

Like many of his contemporaries, Whiting perhaps owed something of his new found freedom to the growing influence of Brecht in England; but probably his own version of "Epic Theatre" was more deeply indebted to the influence of film script writing.[43] The play reads, at times, so much like a film script that one expects to encounter the words "cut to" or "dissolve to" separating short scenes. At times it seems that Whiting solved some of his difficulties by finding theatrical equivalents for predominantly cinematic devices. For instance, D'Armagnac and Grandier discuss the fortifications of Loudun on one side of the stage while a Council of State with Louis XIII and Richelieu takes place on another area of the stage. What occurs is a theatrical version of cross-cutting. Russell realized this, and when he adapted this particular section for his film, he merely followed most of Whiting's dialogue and cross-cut Grandier's appeal to the people with Richelieu's appeal to the king.

Like Huxley then, Whiting used a variety of methods and generic conventions to handle themes, characters, and the broad scope of the material covered, but he did so for his own purposes rather than in imitation of Huxley's method. Unlike Huxley, who attempted through allusions and digressions to relate his major concepts to twentieth century life, Whiting used his knowledge of theatrical history to place his play within an ambience of the past. His language shows that he knows the works of Webster and Tourner; and the sudden juxtaposition of farce with tragedy, which might jolt some modern sensibilities, is simply a convention of medieval mystery cycles, in which the author indulged comic or realistic inclinations along with sacred concerns.[44]

Although his play deals with self-transcendence, the theme so basic to Huxley, Whiting is not really concerned with Huxley's vision or with his message for the future. Rather he is concerned with what he interprets as Grandier's obsession with self-destruction, and the contrast between his method and that of Sister Jeanne des Anges in seeking a meaning to life. Also, for dramatic purposes Whiting limits Huxley's scope, since he cannot include the stories of both Grandier and Surin.

It is wrong, however, to view the play as presenting Grandier as the major character with Sister Jeanne des Anges as the mere catalyst for action. John Russell Taylor claims that Jeanne is reduced to a commonplace and historically incredible character instead of emerging in the central focus.

> The choice of Grandier as centerpiece is obviously deliberate (again, the theme is self-destruction) and the re-distribution of dramatic emphasis consequent upon it is deliberate, but that does not prevent one thinking it basically wrong, since it makes the material seem that much less interesting than intrinsically it is.[45]

This observation ignores much of the tension basic to the play, since Whiting contrasts Grandier's failed quest for meaning through sensation with Jeanne's ascetic denials, which only succeed in spawning her erotic obsessions and fantasies. In order to achieve this tension, however, Whiting significantly alters some of the characters and events as described in Huxley's account.

The opening scenes of the play introduce most of the important characters and present various conflicting attitudes toward Grandier, who quickly emerges not as a man with a unified sensibility bent on achieving the best of the spiritual and sensual worlds, but as a tortured captive of his own passions in the web of the physical world that defined his existence.

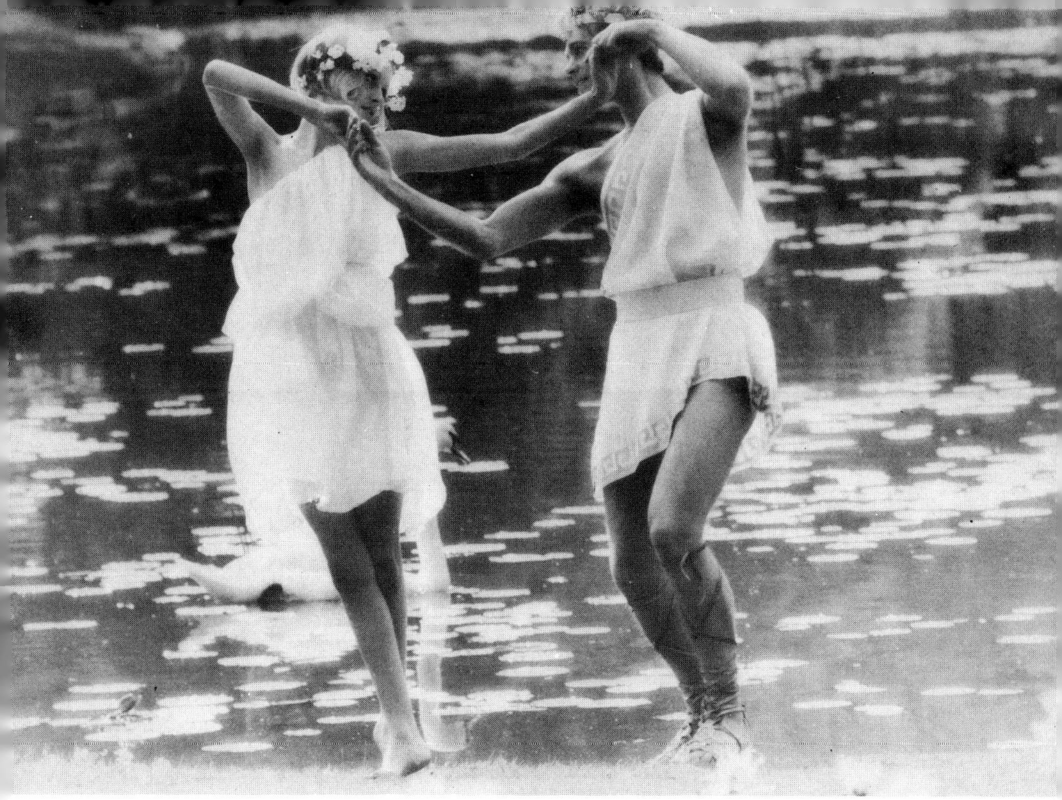

Arcadian idyll – cut from film – *The Boyfriend*

"I could be happy with you if you could be happy with me" – Ken Russell and Twiggy rehearse for *The Boyfriend*

"Fade out on a butchered sequence" – *The Boyfriend*

Tommy Tune teaches Twiggy the hornpipe – *The Boyfriend*

Possessed nuns raving it up in *The Devils*

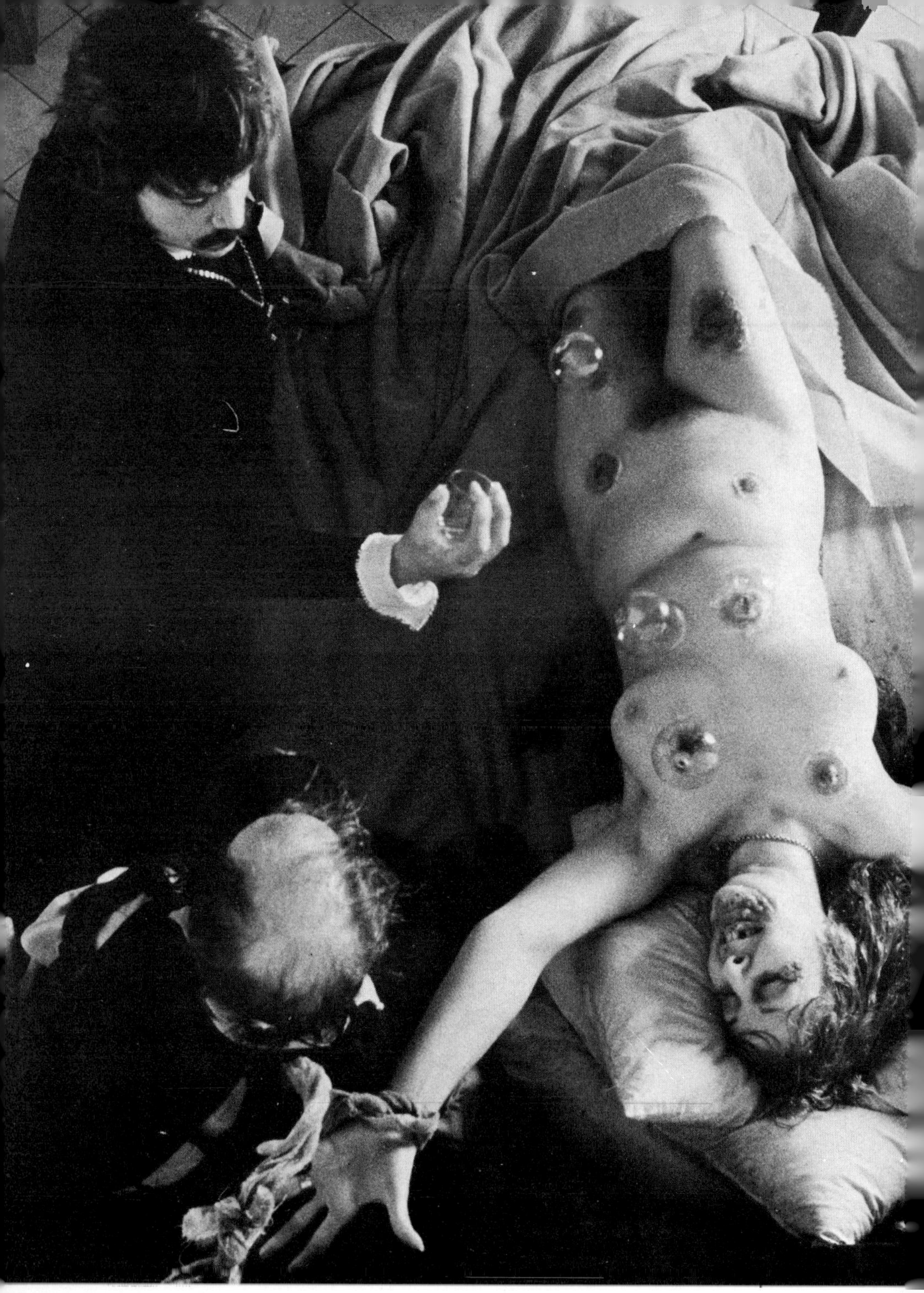

Church versus medical science to save plague victim – *The Devils*

Sister Jeanne (Vanessa Redgrave) at home – *The Devils*

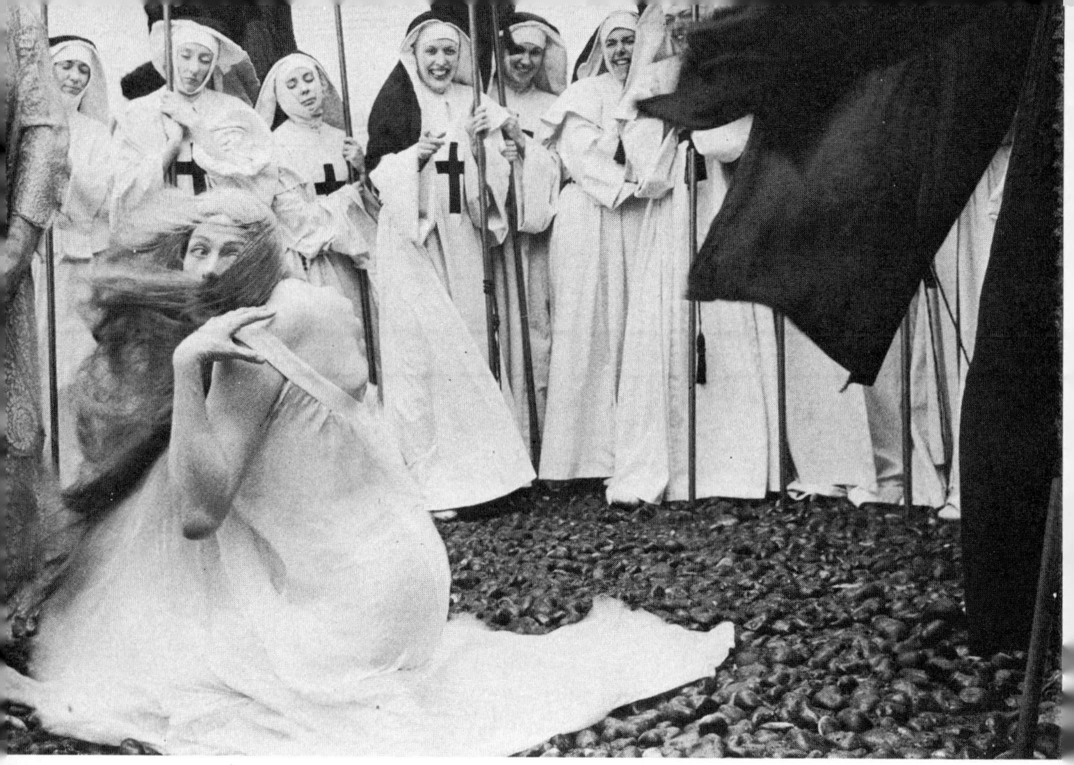

Sister Jeanne dreams of her deformity – *The Devils*

Ken Russell praying for sun in *The Devils*

Driving out the Devils in the Ursuline Convent – *The Devils*

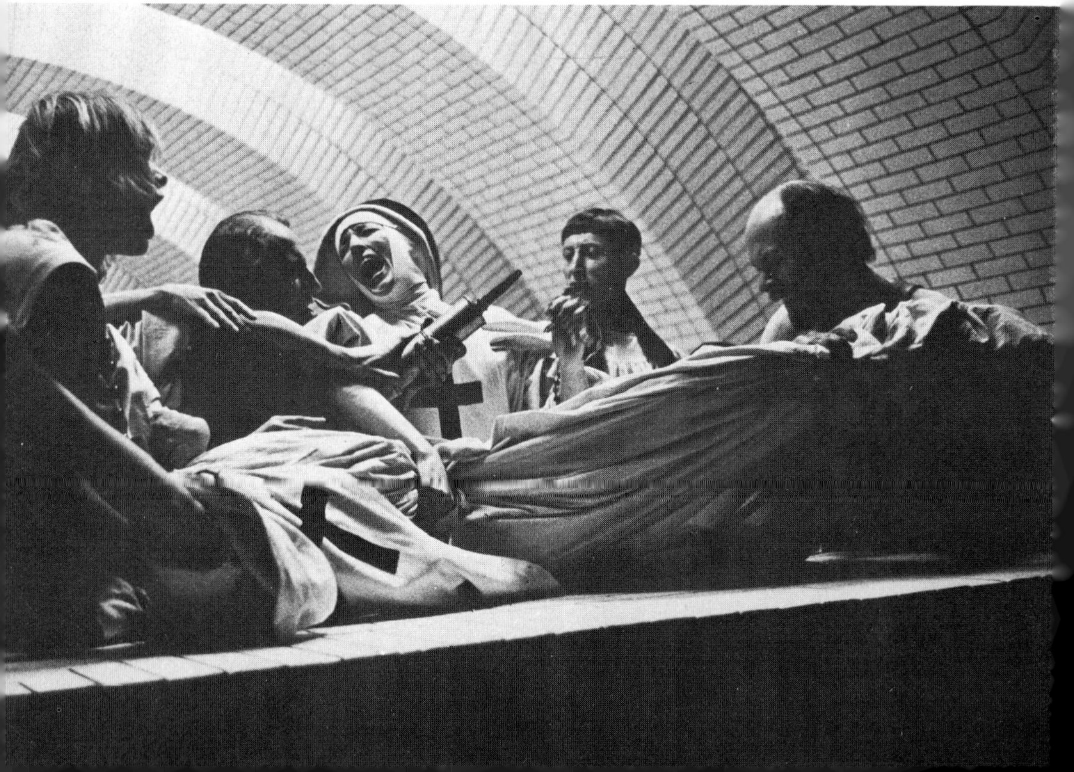

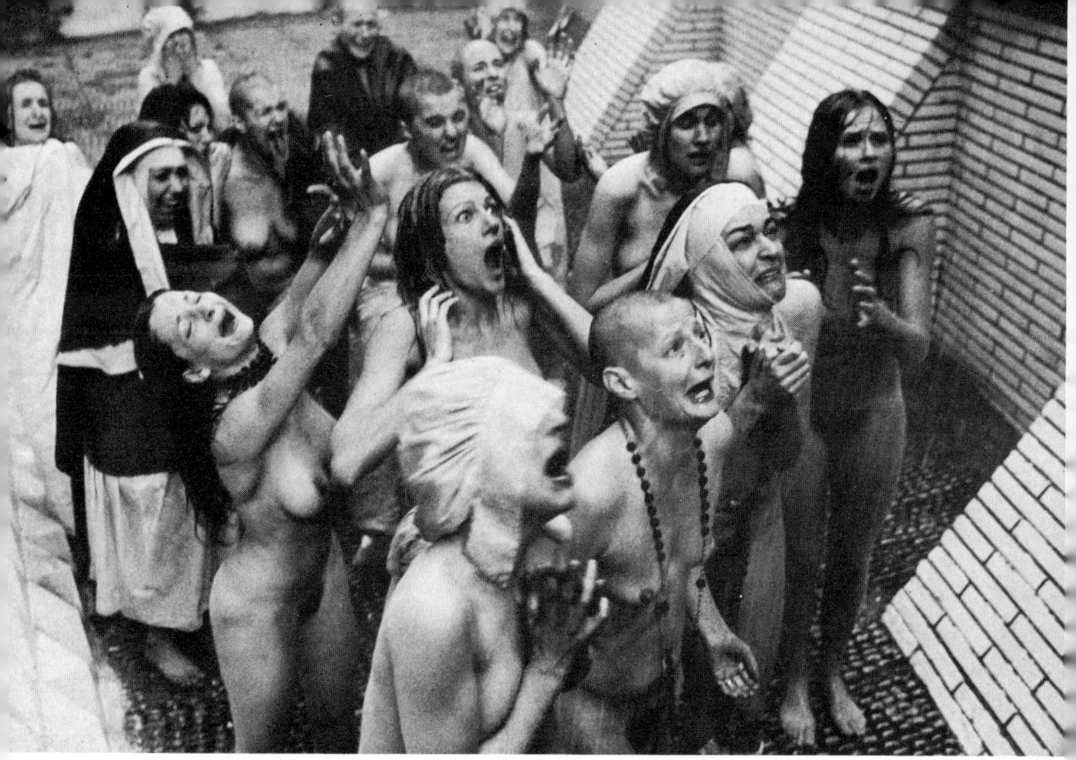

The Sisters watch the Mother Superior's attempted suicide – *The Devils*

Sister Jeanne's prayers are mocked – *The Devils*

Despair at the execution – *The Devils*

"Love versus lust" – Dorothy Tutin as Sophie Brzeska and Scott Anthony as Henri Gaudier in *Savage Messiah*

Oliver Reed as Urbain Grandier in *The Devils*

Ken and Shirley Russell at the opening of *Savage Messiah* in New York 1972

Ken Russell's sons, Alex and James Russell, as extras in *Savage Messiah*

Scott Antony as Henri Gaudier in *Savage Messiah*

Ken Russell's sons, Xavier and Toby Russell as extras in *Savage Messiah*

"Artist with flowers" – Scott Antony as Henri Gaudier in *Savage Messiah*

Ken Russell's daughter, Victoria Russell, in *Savage Messiah*

Madonna and Child carved on rifle butt – "Life in Death" – *Savage Messiah*

"Art is Revolution" – Scott Antony as Henri Gaudier airs his views in *Savage Messiah*

Nude study with pneumatic drill – *Savage Messiah*

> Grandier: O my dear Father, it is the wish of your humble child to come to Your Grace. I speak in the weariness of thirty-five years. Years heavy with pride and ambition, love of women and love of self. Years scandalously marred by adornment and luxury, time taken up with being that nothing, a man.
>
> I prostrate myself before You now in ravaged humility of spirit. I ask you to look upon me with love. I beg that You will answer my prayer. Show me a way. Or let a way be made.
>
> *Silence*
>
> O God, O my God, my God! Release me. Free me. These needs! Have mercy. Free me. Four o'clock of a Tuesday afternoon. Free me.[46]

A few scenes later, the audience encounters Grandier's counterpart, Jeanne of the Angels, who has withdrawn from the physical world but who also, in the form of a monologue prayer, seeks release from the prison of the self.

> Jeanne: . . . You have brought meaning to my life by my appointment to this Ursuline house. . . . Lord, I have had great difficulty with prayer ever since I was a little girl. I have longed for another and greater voice within me to praise you. By Your Grace I have come young to this office. Have mercy on Your child. Let her aspire. Meanwhile, the floors shall be swept, the beds neatly made, and the pots kept clean.
>
> (*Silence*) Mercy. (*Silence*) I will find a way. Yes, I will find a way to You. I shall come. You will enfold me in Your sacred arms. The blood will flow between us, uniting us. My innocence is Yours.
>
> (*Silence: precisely*) Please God, take away my hump so I can lie on my back without lolling my head. (*silence*) There is a way to be found. May the light of Your eternal love . . . (whispers)
>
> Amen.[47]

Once this tension is established, Whiting reinforces it by taking historical personages from Huxley's account and redefining their characters and/or their roles in the tragic events at Loudun. For instance, in both accounts, De La Rochepozay is hostile to Grandier and his cause, but whereas Huxley sees him as a scholar aristocrat who hated Huguenots and who simply believed that the powerful Grandier should be taught a lesson, Whiting's character is a Surin-like figure, an ascetic mystic who rejects any idea of innocence, kindness, and goodness in man, and who sees the ascendency of the devil in any assertion of selfhood.

The next scenes supply the advancement of Grandier's romance with Philippe (Whiting changes the spelling of "Philippe" to "Philippe") and the forging of his political link with D'Armagnac against Richelieu, but some uneasy aspects begin to manifest themselves in Whiting's treatment. D'Armagnac's relationship with Grandier lacks the dimensions of warmth and friendship suggested in Huxley's account. Instead, Whiting's Grandier chooses to side with the Governor in order to help bring about his own destruction. "So let me help you with all the passion of my failure."[48] Whiting mentions nothing of the personal animosity between Grandier and Richelieu, and Grandier's response at this point seems too direct. True, a play must condense, but by cutting down Grandier's vanity and pride, and, by overemphasizing a quest for transcendence that all too quickly becomes identified with a will to self-destruction, Whiting creates a character of limited interest—a character who may sustain himself on an individual level but who fails miserably as an artistic creation functioning on social, political, and historical levels.

Whiting's further presentation of Jeanne also offers some difficulties Thus far, Jeanne has been seen only briefly, and when after Canon Moussaut's death she remarks that there is a young priest named Grandier whom God has put into her thoughts lately, one feels slightly startled. The jump from the opening monologue to the request that Grandier become the new spiritual director is simply too great; and the next short scene, in which Jeanne screams out and only Grandier passing by in the streets hears her, confuses rather than clarifies. Why, for instance, have Jeanne's obsessions led her to choose Grandier? Huxley supplies a number of reasons; Whiting supplies none.

In a first act of 26 scenes, Whiting establishes the situation and the forces which will eventually bring about Grandier's downfall and death, but he does so in such a manner that his two major characters suffer from lack of development and dimension. All seems to be sacrificed for the creation of Jeanne and Grandier as counterpart figures driven by the need for self-transcendence and/or self-destruction.

Whiting continues his particular manipulation of his sources in Act II with the marriage of Phillipe and Grandier. This is the result of combining the characters and functions of Madeleine de Brou and Philippe. Such action could be defended on the grounds of necessary condensation, but the change is also related to the themes of transcendence and self-destruction. Huxley's Grandier found love and peace with Madeleine de Brou and never retreated from his feelings towards her. Whiting's Grandier talks about love, but instead he attempts to reach salvation through a relationship with another human being. The love for Phillipe is merely a means to a greater end, and Grandier makes this position quite clear when he discusses his marriage with the irreverent Sewerman:

> Grandier: Hope of coming to God by way of a fellow being. Hope that the path, which taken alone, in awful solitude, is a way of despair, can be enlightened by the love of a woman. I have come to believe that by the simple act of committal, which I have done with my heart, it may be possible to reach God by way of happiness.[49]

The marriage of Phillipe and Grandier is immediately followed by the purging of Asmodeus from Sister Jeanne's lower bowel, and the suggested contrast is obvious. Grandier's passion leads him to seek his goal through union with a woman. Sister Jeanne's sexual obsession leads her to hysteria and an imagined union with devils.

Jeanne's failure to transcend her ordinary self is quickly evident, and Grandier confesses failure shortly thereafter when he leaves the pregnant Phillipe, but the carefully detailed psychological portrait of the seduction and abandonment found in Huxley's account is again reduced in the play to the conscious motive of self-destruction.

> D'Armagnac: You don't make it easy for your friends, Grandier. Trincant has told me about his daughter. You have your whores. Why did you have to do this?
>
> Grandier: It seemed a way.
>
> D'Armagnac: A way to what?
>
> Grandier: All worldly things have a single purpose for a man of my kind. Politics, power, the senses, riches, pride and authority. I choose them with same care that you, sir, select a weapon. But my intention is different. I need to turn them against myself.
>
> D'Armagnac: To bring about your end?
>
> Grandier: Yes. I have a great need to be united with God. Living has drained the need for life from me. My exercise of the senses has flagged to total exhaustion. I am a dead man, compelled to live.
>
> D'Armagnac: You disgust me. This is a sickness.
>
> Grandier: No, sir. It is the meaning and purpose.[50]

Grandier's quest for death is tempered, however, by the fears of being forsaken or of dying in an insignificant manner. Like Sister Jeanne, he understands that power and love are delusions and that "loneliness and death" are all life offers unless one is able to push beyond somehow. Jeanne's escape "beyond" into a convenient and comfortable hysteria is pitiable, but Grandier's conscious efforts at self-destruction, as presented by Whiting, become annoying.

> D'Armagnac: You are in danger.
>
> Grandier: Thank God.[51]

The last half of the second act deals with the return of Father Barré after the ordinance against exorcisms has been lifted, but since, unlike Huxley's, Whiting's Grandier refuses to defend himself, it becomes necessary for Henri de Condé to serve as the articulate spokesman of Grandier's cause. Whiting attributes an incident in which a visiting nobleman tested the "truth" of the possession through a box of supposedly holy relics to de Condé and even has him eloquently defend the accused priest to Louis and Richelieu in a Council of State. De Condé, however, according to Huxley, was a sodomite prince of royal blood "who combined the most sordid avarice with an exemplary piety. In politics he had once been an anti-Cardinalist, but now that Richelieu's position seemed impregnable, he had become the most fawning of His Eminence's sycophants."[52] For him, there was no doubt as to the "truth" of the possession.

From the larger social and political considerations, Whiting quickly returns at the end of the second act to the development of Grandier, who reveals his latest epiphany to the ever-convenient Sewerman. After being unable to find God through a creative union with another human being, Grandier encounters God in terms of his own being.

> Grandier: I created Him from the light and the air, from the dust of the road, from the sweat of my hands, from gold, from filth, from the memory of women's faces, from great rivers, from children, from the works of man, from the past, the present, the future and the unknown. I caused Him to be from fear and despair. I gathered in everything from this mighty act, all I have seen and experienced. My sin, my presumption, my vanity, my love, my hate, my lust. And I gave myself and so made God. And he was magnificent. For He is all these things.[53]

Act III, however, brings back most of the doubts and fear that have haunted Grandier in the past. With his arrest, the epiphany of the morning vanishes, and with literal night, Grandier endures his dark night of the soul.

> Grandier: . . . This need to create a meaning. What arrogance it is! Expendable, that's what we are. Nothing proceeding to nothing.
>
> Let me look into this void. Let me look into myself. Is there one thing, past or present, which makes for a purpose? (*silence*) Nothing. Nothing.[54]

For the critic Charles Lyons, this speech is perhaps the most crucial in the play, since in it Grandier sees that both the universe and the self are a void and that God and the void are "qualities of his own being. However, God in this sense, is an imaginative construction—in Whiting's sense, a palliative delusion obscuring the present reality or the void."[55] Such an interpretation fails to consider the impact of the visit by Father Ambrose, who convinces Grandier that since he has lived by his senses, he must die by them. As a result, Grandier redefines his quest for meaning in orthodox Christian terms.

> Ambrose: Let Him reveal Himself in the only way you can understand.
>
> Grandier: Yes! Yes!
>
> Ambrose: It is all any of us can do. We live a little while, and in that little while we sin. We go to Him as we can. All is forgiven.
>
> Grandier: Yes. I am His child. It is true. Let Him take me as I am. So there is meaning after all. I am a sinful man and I can be accepted. It is not nothing going to nothing. It is sin going to forgiveness. It is a human creature going to love.[56]

Whereas Grandier finds salvation in this unexpected manner, Sister Jeanne only plunges further downward into depths where she can find neither God nor man. Grandier's last words, "Look at this thing which I am, and learn the meaning of love",[57] have no meaning to her now.

Although keeping the basic facts and at times some of the significant metaphors from Huxley's *The Devils of Loudun*, Whiting frequently departs from his source in order to serve his own purposes. Thus, instead of being a gifted figure very much a product of his times, Grandier becomes a rather unique character embodying the author's preoccupation with the theme of self-destruction. Minor characters, such as D'Armagnac, de Condé, and Mlle. de Brou, are then altered or dropped in an attempt to develop further this basic theme. The end result is that the center of the play cannot hold, and the awkward scenes which try to deal with the social and political dimensions seem curiously disengaged from those presenting Grandier's fate. As Simon Trussler accurately notes,

> There are really two plays here—sometimes separately identifiable, as if the scenes have just got jumbled together, but more often as if the naturalistic hero from one play has got involved with other kinds of characters altogether.[58]

Much of the success of the play comes from the vibrant and impressive prose, but even here, there is a notable drawback. Grandier's eloquence is too severely limited by the over-extending theme of self-destruction, and thus de Condé and D'Armagnac are forced into becoming his articulate mouthpiece. Finally, Sister Jeanne, clearly a counterpart figure to Grandier, is unable to support the thematic and structural weight placed upon her.

Whiting's attempt to adapt Huxley's *The Devils of Loudun* to a dramatic form remains unconvincing to a great extent because the major themes and discernible tone of the original are sacrificed. Ken Russell's film version is extraordinary in that it employs much of the impressive dialogue from the play in order to adapt Huxley's book to the screen, in a manner consistent with the dominant themes and tone of the original, and yet in a manner allowing for the expression of Russell's own unique vision and methods.

NOTES

[1]Aldous Huxley, *Letters of Aldous Huxley,* ed. Grover Smith (New York: Harper and Row, 1969, London: Chatto and Windus, 1969), p. 641.

[2]Cited in Roger Manvell, "You Can Go to *The Devils*", *Humanist,* 86 (November 1971), p. 333.

[3]*Ibid.*

[4]Cited in "*The Devils*", *Filmfacts,* 14 (1971), p. 340.

[5]*Ibid.,* p. 339.

[6]*Ibid.*

[7]Tom Milne, "*The Devils*", *Monthly Film Bulletin,* 38 (August 1971), p. 162.

[8]Cited in *Filmfacts,* p. 339.

[9]See Roger Manvell, "You Can Go to *The Devils*", pp. 331–3; and Michael Dempsey, "The World of Ken Russell", *Film Quarterly,* 25 (Spring 1972), pp. 13–25.

[10]This project never materialized.

[11]Huxley, *Letters,* p. 931.

[12]*Ibid.,* p. 682.

[13]See George Woodcock, *Dawn and the Darkest Hour: A Study of Aldous Huxley* (New York: Viking, 1972, London: Faber, 1972), p. 218. Although Huxley never really established connections in the film industry, he was often well paid for his work and, considering the circumstances, was reasonably active. He began his frequently fruitless role as a scriptwriter in 1938, with a screenplay for a film biography of Madame Curie. He also worked on the scripts of *Pride and Prejudice* and *Jane Eyre.* The projects that he really desired to undertake (a film on the life of Gandhi and adaptations of *Brave New World* and *The Devils of Loudun*) never stood much of a chance. Hollywood producers found his ideas too literary, and even Walt Disney refused his outline for *Alice in Wonderland* on these grounds.

[14]J. M. Cohen, "The Devil and His Works", *Spectator,* 3 October 1952, p. 440.

[15]Anne Fremantle, "Faith Ruptured", *Saturday Review,* 22 November 1952, p. 15.

[16]Huxley, *Letters,* p. 896.

[17]*Ibid.*

[18]Aldous Huxley, *The Devils of Loudun* (1952; rpt. New York: Harper and Row, 1971, London: Chatto and Windus, 1970), p. 278.

[19]Woodcock, p. 285.

[20]Huxley, *Letters*, p. 607.

[21]*Ibid.*, p. 910.

[22]Aldous Huxley, *Grey Eminence* (New York: Harper, 1941, London: Chatto and Windus, 1941).

[23]Aldous Huxley, *Ape and Essence* (New York: Harper, 1948).

[24]Woodcock, p. 246.

[25]Huxley, *The Devils of Loudun*, p. 4.

[26]*Ibid.*, p. 42.

[27]*Ibid.*, p. 31.

[28]*Ibid.*, pp. 38-9.

[29]*Ibid.*, pp. 47–8.

[30]*Ibid.*, p. 75.

[31]*Ibid.*, p. 124.

[32]*Ibid.*, pp. 133–4.

[33]*Ibid.*, p. 173.

[34]*Ibid.*, p. 192.

[35]*Ibid.*, pp. 228–9.

[36]*Ibid.*, p. 260.

[37]*Ibid.*, p. 335.

[38]Aldous Huxley, *The Perennial Philosophy* (New York: Harper, 1945, London: Chatto and Windus, 1969); and Aldous Huxley, *The Doors of Perception* (New York: Harper, 1954).

[39]Huxley, *The Devils of Loudun*, pp. 349–50.

[40]John Whiting (1918–1963) occupied a curious place in the so-called "new drama" in Britain. His relatively small output always managed to be out of touch with the current trend, and his plays touched off extremely hostile critical reactions. *Saint's Day* (1951), for instance, was reviewed by *The Times* as a play "of a badness that must be called indescribable", and this view was echoed by most critics who bothered to review it. See John Russell Taylor, *Anger and After: A Guide to the New British Drama* (Harmondsworth, England: Penguin, 1966), p. 24. Whiting's other plays, *A Penny for a Song* (1951) and *Marching Song* (1954) fared little better critically than *Saint's Day*, and *The Gates of Summer* (1956) never even opened in London. As a result, Whiting voluntarily withdrew from the theatrical scene and devoted his energies to writing screenplays. The favorable critical reaction to *The Devils* (1961), Whiting's return to theater, however, was just short of overwhelming.

[41]John Whiting, "John Whiting: An Interview with Tom Milne and Clive Goodwin", *Theatre at Work: Playwrights and Productions in Modern British Theatre*, ed. Charles Marowitz and Simon Trussler (London: Methuen, 1967), p. 28.

[42] Huxley, *Letters,* p. 897.

[43] Whiting's screenplays include: *The Ship That Died of Shame* (1954), *Castle Minerva* (1955), *The Golden Fool* (1956), *Talk of the Devil* (1956), *The Captain's Table* (1957), *The Reason Why* (1957), *The Gypsum Flower* (1958), *The Gentleman of China* (1960), and *Young Cassidy* (1960).

[44] See Murray Rosten, *Biblical Drama in England* (Evanston, Il: Northwestern Univ. Press, 1968), pp. 20–1.

[45] John Russell Taylor, *Anger and After,* pp. 25–6.

[46] John Whiting, *The Devils* (New York: Hill and Wang, 1962, London: Heinemann Educational, 1972), pp. 21–2.

[47] *Ibid.,* pp. 29–30.

[48] *Ibid.,* p. 33.

[49] *Ibid.,* pp. 55–6.

[50] *Ibid.,* p. 73.

[51] *Ibid.,* p. 77.

[52] Huxley, *The Devils of Loudun,* p. 157.

[53] Whiting, *The Devils,* p. 96.

[54] *Ibid.,* p. 102.

[55] Charles R. Lyons, "The Futile Encounter in the Plays of John Whiting", *Modern Drama,* II (December 1968), p. 296.

[56] Whiting, *The Devils,* p. 105.

[57] *Ibid.,* p. 124.

[58] Simon Trussler, "The Plays of John Whiting", *Tulane Drama Review,* II (Winter 1966), p. 150.

7

The Devils—Russell's Major Achievement

The Film

> I am faithful to what I consider the central idea of every character and situation I tackle.
>
> Ken Russell[1]

In a lengthy interview, Terry Curtis Fox asked Russell how much material for *The Devils* (1971) was taken from John Whiting's play and how much from Huxley's book. Russell's offhand reply reveals much about his attitude towards both works. It helps to support the claim that he was chiefly concerned with the dominant themes of the Huxley account and only employed the Whiting version as a means to return to the earlier treatment:

> It's very difficult to say offhand. I'd say there's about a third from the play, but some of that is superimposed over Huxley, anyway. I suppose mainly Huxley for the atmosphere. I thought the play was rather sentimental. When I first saw it in 1961, I was knocked out by it. Dorothy Tutin played Sister Jeanne, and she was wonderful. Then I read it again just before I started the screenplay. It was very good dialogue, but I thought it evaded the central issue. I thought it soft-centred; it wasn't hard enough.[2]

Russell's approach to the film has been considered a bit too hard for some, but he is quick to remind people that he toned down much of the torments described by Huxley in the original. Russell's film, like Huxley's book, is really a message for the present, and the individual tragedy of Grandier is clearly linked to larger religious and political issues. The subject itself is a perfect one for Russell, in part, because the so-called visual excess of his style at last found especially appropriate content. The theatricality found in all of his films was quite suitable for the reinforcement of key themes, and the bizarre Russell sense of humor found some parallels in both the Huxley and Whiting accounts. Finally, the film found imaginative equivalents to Huxley's method of transcending form: in *The Devils,* Russell combines various art forms to present his vision, and this vision, although very much his own, does more justice to Huxley's concerns than Whiting's play manages to do.

Huxley's work deals not with historical documentation for its own sake; instead, it employs such material to emphasize the biography as a prophetic work dealing with trends in our own time. Russell's film does much the same thing, but with methods many find confusing or revolting. Russell wants his audience to make connections to present day realities, but he also desires that they root themselves in the truth of the events. Grandier's sufferings were not a de Sadian fantasy refiltered through the imagination of the director. They were real, and therefore, a message appears on the screen even before the film's prologue. "This film is based on historic fact. The principal characters lived and the major events depicted in the film actually took place." This announcement for many seems merely a practical joke, but Russell wishes the audience to take it seriously—especially since his biographies are often attacked as inaccurate. The key words in Russell's message are "major events". These indeed did take place; it is the "minor events" which have a basis only in possibility.

Such a minor event is in the court masque which forms the "Prologue" of the film. Russell's research into the court life of the effeminate King, Louis XIII, showed that the masque became popular at court in France during the 1600's and that both Louis XIII and his wife frequently partook in such performances.[3] This information provides the exaggerated situation in the prologue, in which Louis (Graham Armitage) is the central figure in a court masque depicting Botticelli's painting, *The Birth of Venus*, while various members of the court dressed in drag cavort through the audience and gossip. This portrayal is quite functional, however. It provides a stunning visual delineation of the decadence of the court and establishes the theatrical-carnival motif which pervades the entire film. This motif, in turn, is linked to allusions to the plague which exists in the city, both in literal and metaphorical terms, and which Russell employs, not unlike Whiting's less successful employment of the Sewerman, as a controlling structural metaphor.

Aside from appropriately exhibiting the decadence of the court (sexual aberration fittingly opens a film emphasizing sexual indulgence and frustration), the prologue also links the court's moral corruption with the Church. On the visual level, the linkage occurs in shots of courtiers kissing the nuns assigned to assist the physically rotting Cardinal Richelieu (Christopher Logue), and in the cross-cutting between the performing Louis and the bored Richelieu. But dialogue reinforces the linkage emphatically. Richelieu is carried forward to praise the King's originality and to offer assistance in another original creation: "I pray that I may assist you in the birth of a new France in which Church and State are one." The title credit then appears over close-ups of their faces, immediately establishing who in Russell's mind are the real devils.

Richelieu's left-handed sign of the cross to the words "And may the Protestant be driven from the land" again reinforces this sense of a perverse union of politics and religion, and provides Russell with the opportunity, through shock cutting, to show the effects of this pronouncement. There is a cut to a close-up of a decayed corpse with maggots streaming out of eye and mouth openings. A pull-back dolly then reveals that this corpse is tied to a wagon wheel suspended from a long pole. Other such poles form a major part of the *mise-en-scène* as Laubardemont (Dudley Sutton), the executor of this unholy policy sanctioned by Cardinal and King, moves his men toward the walled city of Loudun, which is barely seen in the distance.

Russell then cuts to a long shot of Urbain Grandier (Oliver Reed) against the white brick background of the almost futuristic St. Peter's Church. In fact, the architecture of the entire city is anachronistic—intentionally so, since Russell's film is about a past which warns us about the present and possible future. As such, the anachronisms begin a filmic working out of Huxley's numerous references to twentieth century life—a visual embodiment of perhaps the most crucial aspect of Huxley's *The Devils of Loudun*.

Grandier's first words clearly establish him as the dominant figure in opposition to the policies of Louis and Richelieu: "The religious wars are over. Catholic no longer fights with Protestant." His oration reveals his plan to carry on the ideals of the "late lamented governor". The elaborate *mise-en-scène* (the body laid out in splendor amidst a multitude of large crosses and black banners) and the constantly dollying camera also assist in establishing a marked visual contrast to the preceding sequence, with its maggot-ridden corpses tied to wheels.

In Russell's film, Sainte-Marthe is given the position of governor, and D'Armagnac is eliminated altogether from the script. The real Scevole Sainte-Marthe had never been a governor; he was Loudun's most famous personage, a poet and historian of wide fame who was charmed enough by the cleverness and intelligence of Grandier to welcome him as a frequent house guest. In 1623, Sainte-Marthe died, and Grandier eloquently delivered his funeral oration before the notables of Loudun and the surrounding area.[4] Russell's changes here are significant; he uses an incident grounded in fact, the funeral oration for Sainte-Marthe, but molds it to his specific purpose. Russell's Grandier is a dynamic figure whose motivations for certain actions, such as his attempt to save the walls surrounding the inner city of Loudun, stem from genuine political concerns, and to emphasize this view, Russell dispenses with D'Armagnac so that Grandier can be given full power as governor until a new election is held. Huxley and Whiting, however, interpret Grandier's attempt to save the city's walls in ways rather different from Russell's. Huxley's Grandier loves a good fight and joins D'Armagnac against the forces of Richelieu, in part because of a bond of friendship with the Governor. Whiting's Grandier, on the other hand, responds because of his single-minded preoccupation with the possibility of self-destruction.

The political stature of Grandier during the funeral oration is further enhanced through the functional camera movement, which reinforces the significance of the content of the speech. The camera dollies to Sainte-Marthe's bier for a medium close-up of the body, then swings away to the left before rising upward to encompass the walls which stand only through the "wisdom and humanity" of the deceased Governor. The walls dominate the right side of the screen with Grandier full left. Like his friend, Grandier will attempt to preserve these walls, but physical protection is not enough. The people of Loudun "must build a temple in their hearts". It is here that they fail, and therefore must perish along with the city's walls.

The funeral oration closes with a close-middle shot of Grandier blessing the congregation, an action which, at this point in the film, invites comparison to Richelieu's perverse sign of the cross after the court masque, and which also serves as a repeated visual motif throughout the film. After Grandier descends the stairs to lead the procession, he casually roughs the hair of the altar boys who stand behind Canon Mignon (Murray Melvin). They quickly leave Mignon in order to hold the flowing robes of Grandier, as the snubbed priest casts an indignant glance about him. In Huxley's account, Grandier once snubbed the future Cardinal Richelieu in a similar manner, and thus animosity was clearly a motive for Richelieu's role in the proceedings against this priest. For Russell, however, the actions of Richelieu against Grandier are motivated by political considerations, and thus he slightly distorts this event to supply further motivation to Canon Mignon, a man of secondary qualities who was always forced to stand in the shadow of Grandier.

Finally, Russell presents a number of shots of Grandier leading the procession in the position of honor in order to establish a type of structural unity. This funeral cortège parallels the death journey near the end of the film when Grandier, again the center of attention, is dragged through the same streets to his execution.

Huxley, with the freedom of an extended prose narrative, revealed his characters only as it became necessary or desirable for him to do so. Whiting, given the more limiting framework of a two and a half hour play, introduced most of his major characters, minus Jeanne, in a contrived opening scene. Russell's film, however, limited by time but not by space, manages to present the major personages as we need to know them, but again most of the crucial figures are at least introduced early in the film. Even the *mise-en-scène* of the procession sequence in this sense is revealing. On the right side of the screen stands Philippe Trincant (Georgina Hale) watching attentively, and although the audience does not yet know who she is, it becomes evident, if one bothers to notice facial expressions, that there is a connection between her and Grandier. The Ursuline convent is at the top of the hill that Grandier now approaches, and Russell cuts from a shot of this building in the distance to a medium close shot of nuns struggling on a ladder to see Grandier.[5] Sister Agnes (Judith Paris) announces that he is the most beautiful man in the world, as Sister Jeanne (Vanessa Redgrave), head bent to one side, enters the room to scold the sisters for leaving their devotions. Her words, "Satan is ever ready to seduce us with sensual delights", followed by her hysterical laughter, immediately suggest the disordered frame of mind which manifests itself in the fantasy sequence which follows.

Jeanne's face is, at first, framed by the window bars which isolate her from the outside world, but then the camera assumes her perspective as she sees the approaching Grandier and swoons. The image dissolves into her fantasy. The incense becomes the morning mists, and the black banners and crosses from the procession become white banners held by her own nuns as Jeanne (now Mary Magdalene) descends to meet Grandier (Jesus) who is walking on the water towards her. As she wipes his feet with her hair, a whirling wind blows back her dress and reveals her twisted, reptilian hunchback as the camera rapidly pans the distorted, laughing faces of her good sisters.

This sequence becomes the equivalent of Jeanne's first speech in Whiting's play. Only here, she is provided with adequate motivation—the remarks of Sister Agnes, and the gossip of the women on the street watching the procession—for selecting Grandier as the object of her sexual frustration. The fantasy comes from Russell's imagination, but stands strikingly appropriate—not just because Whiting's Jeanne found it easier to address herself to Grandier than to God, but also because a nun is considered spiritually married to

Jesus. "Take away my hump. Take away my hump. Oh Christ! Let me find a way to You. Take me in Your sacred arms. Let the blood flow between us uniting us. Hmmm Grandier!" This fusion in her mind of Jesus and Grandier runs throughout the film, and serves to clarify some of Jeanne's responses, especially her various uses of the large crucifix attached to her rosary.

Immediately after her fantasy, Jeanne clutches her rosary beads and begins to pray in Latin, presumably to be freed from her enslavement to such fantasies, and Russell uses a sound transition to the physical sexual fulfillment of Philippe Trincant, who, naked on top of Grandier, recites bawdy Latin verses. The dialogue is taken almost verbatim from Whiting, but the impact of the scene is quite different. In contrast to both Huxley and Whiting, Russell's Philippe has little innocence or childlike charm, and her strange make-up further suggests that her knowledge of worldly ways need not be attributable to the good priest alone.

The sequence more clearly reveals the less desirable aspects of Grandier's character, however, namely his vanity and blatant egoism. Grandier shifts from the role of lover to cleric without the slightest difficulty when he finds out that Philippe is pregnant. The sequence is a visual working out of the description found in Huxley's account,[6] and Russell again uses the motif of the sign of the cross to assist him. On hearing the news of the pregnancy, Grandier kisses his fingers, makes the sign of the cross on her forehead, and tells her in all honesty that she must bear her cross with Christian fortitude. He then gets up, dresses, combs his hair, and curls his mustache, all the while discussing the possibility of transcending the body. The tension and irony found in the sequence result, for the most part, from the juxtaposition of the dialogue and the deep focus image of Grandier close-up left with Philippe crying and hysterically beating the bed in the background. The sequence ends with Grandier descending his circular staircase—an image which is repeated at various times throughout the film, most noticably when he discusses with Madeleine her vocation in life, and finally just before he is to have his beard and hair shaved off by order of the court.

Grandier's departure from Philippe takes him outside, where he and the viewer are greeted with a vivid picture of corpses being piled on wagons and of fires consuming plague-contaminated possessions. With Madeleine du Brou's (Gemma Jones) request to assist her dying mother, Russell seizes upon the opportunity, like Huxley, to shock his audience concerning the popular practices of seventeenth century medicine, and to engage in vicious caricature. Ibert (Max Adrian) and Adam (Brian Murphy), while discoursing on the Latin etymology of the names of their cures, place hornets in suction jars to sting the plague-stricken woman. A close-up of such a device on one of Madame du Brou's nipples followed by a shot of her plague-marked face successfully jolt and revolt the viewer, but the impact of the shock is carried even further by the frenzied, dissonant music (again appropriately modern), by the sounds of the woman's screams, and by her final, extended death gurgle.

This sequence especially has been singled out by critics as offensive and sadomasochistic. Even some of Russell's admirers have accepted it merely as an extreme example of Russell's preoccupation with the mutability and decay of the physical world.[7] Neither response, however, really tells us very much. First of all, Russell's "shock treatment" is more subtle than most viewers realize. True, his special effects have improved immensely from the skull mask seen in *Dante's Inferno,* but more is created than merely an edited sequence of close-ups of the hornets and the jar over Madame du Brou's breast. It is the use of sound which helps sustain the impact after we no longer see the image, and it is the carefully recorded sound of Grandier's bones cracking and skin sizzling that increases the horror of two later sequences in the film. Secondly, even if the "shock" technique is expertly achieved, the sequence must function in an appropriate manner or risk condemnation as gratuitous violence with no real substance. But the violence in *The Devils* is functional. Like the violence in Huxley's account, it establishes the callousness of an age and its "dance-of-death" atmosphere, and it forces the viewer to consider the so-called progress of civilization in his own age. More than that, however, Russell finds "shock treatment" the only assuredly effective means of reaching a modern audience.

> People are used to watching television and seeing the Korean War or the Vietnam War or Ireland. I think even that, in the end, becomes associated with fantasy. It becomes a fantasy of reality, of hand-held cameras running down the street. That's why I would never do a modern film like that. People have come to expect that sort of violence. They don't stop eating while its going on. I do want to shock people into a sense of awareness.[8]

The sequence depicting the death of Madame du Brou, aside from presenting the hell-like conditions of plague-ridden Loudun, also allows for development of Grandier as the voice of humanism and reason, a voice strong enough to roust out the likes of Ibert, the chemist, and Adam, the surgeon. Finally, it economically affords an introduction to Madeleine; and Grandier's holding of her hand in prayer against a background of flames and death becomes a strangely lyrical moment which foreshadows their future relationship.

The arrival of Philippe's father outside the house quickly changes the mood, and his attack on the self-satisfied Grandier becomes humorous as Trincant's sword breaks against the chemist's stuffed crocodile with which Grandier defends himself.[9] For many, this episode with Trincant, the rantings of Ibert and Adam, King Louis' "Bye, Bye Blackbird" joke, and the treatment of Father Barré are unforgivable violations of tone and mood. These examples, however, are not inconsistent with the tone of the film but rather essential to it. More damaging to Russell's method is the self-indulgent in-joke which follows as Grandier walks away from Trincant and passes a building with the letters RUSSEL (followed by a cross) painted on it to indicate, presumably, that the inhabitants have been afflicted with the plague. It is this kind of "excess" which pushes the film dangerously close to the ludicrous, not the anachronisms, or the mad comedy which intensifies the films horrors.

The next sequence at the open grave of bodies probably owes much to Peter Brook's production of *Marat/Sade*, but it also clearly evokes the mass burials performed in Nazi extermination camps (as shown in Alain Resnais' *Night and Fog*). Aside from the implied link to our present century, however, the sequence further clarifies character motivation. The dialogue between Mignon and Grandier is taken directly from a discussion between Grandier and D'Armagnac in Whiting's play, but the overly self-conscious attitude towards transcendence found in the Whiting version is here undercut by verbal and visual irony. Grandier's remark that he selects worldly things with the same care that "M. Trincant might select a weapon" should recall the sword which broke in half. Also, Grandier's comment that he has "a great need to be united with God" is followed by a smile which brings forth an accusation of blasphemy from Mignon. The remainder of the confrontation in Whiting is deleted by Russell, as the mood of the sequence shifts. For while Mignon and Grandier have been talking, Madeleine has been walking on the other side of the pit, and the close-ups of her and Grandier suggest the beginning of a greater bond between them.

Madeleine's visit to the Ursuline convent to inquire about the possibility of taking the veil serves as a transition sequence, and provides motivation for a later visit, taken from Huxley's account, to see Sister Jeanne; but the immediate result of this first visit is an attempt to seek Grandier's advice, and he quickly convinces her that as an Ursuline or a Carmelite she would be hiding her "light under a bushel". "Your place is here at Loudun; your vocation to give a shining example of wisdom to all those foolish virgins whose thought was only of perishable vanities." These words echo Huxley's account,[10] but they take on additional impact because of the visual devices employed. The innocence of Madeleine is revealed in the detailed close-ups, and her preoccupation with Grandier is suggested by the moving camera which swirls around her as he walks down a circular staircase before leaving to hear confession.

The confession sequence further clarifies Madeleine's innocence, in part through a juxtaposition to Philippe, which entails screen position and costume. Philippe, screen right, in a temper tantrum, fails to observe the ritual of the sacrament, and Grandier must remind her that she is in "a church and not a market place".[11] Madeleine, screen left, appears in a modest dress and veil, and her "confession" is almost an exact quotation of the words in Whiting's play said by Philippe (but in the play, the characters of Philippe and Madeleine are combined). The emphasis, however, remains on Grandier, the priest—blessing the sinner and forgiving through his priestly powers. The visual treatment of this exchange, namely a series of intercut close-ups, is expected, but the long shot of the priest saying Mass immediately after Madeleine accidentally reveals that she is in love with him underscores again Grandier's role as a priest—an important theme for Russell in this film. The rebuff of the flirtatious "sinner" who follows Madeleine serves a number of functions. It allows time for Madeleine to go to Grandier's house, but more importantly, it undercuts the rank lechery which Huxley's account establishes, especially in its depiction of the cruel seduction of Philippe, and gives another example of the priest's wit. Grandier answers the woman who has forgotten her sins (although she just confessed yesterday) with the remark: "If you have forgotten, perhaps God has as well."

There follows a cut to Madeleine praying at Grandier's house. His confrontation with her closely follows Whiting's dialogue, but the sequence again underscores Grandier's conflict visually. His inner thoughts, "Let us find a way to You together", are presented on the soundtrack while the screen image is that of the crucifix in Grandier's house.

Russell then cuts to the crucifix in the Ursuline convent where the nuns are reciting the rosary. Sister Jeanne announces the fifth sorrowful mystery, "The Crucifixion", and suggests appropriate thoughts for meditation as she moves across the floor on her knees towards the life-size statue of her dying savior. The quick shots of her vision of a nail being driven into a palm shock the viewer but also prepare for the day-dream fantasy to follow. Sister Jeanne is again Mary Magdalene, but this time she stands beneath the cross. The crucified Jesus, however, soon becomes Grandier who descends from the cross to have his stigmata kissed and licked by Magdalene-Jeanne and to roll on the ground with her in sexual delight.[12] Jeanne's terror of her own imagination is cross-cut with her vision which finally ends when she realizes that she has ground the end of her rosary's crucifix so deeply into her own palm that it is bleeding profusely.

In the next sequence Grandier and Madeleine discuss, with lighthearted Jesuitical casuistry, the doctrine of celibacy and priestly marriage. The contrast is obvious: the dangerous perversion of Jeanne's sex-starved imagination is set against the wit and casual tenderness of Grandier's moments with Madeleine. Peace and tranquility, however, are rarely allowed Grandier for any sustained period of time, and the calm is shattered by the beginning of the destruction of the walls. Russell's moving camera and visual composition raise this particular sequence from the level of mere plot development. For instance, when Grandier rings the bell and Madeleine assists him, Mignon is in the background and Philippe on the side (in a medium close shot) staring coldly at her new rival. Grandier's triumph in forcing Laubardemont to back down has its counterpart in Huxley's account, but here with the omission of D'Armagnac, Grandier is given full power as the Governor until a new election; and this fact, aside from increasing the political implications, further elevates Grandier's stature. The low angle shot of Trincant, Mignon, and Philippe witnessing the incident will also be repeated at the end of the film when Grandier is executed in exactly the same place as that of this short-lived victory. Finally, the sequence ends with a visual reference to the cross, an image which Russell will manipulate throughout the film. Here Grandier simply and sincerely blesses the citizens and soldiers who stood with him.

The next sequence depicting the cross-cutting between Grandier's address concerning the walls and King Louis's discussion with Richelieu is taken directly from Whiting, but is here presented very much in the Russell manner, and the transition again is accomplished with the sign of the cross. This time Richelieu crosses himself as King Louis fires a pistol from atop a small bridge. Louis's reply, "Yes", appears to have another function beyond that of answering Richelieu, but at this point, we are not sure what it is. The "Yes" also signals the cut back to Grandier. The camera movement from far shot to medium shot of Grandier parallels the moving camera in the funeral oration sequence, when again the emphasis (both visual and verbal) fell on the preservation of the walls. Here, the words added by Russell to Whiting's dialogue further stress the political implications.

Grandier:
Every time there is a so-called nationalist revival, it means one thing. Somebody is trying to seize control of the entire country. The significance of our walls is that we are self-governing. Richelieu hates this. He deceives the king.

Cut to Richelieu:
If France is to fulfill her own destiny, she must be free within herself.

The counterpointing continues, and although the editing impresses the viewer, it is really the *mise-en-scène* and camera shots which deserve the most attention. The camera moves in closer and closer to the protagonists in both situations: it moves from long to medium shot and finally to a close-up of Grandier addressing the people of Loudun; and the same movement takes place in the King Louis segment—from long shot to medium shot to a close-up of Louis, with a bust shot of Richelieu, Satan-like, whispering apparent deceptions into the King's ear. Also intercut with the Grandier section are shots of the crowd—carefully structured in perspective, but also functional in defining the nature of the conflict. The wheel of destruction, the device for demolishing the walls, is seen in the rear center of the frame, while the front figures screen left are Mignon and Trincant, two who will oppose him on this issue, and the figures screen right are Rangier and Legrand, two characters invented by Russell who staunchly support Grandier and who are later arrested along with him.

The cross-cutting is finally ended by the King's resounding "No" to Richelieu's suggestion that the walls of Loudun be torn down. The camera shot (a close-up of Louis) also breaks the pattern, and we finally see the other meaning of "Yes", a signal to open a large cage containing a man dressed as a blackbird who is forced to "escape" in order to be shot down by the King: "Another Protestant bird for your bag, Richelieu." There follows a dolly to a close-up of the King who looks out at the audience and waves while uttering, "Bye, bye, blackbird". The sequence ends with a medium shot of the bird-man's body sinking in a pond.

For many, this is an offensive or ridiculous scene, but no matter what the reaction, this example is characteristic of Russell's bizarre sense of humor. "Bye, Bye, Blackbird" was also the music played when Isadora caught her scarf in the spokes of the car wheel in *Isadora Duncan*. The sequence, however, is not simply for self-advertisement or a silly in-joke; it functions on a number of significant levels. It is one of the numerous conspicuous anachronisms used throughout to force the audience to see the film in terms of the present and the future, as well as the past. Also, the sequence functions together with other earlier images: the court masque in the prologue to the film presented Louis's favorites as bird figures dressed in gold and silver costumes; here his enemies are stripped of their humanity and reduced to the level of blackbirds in order to be shot by this perverse, decadent ruler. Finally, the laughter of the King is the sound transition to the next sequence of Jeanne laughing hysterically in her room, and this sound links the King's perversions to Jeanne's sex-obsessed fantasies.[13]

Jeanne is composing a letter to Grandier asking him to be the Ursuline spiritual director now that Canon Moussaut has died, and

Russell employs a method of cross-cutting similar to that used in the last sequence. Now he juxtaposes the writing of Jeanne's letter and its aftermath with Grandier's marriage. Russell again uses language from Whiting's play, but he expands the marriage ceremony in a way consistent with his preoccupations and the unifying imagery of the crucifix.

Jeanne's signing her letter to Grandier, "Yours in Christ", and placing it next to the crucifix to which she now prays is cross-cut with Grandier, in a long shot, with a large crucifix in the rear center of the frame as he descends from the altar. The juxtaposition clearly suggests that both Jeanne and Grandier are using Christ for their own purposes—although Russell obviously sympathizes to some extent with Grandier's actions here.

The self-flagellation of Sister Jeanne as she clutches a wooden cross is witnessed by the voyeuristic Sister Agnes, who finds her counterparts in Ibert and Adam spying on Grandier and Madeleine as they seal their marriage by drinking from the chalice of consecrated wine.

From their smiling faces Russell cuts to a nun holding a book from which Baron de Laubardemont reads Grandier's background to Richelieu as the Cardinal is pushed through the halls of the ecclesiastical library on a type of handcart. Russell's treatment of Richelieu is comic, but not without some shreds of historical accuracy. In his last years, the Cardinal found it increasingly difficult to move about freely and had to be maneuvered from place to place by various contraptions. The setting for the library is again anachronistically effective; it appears to be that of a large prison, and like many of our modern governing agencies, appears to have files on just about everyone. The sequence reminds the viewer that although Grandier is surrounded by numerous personal enemies, the main thrust of the attack on him is rooted in politics, and the huge doors with the red crucifix design which swing closed on the sequence reinforce the theme of the perversion of religion by man's egotistical desires.

Russell then cuts to Sister Jeanne watching the mock marriage of Grandier and Madeleine as performed by her own nuns who simply act out the gossip that they have heard. Jeanne's response is visually staggering as she takes her crucifix, also her unconscious phallic symbol, and jams it into her mouth to stifle her moans of jealousy. This extreme reaction justifies, or at least explains, her behavior in the next sequence when Madeleine comes to the convent to return the book and to claim that she now realizes that she has no vocation. Russell again underscores the tension and frenzy of the moment with his moving camera and the *mise-en-scène* of the frames, especially those which contain the bars of the grille separating the two women.

As Madeleine escapes and Jeanne sinks to her bed, she seeks a hidden mirror under her mattress and remarks to herself that Grandier should have seen her first with her "face under its coif, like an angel's peeping through a cloud"—words which are almost an exact rendering of Huxley's description of Jeanne's thoughts.[14] Her reverie is interrupted by the announcement that the new spiritual director has arrived. The mocking "angelic" music and the camera angle which reveals the presence of the director at the last possible moment should make the audience aware of Jeanne's frustration of expectations as Canon Mignon, not Father Grandier, appears at the top of the stairs. Russell's slight distortion here, in that Mignon is appointed rather than requested by the good sisters after Grandier refuses, condenses time, provides further dramatic impact, and supplies both the motivation and the opportunity for her accusation of Grandier, since Jeanne now realizes that he will never see her angelic face. The "sex in the head" which Huxley carefully describes when discussing Jeanne's condition here manifests itself through her play with words. She laughs at the explanation that Grandier has more pressing duties in the town and is obscenely direct when asked what form the supposed incubus takes. She quickly replies "cock" and then "Grandier".

Russell cuts from this nearly hysterical accusation to a tranquil shot of Grandier and Madeleine asleep in positions reminiscent of Gothic *gisant* tomb statues, but this calm is short-lived. There is then a cut to Mignon's face in close-up, hideously distorted through sinister lighting effects, in the hell-like atmosphere of M. Adam's pharmacy. Again most of the words are taken directly from Whiting, but the manner of presentation and the verbal additions reflect Russell's humor. Even after hearing Mignon's statement of Sister Jeanne's accusation, each of the others contend that his gossip or specific claim is the best means to bring about Grandier's destruction. Trincant discusses his daughter's case as proof of fornication, but Laubardemont slyly replies that it would be difficult to ascertain if the pregnancy was "lay or clerical". Philippe also joins this gallery of caricatured conspirators as she stands naked, defiantly spitting out a Bette Davis imitation before being led from the room. The group then huddles together to discuss the possibility of sending for Father Barré. The shot is extreme low angle, and the mist which surrounds them provides the transition for the arrival of Father Barré at the Ursuline convent.

Father Barré is one of Russell's less successful creations. Although not on the same level of caricature as Adam, M. Ibert and King Louis, Barré never reaches the three-dimensional stature of Laubardemont, and even though he embodies characteristics of all the exorcists, one can seriously question Russell's judgment in his madcap presentation of Barré as a "hippie" figure who enjoys the antics of his "possessed" charges. With blue-tinted, wire-rim glasses, long hair more appropriate to present day Soho than to seventeenth century Loudun, and large black and white garden gloves with crosses on the back, Barré might e viewed in a context consistent with the elements of farce, burlesque, and anachronism found in the film, but somehow none of his "trappings" ring true—even in Russell's unique sense of the word. If this is Russell's swipe at Barré acting as a superstar, it is hardly worth the effort, since all too often, Barré (especially as played by Michael Gothard) seems to wrench the film from its major concerns and, as such, to reduce both the horror and the effectiveness of the bizarre humor in the events. Perhaps in this particular instance, Russell has failed to heed Jean Cocteau's aphorism about the need of the artist to know *how* far he can go too far.[15]

If Russell goes too far with Barré, his treatment of the exorcisms and hysteria of the nuns, although considered by most critics to be the supreme excess of the film, is strikingly appropriate. Most of the audience for the public exorcisms wear masks as a kind of prescribed social convention similar to the use of masks in eighteenth century Venice, but even in sixteenth and seventeenth century France, masks were fashionable, especially in court society. "Since the mask protected anonymity, it preserved a residue of mystery, and gave its wearer a pleasurable feeling of otherness and ambiguity."[16] More than merely being historically consistent with the period, however, Russell's use of masks in the film's *mise-en-scène* assists in establishing a frenzied, theatrical atmosphere. Father Barré's entrance is marked by his blessing of the prison-like premises of the Ursuline convent with holy water, and his questions owe much to Whiting's dialogue, but, of course, Jeanne's answers stem from the fantasies that we have seen in the film rather than her more "innocent visions of hell" described in the play and found in Huxley's account.[17] The impact of the sequence, however, is chiefly visual with dialogue merely supporting the image. Laubardemont speaks words from the play originally ascribed to the more sympathetic Guillaume de Cerisay, but here they only reveal the Baron's great desire to form an air-tight case against the priest of Saint Peter's.

The entrance of Ibert and Adam with their giant syringe and their casual remarks ("A bit chilly this morning, but we mustn't complain") introduces the brilliant mixture of horror and humor manifested in the frenzied chaos of the exorcisms. Much of the grotesque humor derives from Whiting's dialogue:

Ibert: As a professional man—

Adam: He speaks for me.

Ibert: I don't like to commit myself.

Laubardemont: Even so—

Adam: Well, let's put it this way. There's been hanky-panky.

Barré: Don't mince words. There's been fornication!

Ibert: Rather.

Barré: Lust! She's been had!

Adam: I'll say.[18]

But Russell liberally blends horror with farce—the blood-stained hands of the surgeon followed by a full shot of the crumbled body of Jeanne, who now, since she realizes that she will be subjected to "forcible colonic irrigation" with holy water, tries to retract by begging for mercy and claiming that she lied about everything. To Barré, this is simply the voice of the Antichrist, and he clasps his hand over her mouth. Jeanne, however, bites him and escapes to pray before the life-sized figure of the crucified Christ, but she is quickly pinned to the altar and spread-eagled before the image of her suffering savior. The horror of the sequence is further enhanced by the extreme low angle shots of the giant clyster approaching as Jeanne's legs are spread apart. There follows a series of quick cuts to shots of screaming nuns, laughing onlookers, and close-ups of Jeanne—all choreographed to dissonant music, extensive percussion, and sirens. The impact is staggering, but this seemingly unbelievable frenzy is taken directly from Huxley's account and is accurately transformed into images. Because of the immediacy of the film experience, the images jolt us more than such effective verbal metaphors as, "Barré had treated her to an experience that was the equivalent, more or less, of a rape in a public lavatory."[19]

The use of farce in this particular sequence is Russell's invention, but rather than mitigating the horror, it merely increases the sense of chaos and panic. Philippe tells the outraged Rangier and Legrand to shut up and spits a wad of gum into her father's hand, but these actions simply seem part of the insane activities which finally cause Jeanne to blurt out that Grandier is responsible for her possession.

Jeanne's uttering of Grandier's name acts as a transition to a quiet, subdued interlude in the midst of hysterical frenzy. Grandier and Madeleine discuss his proposed trip to Paris.[20] The dim romantic lighting and music are similar to that found in the marriage ceremony sequence, and the use of medium close-ups should remind the viewer of the previous shots of Grandier and Madeleine in bed. Grandier refuses to stay in Loudun to clear his name from the slanderous accusations of a half-crazed nun out of fear of losing the crucial audience with the King, and most of his speech about "secluded women" and the unnatural limitations of the ascetic life, although appropriate here, is found in Whiting's play in the somewhat different context of a discussion with Cerisay.

From this tender moment Russell cuts to a medium-close shot of screaming nuns with Laubardemont's voice-over saying that they are in league with the devil. Russell frequently follows lyrical moments with particularly savage ones throughout the film, and, aside from obvious contrast, they serve to undercut almost all of Grandier's hopes and expectations. Laubardemont's address to the accused nuns finds no counterpart in Huxley or Whiting but was devised to emphasize the political aspects of the film. There are, however, similar events in both the play and Huxley's biography. The play, for instance, contains a scene in which Father Mignon, with Laubardemont standing in the background, forces Jeanne to realize that without the voices of the devils in public manifestation she stands condemned to eternal damnation; the voice of Leviathan immediately puts in a word. Huxley's account also makes note of an ordinance published by the Archbishop against public exorcism.

> The prohibition was almost unnecessary; for during the month that followed there were no devils to exorcise. No longer stimulated by priestly suggestions, the frenzies of the nuns gave place to a dismal, morning-after condition in which mental confusion was mingled with shame, remorse and the conviction of enormous sin. For what if the Archbishop were right? What if there never had been any devils? Then all these monstrous things they had done and said could be imputed to them as crimes. Possessed they were guiltless. Unpossessed they would have to answer, at the Last Judgment, for blasphemy and unchastity, for lies and malice. At their feet hell yawned appallingly.[21]

The incident in the film is much more extreme. The nuns are about to be executed by the archers from the city, but it is Laubardemont's rhetoric which demands attention.

> You are accused of being in league with the devil and in obstructing Father Barré's cure of Sister Jeanne. You rebel against the will of the Church, the will of Christ, and the will of His most holy representative, Cardinal Richelieu, and in resisting officers of the crown in the pursuance of their duty, you all are also guilty of treason. You are unrepentant heretics. There is no act more vile. You are traitors. You'll be executed. Now!

Father Barré's revelation from God that the nuns are also victims of possession ("sin can be caught as easily as the plague") comes at a dramatically appropriate time, and Laubardemont claims that they can save themselves yet. "You wouldn't be the first to see the light." Russell cuts away to a close-up of one of the archers. This quick shot suggests the degree to which things have turned against Grandier.

Earlier, the archers had raised their bows at the Baron; now these same soldiers raise their weapons for him.

Father Barré then exhorts the good sisters to scream and to blaspheme, and with his crucifix held high, he plunges into their midst to be pawed and fondled.[22] The results of his exhortations lead the nuns, when back at the convent, to remove their clothes and to give full vent to their sexual fantasies. The shots of full frontal nudity and the more effective *mise-en-scène* found in the British print convey a vision of utter chaos, which, although suggested in the U.S. version of the film, reaches extraordinary heights of hysteria and perversion in Russell's unbowdlerized version.[23] It is a terrifying sequence which is further heightened by being cross-cut with the most lyrical and romantic episode in the film. Grandier rides back to Loudun, while Madeleine walks in a field of flowers as her husband's voice-over reveals the contents of his letter to her. Finally, beside a mountain stream, Grandier breaks bread (after blessing it) and offers it, arms outstretched in a Christ-like pose, to the heavens. The monologue-letter at this point is especially significant, since unlike Whiting's hero who never actually realizes self-transcendence with Philippe, Russell's priest achieves a new response to life.

> Each morning I wake up with a feeling of optimism so strong as to be almost absurd. . . . Strange thoughts come to me. I am like a man who has been lost, who has always been lost. Now, for all kinds of reasons, I have a vague sense of meaning and can think of myself as a small part of God's abundance which includes everything, and I know I want to serve it. I want to serve the people of Loudun. I want to serve you. Pray for us all, especially me.

The consecration of the bread provides a rationale for the shock-cut close-up of Jeanne's face with vomit pouring from her mouth (the shot is longer and more graphic in the British version than in the U.S. version), and although extreme, this shot and the succeeding visuals capture Huxley's description of how the church was turned into a place "like a mixture between a beer garden and a brothel".[24] The feverish pitch and lunatic ravings of the following scenes, although clearly an outgrowth of Russell's visual style and his shock methods of overstatement, also derive from eyewitness observations of the events at Loudun. For instance, Huxley uses Thomas Killigrew's letter to Walter Montague to prove that the "possessed" nuns were no longer regarded as human beings. Killigrew was invited to grasp the limbs of nuns to feel the power and strength of the devil. For Huxley,

> The good father who performs the exorcisms behaves exactly like the proprietor of a side show at a fair. "Step up, ladies and gentlemen, step up! Seeing is believing, but pinching our fat girl's legs is the

> naked truth." These spouses of Christ have been turned into cabaret performers and circus freaks.[25]

Still, Russell surrounds these historical events with his own personal touches, usually of a humorous nature, but even these are consistent with the tone of "gruesome comedy" which pervades Huxley's book. The attempt to create a case to prove Grandier's guilt often revolved around suggestions of witches' Sabbaths and "pacts", which were either "found" in the nuns' cells or vomited up by them.

> But it was Jeanne des Anges who, as usual, outdid all the rest. On June 17th, while possessed by Leviathan, she threw up a pact containing (according to her devils) a piece of the heart of a child, sacrificed in 1631 at a witches' Sabbath near Orléans, the ashes of a consecrated wafer and some of Grandier's blood and semen.[26]

In the film, Ibert, Adam, and Barré examine Jeanne's vomit.

> Barré: Tell me, tell me.
>
> Ibert: That's a left ventricle.
>
> Adam: It's part of the heart of a child.
>
> Barré: Sacrificed at a witches' Sabbath, no doubt.
> Look! A consecrated wafer.
>
> Adam: Yeah, blood, thick blood, blood of a man.
>
> Barré: Yeah, Grandier.
>
> Ibert: That slimy stuff could only be semen.
>
> Barré: And what's that?
>
> Adam: That's a carrot.

The absurdity of this analysis is underscored by Huxley through irony and sarcasm, but Russell's addition of the carrot achieves a similar effect.

> The inclusion of the comic line about the carrot was typical of many deliberate ludicrous touches throughout the film, designed to point out the nonsensical irony of these horrors being committed in the name of God. The church had her vomit analyzed but it was done, not by a surgeon as we understand the term today, but by a barber and a grocer. The whole film was conceived as a black comedy. . . . What the film is saying is that this would be a terrible joke if it weren't all so horrible and hadn't actually happened. I find it extraordinary that Grandier was convicted and burnt on the strength of ludicrous statements which even a young child would find implausible these days in a fairy story.[27]

The sequence depicting the Duke de Condé provides further

examples of Russell's method of shaping material from his sources. Henri de Condé, a member of the royal family and notorious sodomite, did come to Loudun, but he left believing in demonic possession. It was another visiting nobleman who offered Father Barré the box of "exceedingly holy relics". In Whiting's play, the two figures are combined, and the character of the Duke expanded to the point that he becomes Grandier's most eloquent defender and perhaps even something of a parallel figure to the libertine priest.

> De Condé: Mother, I am often accused of libertinage. Very well. Being born so high I have to stoop lower than other men. Soiled, dabbling myself, I know what I am doing and what I must give. I'd say you'll have your wish about this man Grandier, seeing the way the world goes. But do you know what you must give? (casually) Your immortal soul to damnation in an infinite desert of eternal bestiality.[28]

Russell attributes most of Condé's more eloquent responses to Grandier himself and reduces the Duke simply to another example of the court's decadence. True, in the film, he is the cynical visitor who fulfills the task of the nameless nobleman in the Huxley account, but his physical appearance is so close to that of the King that some viewers confuse their identitites.[29] Also, although many of his lines concerning the supposed box of relics are taken directly from Whiting's play, Russell's visual emphasis in this sequence is on the decadence and ridiculousness of the events.[30] The play on words is frequent and obvious. While the Duke de Condé addresses Father Barré, a nude, hysterical nun flings herself at the exorcist and screams "Love me. Love me." Barré's reply to Condé, "I am at your service", may also be construed as a response to the good sister's request. Some viewers might argue that these hyperbolic examples destroy any semblance of fidelity to the original sources, but they are merely part of Russell's attempt to capture the atmosphere verbally depicted by Huxley.

> And over everything, like a richly smelly fog, hangs an oppressive sexuality, thick enough to be cut with a knife and ubiquitous, inescapable. The physicians who . . . visited the nuns, found no evidence of possession, but many indications that all or most of them were suffering from a malady to which our fathers gave the name of *furor uterinus*. The symptoms of this disease were "heat accompanied by an inextinguishable appetite for venery" and an inability, on the part of the younger sisters, to "think or talk about anything but sex".[31]

The chaos of the scene with its mad cavortings, numerous crosses, and swinging censorium provides the necessary theatrical backdrop for the exorcists' rituals. Condé's offering of the box containing a phial of the blood of Jesus Christ is accepted, and the "devils" are put to flight. The humor of the incident is underscored visually by Russell's close-up shots of the nuns swirling about their out-stretched tongues as the demons depart. The mock angelic music (the same as that played when Jeanne ran to meet the new father confessor) prepares the audience for the revelation that the box is empty. Condé, however, makes no criticism of Jeanne in Russell's film; he simply tweaks her chin and tells her to "have fun".

Barré vainly attempts to impose order, but he is quickly smashed over the head with a large wooden cross as the frenzy reaches its most extreme state. In the British print, Sister Agnes madly rubs her hand up and down a huge phallic candle, and the actions of the deranged nuns are presented for a few seconds more before the cross-cut to Grandier. This frenzy led to the now deleted rape of Christ sequence.

> The naked nuns tear down a wooden figure of Christ and throw themselves on it, having it in every possible way. . . . Both Warner Brothers and the censors thought it was too strong so I took it out. Short of burning the entire film I had no choice. But it was really central to the whole thing, intercut as it was with Grandier finding both himself and God in the solitary simplicity of Nature. Over-ripe, perverted religion going as bad and wrong as it can possibly become, with the eternal truth of the bread and the wine and the brotherhood of man and God in the universe. Try getting the Hollywood heavies or the Festival of Light to swallow *that*![32]

Basic as this sequence may be to Russell's pattern of imagery in the film, it is not without some slight factual support for inclusion—even on a literal level. Huxley quotes from *Histoire des Diables de Loudun* by Guillaume Aubin, a Protestant pastor who lived in Loudun and was acquainted with many of the figures involved. Claire de Sazilly (Sister Claire)

> se trouva si fort tentée de coucher avec son grand ami, qu'elle disait être Grandier, qu'un jour s'étant approchée pour recevoir la Sainte Communion, elle se leva soudain et monta dans sa chambre, où ayant été suivie par quelqu'une des Soeurs, elle fut vue avec un Crucifix dans la main, dont elle se préparait. . . . L'honnêteté [adds Aubin] ne permet pas d'écrire les ordures de cet endroit.[33]

The chaos of the exorcists' activities is again cross-cut with the tranquility of Grandier's return journey to Loudun, but the transition is especially appropriate, even considering the gap left by the deleted sequence. We move from the false relic of Condé to the transubstantiation scene in which Grandier and Madeleine drink from the chalice, while the words of Grandier's letter are heard as a voice-over.

> I know I am a weak, bad man, but after this journey, I may find the strength to change, to summon towards myself the good will and wisdom that lies in the people of Loudun. The king has secured our stones. Now we have to show him that the city is the strength that lives in the hearts of men. That greed and dissension will never destroy her, and with God's help, we will change her walls to terraces that have the colour of stars.

Russell's cut to a low angle shot of the skeleton on the suspended wheel just outside the city gates hints that Grandier's vision of the New Jerusalem will never come to pass.

Grandier's entering of his own church, where the public exorcisms are now taking place, is conceived in a manner to parallel Jesus's rousting of the money changers from the temple. This confrontation is Russell's invention, and Grandier's rhythmic verbal response is probably the best original dialogue in the film.

> You have turned the house of the Lord into a circus, and its servants into clowns. You have seduced the people in order to destroy them. You have perverted the innocent.

Madeleine de Brou's defense of her marriage pushes Sister Jeanne into further accusations against the priest, and finally Grandier is arrested. Again the parallels to Jesus are obvious as Grandier pleads, "Forgive her. Forgive her. She has been broken by the priests", while being brutally dragged from the church.

In the next sequence, Grandier's tongue is pierced to detect marks of the devil, but Russell quickly cross-cuts to Jeanne in the convent courtyard as she attempts, in Judas-like fashion, to hang herself. This incident is only a slight bit more dramatic than Huxley's account in which she stood in the rain for two hours with a candle in her hand and a rope around her neck and later knelt before Laubardemont to confess that she had accused an innocent man. Russell then cuts back to Grandier (out of focus), who staring at the torture device (sharp focus) mumbles about his need for God and makes another verbal allusion: "I thought I had found You, and now You have forsaken me." Mother Jeanne then confesses to Mignon and Barré that she has wronged an innocent man. Barré, at this point, decides that he must resort to other measures, since the exorcisms have failed, and while we hear off-camera moans from Jeanne, the camera focuses on Mignon whose eyes reflect astonishment at what he sees. Unfortunately, it is a cheap trick which perhaps misleads rather than tantalizes the audience.

The dialogue with Grandier, after Laubardemont and his soldiers enter the priest's house, is drawn from various characters found in Whiting's play (Bontemps, Father Ambrose and Laubardemont), but again the impact of the sequence is chiefly visual—with shock-cutting to complement lines of dialogue ("You are going to be tortured"—close-up of rifle butts smashing a statue). This destruction of Grandier's possessions, however, is merely the beginning of the process through which Grandier, the sinner, progresses from vanity and pride to humility and forgiveness.

At his trial, Grandier is dressed in the same vestments as those worn during the solemn moments of Saint-Marthe's funeral. Only now he is the subject of derision, laughter, and scorn. The accusations by Laubardemont are directly taken from Whiting's play, especially the Council of State scene near the end of Act II, and Grandier's reply owes much to Henri de Condé's speeches from the same scene. The differences, however, reveal Russell's intensification of the political implications in the film.

> De Condé: For the love of Jesus Christ, if you wish to destroy the man, then destroy him. I'm not here to plead for his life. But your methods are shameful. He deserves better. Any man does. Kill him with power, but don't pilfer his house, and hold evidence of this sort against him. What man could face arraignment on the idiocy of youth, old love letters, and the pathetic objects stuffed in drawers or at the bottom of cupboards, kept for the fear that one day he would need to be reminded that he was once loved? No. Destroy the man for his opposition, his strength or his majesty. But not for this![34]

> Grandier: For the love of Jesus Christ, if you wish to destroy me, then destroy me. Accuse me of exposing political chicanery and the evils of the state, and I will plead guilty, but what man can face arraignment on the idiocy of youth, old love letters and other pathetic objects stuffed in drawers or at the bottom of cupboards. Things kept for a day when he would need to be reminded that he was once loved.

Russell also makes clear that the heretical nature of Laubardemont's and Barré's doctrine that "when duly constrained the devil is bound to tell the truth" is a total perversion of Christ's teaching, which at this point in the film Grandier represents and defends. The theological issue in question is dismissed out of political expediency, and again Grandier's speech makes this clear.

> This new doctrine . . . especially invented for this occasion is the work of men who are not concerned with fact, or with law, or with theology, but a political experiment to show how the will of one man can be pushed into destroying not only one man or one city, but one nation.

The power of these words, however, is reinforced by the effective use of close-ups and the director's constantly moving camera.

This speech causes the court to remove the prisoner, but before departing, Grandier, in a last act of grandeur, blesses both his accusers and those in attendance at the trial. It is a touching and majestic moment, but only when seen in the context of the numerous blessings and cross motifs found throughout the film. Finally, the lingering long shot of Grandier leaving the courtroom will be paralleled by this same shot of his return—physically humiliated (shorn of all his hair and dressed in a common smock) but still intellectually and spiritually triumphant.

The sequence depicting the shaving of Grandier's beard and head is taken directly from Whiting's play, but here it is meant to remind the viewer of previous moments from the priest's life as presented in the film. The close-ups of his arms being clamped into the chair take us back to those recent tortures when Ibert sought the "marks" of the devil. The seeing of himself in the make-shift mirror suggests the change that has taken place since he dismissed Philippe's pregnancy while carefully combing his hair and twirling his mustache.

Grandier's speech back in the courtroom after the sentencing is again drawn from Whiting, but it is drastically condensed, which perhaps even increases its impact. To some extent, it becomes more of a prayer than the usual last words of the accused, and Russell forces our attention to the words by using a bust shot and keeping his camera stationary. Laubardemont's immediate haranguing of Grandier allows the parson to voice again the political reasons for his execution, but Barré also joins the attack. His non-stop talking, a spitting out of words at Grandier, is filmed effectively in medium shot foreground, while in the background the gallery erupts in violence.

As Russell has noted on a number of occasions, the torture of Grandier in Huxley's account is far more detailed and horrible than what he presents in the film. "But the word has to be translated, interpreted, if necessary censored—the image is immediate, irrefutable."[35] Russell, however, does not rely on the image alone. Sound, in this case the cracking of bones, assists in conveying the realism and horror of the incidents. Grandier's legs were stretched out on the floor, and the portion from his knees to his feet were enclosed between four oaken boards, two of which were movable. Thus by driving wedges into the space between the movable sections, it was possible to crush the legs against the outer framework. There is a quick close-up of the legs, but the effectiveness of the sequence really rests with the close-up and bust shots of the major figures. It is important that we see Grandier's face, which succeeds in revealing his agony and strength much more than shots of blood and crushed bones.

Russell's use of the historical fact of Louis XIII changing his mind about Loudun's wall finally manifests itself in this sequence. In the autumn of 1633, the King actually reversed his decision concerning the walls, but in the film, Russell telescopes and condenses time in order to emphasize the political theme and to heighten dramatic impact—the destruction of the walls at the moment of Grandier's death.[36] But to prepare the viewer for this event, Laubardemont adds to Grandier's physical torment, by teasing him with the news of the King's decision.

> Laubardemont: Do you know that the King has gone back on his word because of your crimes? The walls will come down, the city will be destroyed.
>
> Grandier: You have lost.

Russell then cuts to the processional in which Grandier is pulled on a make-shift stretcher by a donkey. This journey, as previously suggested, parallels the funeral procession of Saint-Marthe, and the visit to the gates of the Ursuline convent parallels Mother Jeanne's fleeting glimpse of him in the opening of the film. The motif of theatrical imitation of life found throughout the film (Louis' "Birth of Venus" masque, the nuns', re-enactment of Grandier's marriage, and the exorcism as theatrical side show) is also represented here in a dance-mime depicting the major characters' supposed actions. Finally, the banners and crosses which provided so much of the *mise-en-scène* for Saint-Marthe's funeral again decorate the square.

The sequence depicting Grandier's death, then, incorporates many of the motifs found throughout the film, but it is also a moving tribute to Grandier which makes full use of the film medium. Whiting must forego the execution scene in his play, and Huxley's account, dramatic as it may be, is notable for the description of the events which occur immediately after the burning.[37] Russell, however, shows everything—including close-ups of his hero's blistering, burning flesh—but the entire sequence of orchestrated chaos reflects the perversion that has brought about this unjust action. In the midst of the constantly moving camera and close-middle shots of the nearly hysterical exorcists, Grandier, to the very last, remains the spiritual and political leader of the city.

When Barré refuses to give Grandier "the kiss of peace", the carnival attitude of the crowd prevails. Mignon, to quiet them, finally does so, but the kiss only causes the crowd to chant "Judas, Judas". For some viewers, this incident is too contrived, especially given all the Christ parallels suggested throughout the film. The episode, however, was taken directly from Huxley's account, where Father Lactance finally kissed Grandier.[38]

In the film, the response of the crowd causes Barré to start the fire before Grandier can be strangled by the executioner, and the following shots depicting Grandier's last moments remain for many viewers the most memorable in the film: the medium close shots of the burning Grandier, the close-ups of the hysterical crowd who seem to be engulfed in the flames instead of looking at them, the shots of Trincant's balcony, the close-ups of Philippe's smiling face, and then back to a close-up of Grandier. The frenzied cross-cutting continues until Grandier, now burning alive, gives his final message against the background of the visual chaos of the city and the dissonant music score.

> Don't look at me. Look at your city. Your city is destroyed. Your freedom is destroyed also. . . . If you would remain free men, fight or become their slaves.

For the inhabitants of Loudun, it is too late; their city as presented by the filmmaker has become a kind of hell, and they are its lost souls. Laubardemont then gives the signal for the walls to be blown-up to underscore the apocalyptic effects of the sequence.

Russell, however, does not end the film here. Laubardemont's discussion with Mother Jeanne supplies some necessary details about the fate of Mignon and Barré and suggests what will become of her. The presentation of a souvenir, one of Grandier's bones, provides the transition to the final shots of the film. The executioner shovels Grandier's remains to the four winds, as Madeleine leaves the city. The color is drained from these last frames, as she climbs over bricks and through a section of the destroyed wall and down a road which is lined with the corpses of Protestants on suspended wheels. It is a haunting image which evokes Pieter Bruegel's *The Triumph of Death.*

The Devils stands as Russell's major achievement, in part, because the flamboyance of his style is so perfectly suited to the film's subject matter. The theatricality of the images and the performances, for instance, are strikingly appropriate to the exotic historical characters in the film. Russell's love of extravagance also functions in assaulting his audience with the excesses of this story, and his methods of shock cutting effectively jolt the audience out of the comforts of detachment and into an awareness of the horrors of religious and political exploitation. His outrageous sense of humor meaningfully mirrors the attitude of black comedy found in Huxley's account, and even his use of hyperbole, so often misunderstood by critics, matches the extremes of the historical events themselves.

This film, perhaps more than any other, also best reveals Russell's genius as a creator-adaptor. He remains faithful to all of the major events in Huxley's book, captures the tone of the original, and, most importantly, delineates the major themes of the prose account in methods appropriate to the film medium. He also forcefully presents his own attitudes and responses, but in a way which never violates Huxley's vision. Finally, unlike John Whiting, who failed to control the unity of his play adaptation, Russell shapes the material from Huxley's somewhat diffuse biography into a carefully structured work of art, which achieves unity through allusions, motifs, imagery, and parallel shots.

The fact that *The Devils* is his most accomplished film to date is even acknowledged by Russell himself. " . . . *The Devils* is the most successful film I've done, insofar as what I expected is there. The effects I aimed at seemed to work."[39]

NOTES

[1]Cited in Terry Curtis Fox, "Conversation with Ken Russell", *Oui,* June 1973, p. 103.

[2]*Ibid.,* p. 105.

[3]See Ken Russell, "Ken Russell Interviewed by Colin Wilson: Part 2", CBS telecast on *Camera Three,* 30 September 1973.

[4]Aldous Huxley, *The Devils of Loudun* (New York: Harper and Row, 1971, London: Chatto and Windus, 1970), p. 26.

[5]Compare this example to the cut from Laubardemont and his enslaved Protestants to Grandier's oration.

[6]Huxley, *The Devils of Loudun,* p. 38.

[7]See Michael Dempsey, "The World of Ken Russell", *Film Quarterly,* 25 (Spring 1972), 13–25; and Stephen Farber, "*The Devils* Finds an Advocate", *New York Times,* 15 August 1971, Arts and Leisure Section, p. 1, col. 6 and p. 9, cols. 1–2.

[8]Cited in Fox, p. 105.

[9]A stuffed crocodile was frequently found in an apothecary's shop. See Huxley, *The Devils of Loudun,* pp. 43–4.

[10]*Ibid.,* p. 47.

[11]The irony of this line is notable given what happens later in this church.

[12]The use of black and white film and the grainy quality of the image suggest that Jeanne's fantasy is meant to parody such motion pictures as C. B. DeMille's *King of Kings* (1927).

[13]See Russell's comments in John Baxter, *An Appalling Talent/Ken Russell* (London: Michael Joseph, 1973), p. 206.

[14]Huxley, *The Devils of Loudun,* p. 113.

[15]Cocteau's aphorism is used in a different context by Roger Manvell, "You Can Go to *The Devils*", *Humanist*, 86 (November 1971), p. 333.

[16]Otto Bihalji-Merin, *Great Masks* (New York: Harry H. Abrams, c. 1971), p. 98.

[17]Huxley, *The Devils of Loudun*, pp. 130–1.

[18]John Whiting, *The Devils* (New York: Hill and Wang, 1962), p. 68.

[19]Huxley, *The Devils of Loudun*, p. 124.

[20]Russell condenses events that occurred over a number of years into what seems to be a few months, and he abandons or significantly alters events (the numerous appeals, the return of Barré to Chinon, the changing of the King's mind about the wall, the recalling of Barré, and the involved struggles between secular and ecclesiastical courts) for both dramatic and thematic purposes.

[21]Huxley, *The Devils of Loudun*, p. 155.

[22]The portrayal of Father Barré is again open to question here. At times, he seems to be a sincere, if foolish and ultimately dangerous, individual who fears that Satan's legions are everywhere. On other occasions, however, he seems to be consciously in league with Laubardemont.

Huxley notes that we know nothing firsthand of Father Barré's state of mind, but using accounts of the other exorcists and Father Surin's writings, Huxley suggests that the priests were constantly subjected to sexual temptations.

> At the center of a troop of hysterical women, all in a state of chronic sexual excitement, he was the chartered Male, imperious and tyrannical. The abjection in which his charges were so ecstatically wallowing served only to emphasize the triumphant masculinity of the exorcist's role. Their passivity heightened his sense of being the master. In the midst of uncontrollable frenzies, he was lucid and strong; in the midst of demons, he was the representative of God. And as the representative of God, he was privileged to do what he liked with these creatures of a lower order—to make them perform tricks, to send them into convulsions, to manhandle them as though they were recalcitrant sows or heifers, to prescribe the enema or the whip.

See Huxley, *The Devils of Loudun*, p. 127.

[23]The U.S. version of *The Devils* is only two minutes shorter than the British print of the film, but a number of short graphic shots have been removed. Also, a different take of the sequence depicting Henri de Condé's visit to Loudun is found in the U.S. version.

[24]Huxley, *The Devils of Loudun*, p. 157.

[25]*Ibid.*, p. 178.

[26]*Ibid.*, p. 169.

[27]Baxter, *An Appalling Talent*, pp. 202–3.

[28]Whiting, *The Devils*, p. 90.

[29]After a recent viewing of the film I came to realize that the masked Duke *was* in fact the King incognito, which makes his behavior and the general treatment of the sequence totally consistent with what has gone before.

[30]*Ibid.*, pp. 83–90.

[31]Huxley, *The Devils of Loudun*, p. 129.

[32]Baxter, *An Appalling Talent,* p. 210.

[33]Huxley, *The Devils of Loudun,* p. 204.

[34]Whiting, *The Devils,* p. 93.

[35]Baxter, *An Appalling Talent,* p. 202.

[36]Parallels can be found between this moment in the film and the end of Carl Dreyer's *La Passion de Jeanne d'Arc* (1927).

[37]Huxley, *The Devils of Loudun,* pp. 240–8.

[38]*Ibid.,* p. 240.

[39]Cited in John Baxter's first draft of *An Appalling Talent/Ken Russell,* TS.

8

Savage Messiah

Truth Through Exaggeration

> In Art one must exaggerate; as the sculptor deepens a depression, or accentuates a relief, so the writer accentuates a vice, diminishes some quality, according to his needs; and it is only here that the imagination comes into play. Grandiosity, sublimity and luxury with which you reproach me goes with that necessary exaggeration of the facts which helps to secure greater truth, and that is what I mean by a well-thought-out copying of nature.
>
> Henri Gaudier-Brzeska[1]

Russell claims that a new film is often a reaction to the previous one, and this was certainly the case with *The Boy Friend* (1971). According to Russell, "*The Devils* left many of us weak, miserable and shattered",[2] and when MGM proposed that he direct Twiggy in a film version of *The Boy Friend*, he accepted and immediately cast many of those who worked with him on *The Devils* (Max Adrian, Murray Melvin, Georgina Hale, Brian Murphy, Graham Armitage, and Catherine Wilmer) in his adaptation of Sandy Wilson's musical.

Even though the play *The Boy Friend* (1953)[3] is merely a light, charming parody of musicals from the twenties, Russell's approach to his source material was as ambitious as ever. He created a complex "show-within-a-movie" framework for the film, after taking Twiggy to see an amateur production of the show. "The cast got wind that I was there and played up to the hilt. I was sitting in the audience, mentally visualizing how I was going to direct the film version, when the idea came to me."[4] The structure of the film, however, also owes much to the tripartite perspective that Russell manipulates in so many of his adaptations. In this instance, the performance of the play by the provincial theatrical troupe captures the facts (here the lines of the play itself). The backstage sub-plots and the fantasies of Max (Max Adrian), Tony (Christopher Gable), and Polly (Twiggy) reveal how the characters view themselves; and De Thrill (Vladek Sheybal), a parody of Russell himself, reflects Russell's own vision of how the material should be presented. The backstage drama also mirrors the plot and characters of the play itself, and reality and art merge when Tony and Polly declare their love for each other near the end of the performance. The complexity of the film is further increased by production numbers within production numbers and a surprise comic ending. Finally, the film could even be viewed as Russell's capsule history of the Hollywood musical, since he incorporates tributes and pastiches to such films as: *42nd Street* (1933), *Flying Down to Rio* (1933), *The Wizard of Oz* (1939), *Singin' in the Rain* (1952), and *The Bandwagon* (1953).

The Boy Friend was a film fraught with difficulties. It was under-budgeted at $1·7 million, and the technical experience and expertise for making this kind of film were simply not available in England. The same held true for physical facilities. The roof at Elstree Studios, for instance, simply wasn't high enough to shoot certain production numbers. Finally, to make matters worse, Russell had a number of serious quarrels with members of the cast and crew.[5] As a result, this supposedly pleasant diversion from the "horrors" of *The Devils* turned into a nightmare.

In reaction to the difficulties of a large-scale film production, Russell next turned his attention to making *Savage Messiah* (1972), a small, privately financed film.

> I wanted this film to be totally different, away from the big companies and back into the small studio; back to the BBC sort of style with a small unit. I mean it's as small as can be. And of course it's a very romantic film, but not at all sensual; very austere actually. It's more a film about art and various aspects of art and attitudes to it—lay attitudes—than anything I've made before.[6]

Savage Messiah was greeted with the usual response to Russell's work—a few short, tentative appreciations, a few mixed reviews, and a barrage of passionately abusive, unfavorable reviews.[7] The critical diatribes hurled at *Savage Messiah* were similar to those brought against *The Music Lovers* and *The Devils*, and although just about all the critics agreed that this latest film was comparatively restrained, their wrath in no way decreased. Robert Hughes, for instance, claimed that "Russell is a director whose appetite for excess verges on petulance" and whose major enterprise is the "disembowelment of history".[8] In her review, Pauline Kael used the film as an excuse to make a particularly savage attack on the director, who has so often in interviews referred to her as "a shrilling, screaming gossip".[9] She claimed that he is a filmmaker who has little command of film technique and whose movies "cheapen everything they touch".

> He's a one-man market-place, a compulsive Hollywoodizer, and his images of the artist's suffering are frantic versions of Hollywood's. This movie is like a continuation of *The Music Lovers*, but now it's all random buffoonery. . . . He's not trying to deal with the age any of his artist subjects lived in, or the appetites and satisfactions of that age, or the vision of a particular artist; but is always turning something from the artists' lives into something else—a whopping irony, a phallic joke, a plushy big scene.[10]

Unlike Hughes and other critics who showed little knowledge of the historical figures presented in the film, and less about Russell's methods, Miss Kael at least did her homework on Henri Gaudier-Brzeska, the subject of *Savage Messiah*; but unfortunately, in her haste to condemn the director, she frequently distorted or misunderstood key episodes in the film.

Like the subjects of so many of Russell's earlier films, Gaudier-Brzeska was an artist in conflict with the external world, but unlike most of these other figures, he was never overly conscious of the fact that he was such an outsider; and his youth provided energy and an intensity with which to proclaim revolutionary attitudes.

> Yes, it *is* much the same as much of my earlier work—the artist at odds with his society and all that—exactly the same as them all perhaps, but Gaudier-Brzeska is a vastly different character from any of them. Much younger, more revolutionary, more anti-establishment and everything. He may have turned into *the* great antithesis of all that of course as they all did because most of the other people mixed up with him became very restrained and conservative as life went on, even reactionary, but that's always the way, isn't it.[11]

Perhaps because Gaudier-Brzeska did not live long enough to stagnate or to slip into a secure conservatism, or perhaps because—like Blake—he never doubted his own artistic judgments or feared the scorn of detractors, Russell uses this "quiet little film" to encapsulate many of his own views on the role of the artist in society. Many of the concepts come directly from Ede's book, but much, as might be expected, builds from where the book stops. In some respects, the film becomes an accurate portrait of both Henri Gaudier-Brzeska and Ken Russell.

Savage Messiah, however, is also a film which depicts a strange

Platonic love affair, and the brief note ("the story of a young French artist and the Polish woman he met just before World War I") after the title reinforces this fact. Russell, like Ede, begins his portrait with this meeting because he sees the strange relationship with Sophie Brzeska as the necessary catalyst for his protagonist's creative activity. This attitude is established early in the film when Henri tells Sophie " . . . but sometimes I don't think that I'll be able to do what I want to do, on my own". The film's structure and the dominant pattern of visual rhythms, although less complex than in other Russell films, emphasize the uneasy Platonic union these two very different individuals form against the forces of a hostile, external world.

There have been only three books written about Gaudier-Brzeska: Ezra Pound's *Gaudier-Brzeska: A Memoir,* Horace Brodzky's *Henri Gaudier-Brzeska 1891–1915,* and H. S. Ede's *Savage Messiah*; and although Christopher Logue's script uses material from all three accounts, it is most clearly an adaptation of the Ede biography, which consists, for the most part, of letters written by Henri interspersed with commentary by the author. Ede did have access to Sophie Brzeska's diary, but as the preface notes, little is quoted because "the Diary is too diffuse, and too personal to Miss Brzeska to allow of a direct translation".[12] As a result of this method, those periods when Henri and Sophie were separated seem to be stressed a bit more than they should be, but the frequent letters from Henri do provide an excellent opportunity for him to articulate his various attitudes toward art and its role in the past and present world.

Henri Gaudier was born on October 4, 1891, at St. Jean de Braye, near Orléans, France. His father was a carpenter whose ancestors, according to legend, worked on the cathedral at Chartres, and Henri became interested in drawing and tool work at an early age. His parents, however, were anxious that he should have a successful business career, and he went from Orléans to University College, Bristol. After work in a business firm in Bristol and brief periods of residence in Nuremberg and Munich, he journeyed to Paris where in 1910 at the St. Genevieve Library, he met Sophie Brzeska, an emotionally battered, high-strung Polish woman who was twenty years his senior.

Their friendship grew rapidly, and later that year, while staying at his parents' home, Henri invited Sophie to come and live in a cottage nearby. This harmonious arrangement was soon disrupted, however, when an anonymous letter falsely accused Sophie of using her rooms "for the improper reception of men".[13] Disgusted by bourgeois persecution and harassed by Henri's coming military obligations, the couple left for London in late 1910. There, "the two were to live together under the name of Gaudier-Brzeska, as brother and sister; each in his or her way passionately fond of the other, but seldom rising sufficiently above the daily grind of poverty to be able fully to appreciate each other's friendship".[14]

In London, Henri found work as a typist and foreign correspondent, and Sophie began a series of unfortunate posts as a governess which took her to Felixstowe, Frowlesworth, and Dodford. Interspersed with these positions were extended periods when she returned to London and lived with Henri, but it was not until January 1912 that these lonely people made any serious or significant friendships. Henri wrote to Haldane Macfall, whose writings on art appeared in the *English Review*, and through him, they met Enid Bagnold, Lovat Fraser, Middleton Murry, and Katherine Mansfield. Henri attempted to reach a fulfilling friendship with Murry and Mansfield, but Katherine was so repulsed by Sophie that this idea soon became impossible. Finally, sounding much like D. H. Lawrence, who also had a frustrating friendship with Murry, Gaudier composed a letter to end the relationship. "I loved you innerly and still sympathize with you as a poor boy chased by the Furies, but I must reproach you your lack of courage, discrimination and honour. Katherine Mansfield I never wish to see any more."[15]

For the next two years, although often in poverty, Henri worked at a feverish pitch on his drawings and sculpture. During this period, he received encouragement and/or friendship from Horace Brodzky, Jacob Epstein, Frank Harris, Roger Fry, Wyndham Lewis and Ezra Pound. The link with Pound and Lewis resulted in Gaudier's association with the Vorticist movement, and he even wrote two short theoretical essays for the first issues of *Blast*, Lewis's short-lived journal. Also in 1914 and 1915, his work was exhibited with the London Group and with the Allied Artists Association.

The outbreak of the war took the Gaudier-Brzeskas by surprise, and Henri quickly decided to return to France to fulfill his military obligations. "One has to die sometime; if it is in bed or in the war, what does it matter?"[16] When he arrived in France, however, he was treated as a deserter and imprisoned. On his first night in jail, he chiselled a bar loose, escaped, and returned to England. Later in September of 1914, he obtained a satisfactory passport and returned to France. At the front, he received two field promotions for gallantry but still found time to make carvings from scraps of wood and rifle butts. Finally, during the attack on Neuville St. Vaast, he was killed in the early afternoon of June 5, 1915.

Sophie was in London when she heard of Henri's death and blamed herself, in part, because in her last letter to him, she again rejected his proposal of marriage and complained bitterly of her life in England. She felt her letter "had perhaps driven him into danger",[17] and for the next seven years, she wandered the streets of

London trying to convince herself that he wasn't dead. She was finally put into the Gloucestershire Asylum, where she spent the last three years of her life until her death in 1925.

Ede's book has no complex structure of its own or sense of organic form growing from a particular method of treatment. It provides only the essential information, and its author avoids speculation and remains content to refrain from personal comment beyond that which is absolutely necessary. The result, from the perspective of the art of the biographical form, is, at times, an unsatisfying and all too frequently dull account, but Logue and Russell in their portrait of the Gaudier-Brzeskas, speculate widely, interpret freely, fill in gaps suggested by Ede's work, and elevate some of their protagonists' fantasies to the level of reality. As a result, they fail to capture the pace and tone of Ede's account, but instead succeed admirably in capturing the essence of the historical characters whose lives they are presenting in film form. Also the intensity, enthusiasm, and child-like exuberance of Henri, which are documented ever so frequently in both Ede's and Brodzky's accounts, are appropriately complemented by Russell's flamboyant style of filmmaking.[18]

This, however, does not mean that Russell's film is in no way faithful to Ede's biography. The opening of the film, for instance, is a remarkably accurate visual representation of Ede's description of the meeting between Henri and Sophie. Ede presents Sophie as a neurotic, independent woman who set before her on the library table all her paraphernalia with meticulous precision and who generated all kinds of speculation from the young men who frequently sat at the same table. A flirtation of sorts began with a Russian student who often used the table, and the other students there "gave her encouraging looks, hoping that they, too, might be drawn in. . . . Henri Gaudier was the most assiduous of those. He always managed to sit by her side, putting his books quite close to hers."[19] One day after showing her his book of drawings, he waited for her at the door, and they walked some distance together. Later Sophie let him walk her as far as her hotel, and after many such walks they finally decided to visit the Louvre together.

Russell's opening sequence vaguely suggests the flirtation idea through Henri's exchange of winks with a fellow student, and Russell replaces the book of drawings with a folded paper bird, but otherwise he introduces his characters much as Ede does, except for a more obvious portrayal of Sophie's "matter-of-fact order" and Henri's forwardness. Immediately after this sequence, however, Russell creates a vignette which not only expresses the charm and energy of Gaudier, but also establishes the central motif of external rejection versus belief in the self.

While talking to Sophie (Dorothy Tutin) about his genius and his ability to create beauty, Henri (Scott Antony) leaps upon a group of conventional statues around a fountain and proclaims to the public his views on art. "Art is dirt. Art is sex, and art is *revolution*." The police, of course, care nothing about art but much about public morality, and Gaudier is forced to flee. This fabricated episode then sets up a visual patterning which will be repeated throughout the film, for although in conflict with each other (Sophie, who is writing a book entitled *Truth: A Novel of the Spirit*, claims that "art is above sex"), the Gaudier-Brzeskas battle together against the limitations and hostility of the outside world.

Henri's theatrics and his free-wheeling declaration of epigrammatic insights on art while engaging in gymnastic feats, although typical of Russell's portraits of artists, appropriately serve to capture visually the description of Henri as a faunlike creature of boundless energy suggested by Pound, Brodzky, and Ede. Also, such scenes allow Russell to present some of the views on art found in Henri's letters in a more dramatic context.

Much of the dialogue between Sophie and Henri in the film is suggested or inspired by letters or descriptions from one of the biographies. Even a casual line such as Henri's reply to Sophie's remark that she does not like men ("Oh, I do. Sometimes I think men are more beautiful than women."), for instance, is often dismissed by critics as Russellian fabrication. The line, however, is not meant to suggest latent homosexuality, nor is it meant to be sensational. It simply reflects observations from Henri's letters.

> He [a Hindu seen in Kew Gardens] walked like a tiger, proud and haughty, with eyes that flashed like steel. I think he was the most lovely man I have ever seen, the sight of him made me wild with pleasure; and would you believe it, the English, with their hideous mugs, laughed like idiots as he went by. In this country it's a kind of crime to be beautiful.[20]

Even the sequence at the Lartique Gallery in which Sophie catches Henri forging a Fragonard is not without some basis in fact. Ezra Pound claims, and Ede accepts this information, that while in Munich, Henri was gainfully employed in the production of faked Rembrandts.[21]

Russell's chief method for the delineation of Sophie's character in the early section of the film is a monologue based on the events of her past life as described by Ede. The language of the script at this point owes much to the second chapter of *Savage Messiah*, but again Russell employs source material only for his own purposes. The sequence is more than the mere revelation of Sophie's frustrations; it is also an attempt to suggest something of Henri's drawing methods. While chopping vegetables, Sophie pours forth her life story at breakneck speed: "Girl, she said, girl, better find a man as stupid as yourself. Writing? Writing? Put that book down. However will we get rid of you? I am sure I do not know." Henri listens from a chair and begins to sketch her, and we, the audience, begin to see her as he does. The bust shots, the intense close-ups of her head and hands, the occasional re-establishing full shots of Henri, and the final glimpse of the drawing simulate the creation of a sketch.

The following sequence, however, owes little to factual evidence, except that it is known that Henri had an interest in primitive art and that he and Sophie visited the Louvre together shortly after their agreement to establish an "artistic companionship". The dialogue as they walk to see Henri's "real" mother, the Louvre, may be an attempt to expose some of Henri's ideas about the relationship of the present to the past in art, but in no way does this brief exchange even hint at the complexities of the historical Henri's Bergsonian theories. The entire sequence itself, however, helps to establish the motif of rejection basic to the film. The improperly dressed Henri wanders through the rooms amidst lifeless paintings viewed by lifeless people presented in "cut-out" fashion, and finally, after being pursued by two guards, he climbs atop a huge stone head from Easter Island and lectures in flamboyant fashion to staid onlookers enjoying the so-called benefits of cultural democracy. "Art is alive. Enjoy it. Laugh at it. Love it or hate it, but don't worship it. You're not in church." Needless to say, both Henri and Sophie are forcibly ejected—and humorously enough right into the midst of a passing funeral procession. As a result of this treatment, they decide to visit Henri's "natural" mother; but she treats them little better.

The removal of Sophie from a cottage near the home of Gaudier's parents is fact, but Russell's method of presentation clearly parallels the Louvre episode and visually reinforces the rejection motif. True, Sophie's discussion with Henri concerning the loneliness of her past life and her inability to kill herself because she was afraid of the worms and the dark comes directly from Ede's account, as does the anonymous letter accusing her of "the improper reception of men". Russell, however, presents Henri's mother as the culprit and stresses the violent reaction of Henri to such an accusation.

The London phase of the lives of Henri and Sophie is condensed by Russell for reasons of time and to achieve the kind of dramatic structure necessary for film. For instance, Sophie's jobs away from London are condensed into one period, and the couple reside throughout at the Putney Arch studio (which the historical Henri found only in the last year of his life in London). Still, many of the short sequences depicting their early life in London (Sophie begging with "her baby"—a doll wrapped in a shawl, Henri translating letters for his Norwegian employer, and Henri visiting a five-bob whore but doing nothing except sketching her) were constructed from a factual base and reshaped by Russell to reinforce the dominant motifs of rejection and conflict which permeate the film.

If the Gaudier-Brzeskas stand in marked contrast to bourgeois conventionality, they are not exactly the darlings of the bohemian world either. It is clear that Henri attended dinner parties similar to the one given by his friend Corky. "A Russian actress ——, a woman with a monocle and pretty stupid, asked in French to explain to her futurism and cubism. When for a joke I made her believe that it had to do with homosexuality, she asked me to go and see her on Thursday evening."[22] But Russell's caricatures of Corky's associates are extreme, perhaps even for him. Indeed, unlike *Dante's Inferno*, in which he offered various, and at times quite unflattering, portraits of the most celebrated members of the Pre-Raphaelite Brotherhood, Russell avoids exact characterizations of any of the Vorticist group and their associates; instead, he creates a glimmering gallery of malicious, decadent, pompous fools led by an epicene art dealer named Shaw, whose sole function seems to be "to depress art".[23] The remainder of the group, minus Corky, are presented as poisonous poseurs who possess neither talent nor character when compared to the Gaudier-Brzeskas, who are the only three dimensional characters in the film, as well as the only characters with real names.

Tom Buff and Kate at times suggest Middleton Murry and Katherine Mansfield, and Mavis Coldstream could have been inspired by Enid Bagnold, but perhaps it is wiser to look at these figures as mere stereotypes. Corky (or "Porky" as he is referred to in Logue's script and on various occasions in the film), on the other hand, is a composite character modelled on Horace Brodzky and Haldane Macfall. Clearly, the first dinner sequence with Corky is drawn from Brodzky's account of his early meetings with Henri and Sophie. The food was frequently made in large quantities and then reheated each night until it was gone, and frequently the conversation concerned Henri's impractical actions.

> She called him "idiot" when he smilingly gave away a carving that he had sweated over for days, and at a time when he was without food, and when he did sell a work, he was often cheated out of the money.[24]

Finally, Brodzky notes that Henri had no social graces and insufferable eating habits ("one never 'dined' with him—that was too polite").[25]

Russell ends the dinner sequence with a wild escapade in which Henri pretends to smash his own ear with a hammer and then runs around the studio before Sophie finally catches him and discovers the hoax. One's first inclination might be to suggest that Russell the prankster has fabricated the episode for his own fun, but he was merely fashioning his distinctive vision of Henri through a careful selection of appropriate biographical material. In fact, in this particular case, the visual rendering, although done in typical Russell fashion, is remarkably similar to Brodzky's account of the incident.

> One evening while working at his bench he told me that he longed for ear-rings, and in fact he would pierce his ears this very evening at once! Sophie was horrified, and called him "abominable," while I was greatly amused.
>
> Having selected a chisel with a fine pencil point, and clasping a hammer in his right hand, he lowered himself into a stooping position until the lobe of the ear was level with the edge of the bench. . . .
>
> He then placed the top of the chisel on the flesh saying, "Ready," gave a smart tap with the hammer, "ping!"
>
> In an instant Brzeska dropped the tools, grabbed his ear, yelled and danced round the studio cursing his agony. Sophie chased him and he eluded her. And then began a mad tearing round the studio, until Sophie was exhausted, being unable to capture him. The air was full of "*psharchref*" and other strange language, and dust. And Sophie cursed and called him "*abominable*." And all the time Brzeska held his ear with a handkerchief and moaned. He wouldn't come to her. And then she coaxed him in a soft voice, and eventually she grabbed him, and examined his ears, first one and then the other. And when she had convinced herself that Brzeska had played another trick upon her, and that he had not touched his ear at all, she gave him a resounding slap in the face.[26]

Although Corky and his associates have a basis in historical fact, one might suspect that Shaw, the poseur and parasite who lives off the arts, is wholly a Russell creation. But this is not the case. Shaw, a universal figure whose existence plagues the serious artist at every turn, "was based on Roger Fry, the guy who exploited Gaudier and the whole vortex group".[27] While counterpointing Henri's values, Shaw also functions in the film by setting up one of the key sequences. He baits Henri into an offer to show him a non-existent statue, and Gaudier, with assistance from Corky and Sophie, steals a suitable piece of marble from a graveyard and in a frenzy of work creates "Torso" in a mere six hours.

The incident is obviously exaggerated, but again it is not without foundation from Gaudier's life. Ezra Pound notes that when passing a certain cemetery, Henri often marvelled at the waste of good stone, and Frank Harris tells the story that Gaudier created his first carvings when Jacob Epstein told him that he would come to see his work. "So Gaudier at once went out, got three small stone blocks, and by working more or less night and day had something ready by Sunday."[28] Also, the babbling-lecture to the yawning Corky and the sleeping Sophie has a parallel to historical fact. On one occasion, Brodzky spent the night with Gaudier but found it was impossible to sleep. Brzeska needed an audience and talked into the early hours, hammering away at some stone and explaining his actions to his half-asleep companion.[29]

In the film, the "Torso" sequence allows Russell to show that artistic achievement is "usually five percent inspiration and ninety-five per cent perspiration and hard slog"[30] and to present a context for Gaudier's monologue, which reveals some of the artistic attitudes held in common by both Gaudier and Russell.

Henri philosophizes and chips away at the marble stone, and as the rhythmic ticking of the chisel accompanies his voice, the constantly moving camera sweeps in an 180° angle, then slowly up, then down; all with the net effect that the audience begins to see the form take shape. Also, the superb lighting and the *mise-en-scène* of the sequence allow the viewer to gain some sense of the texture of the stone itself.

For Henri, each blow must be true, and because of that, "every blow is a risk". Art, however, is not something magical or mystical, as Henri explains in his monologue.

> You can always tell a bad artist, like a bad doctor, by the fact that he tries to surround his words with some hocus-pocus. Sure there's a mystery, but there is as much a mystery to the one who is doing it as to the one who is looking at it. . . . But, by and large, it would be wrong to be taken in by that solitary genius stuff. Of course, I do it because it pleases me. There is nothing wrong with that. But if it don't give me a lot doing it, how the hell is it going to give anything to anybody else. That's the mystery, Porkums.
>
> Why anybody else wants to look at the work someone like me does and give good money for it—*Amazing*. Why don't they just do their own? I'm not interested in somebody else's work, unless I can steal from it—unless it gives me something I can use. And yet, if there isn't somebody there to see it, then "*zut*" as my divine sister would say, just a lump of stone. Put St. Paul's Cathedral in a cardboard box, and what have you got? A heavy box.

Russell's Henri Gaudier, the man, is as much passion as perspiration. Although Henri completes the torso piece in a single night, Shaw does not bother to keep his appointment, and Russell again fabricates an incident which adds to the visual rhythm and the structural pattern that subtly unifies the film.

Henri carts his newly created piece to Shaw's and then proceeds to throw it through the gallery window, and the following short, ironic scene, depicting Henri being forcibly removed from a cell and the jailhouse itself, is filmed in a fashion parallel to the expulsion from the Louvre. Yet another variation of this motif occurs only a few scenes later when Henri and Gosh Boyle are thrown out of the Vortex, Shaw's anachronistically garish nightclub.

Gosh Boyle, Russell's most outlandish female character in the film, is little different from Shaw, and just as he is used to counterpoint Henri, Gosh contrasts with Sophie—at all levels from social to sexual. Both women, for instance, sing ridiculous songs. The historical Sophie often sang her Polish folk melodies for guests, and Russell's Sophie sings about the lives of two fleas as a commentary on her own existence, as a half-insane cry from the depths. Gosh's plea of "Votes for Women", on the other hand, is merely a faddish attempt to save herself from boredom, and Russell ruthlessly ridicules Gosh not because she is a feminist, but because she is a shallow, spoiled fool with silly illusions of grandeur. When nude descending a staircase and dancing à la Isadora Duncan, she rhapsodizes on her creative ambitions. "I don't care what I do so long as it's creative. I want to leave something behind me that was never there before." The fully clothed Henri replies, "Lavatory is outside." Later in the film, however, Gosh finds her "creative outlet" by designing the handbag she takes with her to the front—which, if nothing else, will relieve the tedium of her life as a civilian.

Like Shaw and the others, Gosh Boyle is also drawn from a real character in Henri's life—a young woman who agreed to sit for him but who, after a short time, left for Paris. When she returned, she

> came back with sensational tales of how she had danced naked, greatly to the delight of the artists; how Isadora Duncan had wanted to meet her, and how several theatres had offered to engage her. Also Modigliani had wanted to sleep with her, but she had refused because he drank and had no money.[31]

Henri was charmed by her unconventionality and told Sophie that he intended to make love to this woman. Sophie replied that she must be allowed to stand behind a screen when this event took place. Finally, after a few weeks Henri brought his model to see Sophie.

> Miss Brzeska was feeling particularly irritated by the noise around her, had stopped her ears with cotton-wool, and was sitting right up against the wall, with her back to the room, so as not to see its bare misery, and was singing at the top of her voice.[32]

Russell, in his film, treats Sophie's remark about standing behind the screen as literally happening, and also includes much of the material from Sophie's actual meeting with Henri's model. The result is, of course, an exaggerated and humorous scene, but one which also incorporates a number of recurring themes and motifs (the "Two Fleas" song, the incomplete sexual encounter, and the strange bond between Henri and Sophie which can't be understood by outsiders) that again function in terms of the film's structure.

For purposes of condensation, Russell also makes Major Smythies, who actually commissioned a bust from Henri, into Major Boyle, Gosh's father. There is, however, much more involved here. The action of the sequence involving the creation of the bust is again based on fact,[33] but the dialogue as presented in the film has little to do with the war views of the real Henri. Instead, this sequence is an attempt on the part of the filmmaker and the script writer to force the audience to respond directly to certain issues which existed both in Henri's time and the present. Major Boyle is appalled that "some young men would rather go to jail than go to war", and he criticizes "too much education" because it leads to "fancy ideals, like art". Obviously, the dialogue again stresses the role of the artist as an outsider attacked by the prevailing forces of a society which can never fully understand or respect his achievements.

Two other notable sequences in the film also merge biographical facts with Russell's unique vision and style. First, Shaw's nightclub, Vortex, has its parallel in the Café Royal, where Horace Brodzky first heard the news of Henri's death at the front, but as it is conceived in Russell's film the club functions as the vehicle for a satirical thrust at the entire Vorticist movement, and as the basis for an attack on our own culture. This anachronistically designed set (reminiscent of a modern discothèque) suggests that the decadence and hypocrisy which masquerades as art is as much a part of the present as of the past. Second, the seaside holiday, although of major emotional importance to the Gaudier-Brzeskas and presented as such in the film, also provides Russell with his obligatory transcendence sequence where Henri, high atop a cliff of marble slabs, shouts exuberantly of his talent and dreams to his "real" father, the Sun.

Exaggeration for thematic purposes and to create structural patterns of visual rhythm is by no means the only effective technique in this film. The use of close-middle shots and space play, the manipulation of setting, and the employment of music for purposes of contrast and allusion are subtle devices which have gone unnoticed by those reviewers who claim that the film is "very poor technically".

Russell makes extensive use of close-up shots in all his films, and *Savage Messiah* is no exception. When filming Henri and Sophie, however, he frequently opts for the close-middle shot, presenting them in the frame together. This is done so frequently that the right side of the screen becomes associated with Henri and the left side with Sophie; and thus the idea of the two as a unit against the outside world is spatially supported. When Henri is with Gosh Boyle, Russell rarely includes them in the same frame, and when he does, he tends to avoid the close-middle shot. Only once, for a brief instant, does he employ this shot, but even here Gosh does not usurp Sophie's area of the screen.

Setting is also used to suggest the pressures brought against the protagonists by the external world. Only twice do we see the Gaudier-Brzeskas free from the confines of the city. The first is a moment of serenity at Henri's parents, and the second a moment of grandeur when, on holiday, they journey to the seacoast. These times, however, are short-lived, and the bulk of the film emphasizes the poverty these two people endure. Russell has often complained that color glamorizes films—even scenes of squalor, and this is probably true, but his use of lighting and the cramped setting at the Putney Arch studio create an atmosphere which effectively imprisons his characters.

Finally, it is necessary to mention the *mise-en-scène* of these sequences. The open space in front of the arch is a haven for beggars ("If you live in an age of beggars, you must draw beggars"), and the final resting place for Henri's last unfinished sculpture piece. Above this area, the iron-barred grate allows for a glimpse of the concerns of the external world: demonstrators against the coming war, cannons on the way to the front in France, and parade bands playing marching songs.

Russell also distorts the historical Henri's enthusiasm about fighting in the war in order to suggest again that society impinges on the artist, try as he may to see his own effort as equal in importance to politics and social activity. Russell's Henri, who considers his work significant and beneficial to people ("I am responsible, and I don't care what they say. Things are beautiful, and that helps"), finally decides to enlist only after he discovers from a passing newsboy that the Germans have bombed Rheims Cathedral. Even Gaudier-Brzeska cannot totally remove himself from the society around him, and Russell emphasizes this fact by a significant shot from the street level down into the basement space as Henri reaches his hand through the grate for a copy of the newspaper. At the very end of the film, Sophie stands alone with Henri's unfinished sculpture in this open space outside the studio, while the marching soldiers returning from the war are seen through the outside grate. Thus Russell again forces his viewers to acknowledge the conflict which has been so dominant throughout the film.

This conflict is also suggested in other ways, as in the use of music in the film. The forces of conventionality are frequently represented by military band music for instance, while a bouncy but dissonant piano accompanies the decadent, bohemian types. Henri and

Sophie, on the other hand, are associated with the music of Debussy and in one particularly effective sequence with the music of Alexander Scriabin. The two spend an afternoon sketching and writing while sitting near a pond. They look at each other and clasp hands. The long, lingering close-up of the hands—one young and smooth between two thin and worn—is accompanied by the sounds of the opening of the third movement of *The Divine Poem*. This music, according to Scriabin, describes the evolution of the human spirit which, after struggling through intellectual and sexual doubt, reaches a mystical state. "The spirit is now released from its former ties of submission to a higher force . . . it creates its own world by its own creative Will."[34]

The sequence with its central images of the clasping hands serves as an aural/visual manifestation of the Platonic link between Henri and Sophie, and as a necessary prelude to the pledging of troth and the exchanging of last names; but more than that, it is also part of another visual motif which reveals conflict through contrast. The title credit is set off against Henri's drawing of the bones of a hand, and close-up shots of hands abound in the film—Henri chiselling a stone or sketching, Sophie writing or chopping vegetables, or their hands clasping together. In contrast, we have the bejewelled fingers of Shaw squeezing grapes, the waving hands of Gosh in imitation of a new dance movement, and the hands of the glittering, painted dancers in Shaw's club who cavort about while Corky reads Henri's final letter.

This sequence at the pond between Henri and Sophie is entirely Russell's invention, and serves as an excellent illustration of his working methods with scripts by other writers.

> I usually tell them [script writers] how I would like the story. We discuss it; they will say why they don't like something or how they think something can be improved or come up with their own idea. They read it to me, and we revise as we go along. Usually, when I'm shooting, I revise yet again according to the necessities of the day. I believe in using what is available, and when I've changed my mind, I rewrite the whole thing. They know how I feel and they know my work. They've seen all the films. It's a very good relationship.[35]

Russell clearly changed his mind about the pond sequence, but more importantly, the changes reveal his overriding desire to communicate whenever possible with sound and image rather than with words. Russell transforms the verbal essence of the sequence into a series of effective images supported by sound. This process, no matter what the subject matter of his films, remains the one constant in Russell's methods of adaptation.[36]

Although *Savage Messiah* is a vastly underrated film, it also contains some damaging faults. Things have become easy for Russell, and in this film, he seems content to repeat himself, rather than to tackle new artistic problems. The dinner sequence at Corky's, for instance, owes something to the "fig-eating" lesson from *Women in Love*, and staged poses and facial expressions suggesting awe, transcendence, or concern wear a bit thin after seeing them repeatedly in Russell's films. Russell himself appears to have sensed something of this problem, and purposely avoided most of his usual actors, with the exception of Judith Paris (Kate) and Ben Aris (Tom Buff). Unfortunately, inexperienced Scott Antony, the male lead, flattens out the character of Henri and can't match the subtle, nearly flawless performance of Dorothy Tutin as Sophie.

Finally, it is necessary to mention the uncommon restraint which Russell exercises in this film. There are no great war sequences, only a single photograph showing Henri, the soldier, as he points to a carving made out of the butt of a captured rifle. Russell never mentions the fact that Sophie loses her reason and dies in a madhouse. Instead, the film sacrifices such high drama, ending with a striking exhibition of the major pieces sculpted by the man whose life we have just seen. Even here, Russell significantly alters Logue's script. In the first draft, the exhibition is held before Henri's death, and he is present to comment on spectators' responses to his work.[37] In the shooting script, the exhibition takes place after Henri's death, but the emphasis remains on the verbal responses of the people in the gallery. In the film, there is no dialogue; only the music of Debussy accompanies the images. True, many onlookers giggle at the pieces or just pass casually by, but we, the film audience, see these works in a different way, and Russell's filming allows us full appreciation. There is little camera movement, but there are multiple light sources, and the pieces frequently rotate on turntables. As a result, light reveals the form of many pieces and provides a sense of their texture. Gaudier-Brzeska's art, like the paintings of Rousseau and the music of Delius, survives the man; but the last shot of Sophie standing next to the large, barely chiselled stone reminds us of the unfulfilled potential of the man.

Possibly, Ken Russell was attracted to Henri Gaudier-Brzeska as the subject of a film biography because, as he noted in an interview with Peter Buckley, "one recognizes in him what one hopes one might aspire to oneself. He had marvellous things to say about art, very simple, straightforward things, and he knew he was good."[38] In *Savage Messiah*, Russell presents the views of Gaudier-Brzeska and exposes some of his own attitudes towards art. In doing so, he creates the least ambivalent and most glowing portrait of any of his artist heroes.

NOTES

[1]Cited in H. S. Ede, *Savage Messiah* (New York: Avon Books, 1972, London: Gordon Fraser, 1971, pp. 60–1.

[2]John Baxter, *An Appalling Talent/Ken Russell* (London: Michael Joseph, 1973), p. 211.

[3]Sandy Wilson, *The Boy Friend* (Harmondsworth, England: Penguin, 1959).

[4]Cited in "*The Boy Friend*", Filmfacts, 14 (1971), p. 470.

[5]See John Baxter's first draft of *An Appalling Talent,* TS.

[6]Cited in Peter Buckley, "Savage Saviour", *Films and Filming,* October 1972, p. 14.

[7]In the *New York Times* of November 26, 1972, the column "What's New at the Movies?" lists two favorable reviews (Wolf and Zimmerman), four mixed reviews (Kathleen Carroll, Sarris, Crist and Drew), and 13 negative reviews (John Simon, Arthur Knight, Canby, Winsten, Kissel, Shalit, Harris, Lyons, Kael, Schickel Reed, Taylor and Gelmis).

[8]Robert Hughes, "Erratic Bust", *Time,* 20 November 1972, p. 98.

[9]Cited in Buckley, p. 15.

[10]Pauline Kael, "Hyperbole and Narcissus", *The New Yorker,* 18 November 1972, pp. 225 and 228.

[11]Cited in Buckley, p. 14.

[12]H. S. Ede, "Preface", *Savage Messiah,* p. 7.

[13]H. S. Ede, *Savage Messiah,* p. 32.

[14]*Ibid.,* p. 33.

[15]*Ibid.,* p. 90.

[16]*Ibid.,* p. 155.

[17]*Ibid.,* p. 160.

[18]It should be noted that Russell was not entirely happy with Logue's first draft and made significant changes before the adaptation reached the shooting script stage. Michael Dempsey, in "Savage Messiah", *Film Heritage,* 9 (Winter 1973–4), notes that "Logue's first draft, besides omitting the antiwar demonstrators, also omits the film's warmongering Gosh, the newsphoto, and Major Boyle. (For him it substitutes a daffy eccentric, Lady Hilarity, who has turned her house into a military shrine and dresses up like Florence Nightingale.)"

[19]Ede, p. 11.

[20]*Ibid.,* p. 61.

[21]*Ibid.,* p. 27.

[22]*Ibid.,* p. 126. Compare these lines to the following extract from Logue's shooting script.

> 33 Porky's flat. Int. Night
>
> People sitting round listening to the gramophone. The source of the music. Gaudier is still drawing.
>
> Gaudier: A tiger burning in the day—a woman's body burning in the night.

Sensual, kaleidoscopic lights and shades but with sounds instead of tones.

Kate: That's one vision I suppose. But it sounds more like Blake than Debussy.

Buff: I don't smell tigers, but it reeks of sex.

Sophie: I see lights.

Mavis: I thought it was a ballet about homosexuality.

Buff: Just what you'd expect from the Diaghilev set.

Shaw: They say he's had every little boy in the corps de ballet.

Kate: Do you associate impressionism with homosexuality, Mr. Brzeska?

Gaudier: It's a lot of cock.

[23]Possibly because of the legal difficulties with *The Dance of the Seven Veils*, Russell decided to avoid any libel action by simply dealing with the minor figures as stereotypes.

[24]Horace Brodzky, *Henri Gaudier-Brzeska 1891–1915* (London: Faber and Faber Limited, 1933), p. 28.

[25]*Ibid.*, p. 50.

[26]*Ibid.*, pp. 56–8.

[27]From Russell's undated letter commenting on an early draft of this chapter.

[28]Ezra Pound, *Gaudier-Brzeska: A Memoir* (New York: New Directions, 1970), p. 76.

[29]Brodzky, pp. 50–2.

[30]See "Many Stories in One", *MGM Pressbook for Savage Messiah* (Metro-Goldwyn-Mayer, Inc., 1972).

[31]Ede, p. 150.

[32]*Ibid.*

[33]Brodzky, pp. 77–8.

[34]Cited in Faubion Bowers, *Scriabin*, Vol. I (Tokyo: Kondansha International Ltd., 1969), p. 341.

[35]Terry Curtis Fox, "Conversations With Ken Russell", *Oui*, June 1973, p. 102.

[36]In a recent interview, Russell claimed that he is happiest when "doing music and visual things".

> I associate dialogue with plays rather than films. The film of mine that was least successful was *Savage Messiah* which, although worthy, wasn't cinematic enough. I leant too heavily on the script; it could have been a radio play.
>
> I prefer to write my own scripts. I'd be the first to admit that I can't write as well as my writer-friends, but I can express on film things that I can't explain to them so that they can put it into their dialogue for the scene to work.

See John Walker, "Ken Russell's New Enigma", *The Observer Magazine*, 8 September 1974, p. 55.

[37]Dempsey, p. 16.

[38]Buckley, p. 13.

9

Mahler

Further Experiments With Metaphor and Personal Vision

> Composers are the nearest to doing what I'm trying to do; to express the inexpressible, or rather, to investigate it, to plumb the unplumbable, the divine mystery.
>
> Ken Russell[1]

Savage Messiah was a comparatively restrained film with somewhat limited objectives, but *Mahler* (1974), Russell's next biopic harkened back to *The Music Lovers*, where he fused history, myth, music, and personal vision into a carefully structured, organic work of art. In *Mahler*, however, Russell sacrifices concerns with organic unity to press this synthesis even further. In some respects, it is Russell's most experimental work to date, but it also emerges as a curious mixture of grand moments and unfortunate miscalculations.

Like so many of the subjects for his films, Gustav Mahler was considered as an appropriate protagonist for a Russell biopic some time before the film was actually made. As early as 1970, Russell expressed a desire to film the Austrian composer's life. This remark, in turn, prompted film critic Alexander Walker to reply that he would come after Russell with an elephant gun if he ever made such a film; and this claim provided some of the basis for one of those notorious confrontations between Russell and Walker on the BBC Film Night Program.[2] Plans for the film, however, never seemed to materialize.

> I'll get a letter from Anna Mahler saying "I'm back in London. I'd like to see you" and I think: My God, I *must* do that film. For a whole

> day it's going to be my next film, then I think of something else and the Mahler vision recedes. They all keep recurring year after year, these ideas; new ones come and go, but when the final choice has to be made it always seems inevitable.[3]

Perhaps Russell's decision to begin shooting a film biography of Mahler in 1973 was inevitable, but one suspects that being out of work for over a year also played a role. After the failure of a number of projects, an offer came to make a film on Mahler as an English-German co-production "for the video cassette market".[4] The project as originally conceived fell through, and the large budget had to be scaled down considerably when Goodtimes Enterprises took over the project alone. Russell, however, gathered Dick Bush and a number of his other regulars to shoot the film in only nine weeks, and the results were stunning enough to earn the film the 1974 Cannes Award for Best Technical Achievement.

Beginning with the Strauss film, Russell emphasized his own personal response to the music and to the protagonist of his composer biopics, but this emphasis is even greater in *Mahler*, perhaps because the composer and the filmmaker have similar artistic sensibilities. Both, for instance, have paid tribute to the value of exaggeration in art, and both have created some of their greatest works by reshaping the texts of others to fit their own artistic conceptions. For Mahler, the assimilation of music and ideas from various divergent sources became crucial to his development of a revolutionary orchestral idiom. "Synthesis", writes biographer Kurt Blaukopf, "is the essence of Mahler's philosophy in his symphonies, combining in a uniquely personal manner philosophical concepts, ecstatic confessions, expressionist outbursts and the poetic innocence of . . . Romanticism."[5] Much the same can be said for Russell, who in his chosen medium achieves synthesis through the assimilation of influences from a variety of sometimes unlikely sources. Finally, there are even a number of similarities in their personal lives: both men pursued their own particular artistic visions without regard for the hostile attacks on their work, and both men converted to Roman Catholicism. Alma Mahler, in her memoirs, suggests that Gustav always had a leaning towards Catholic mysticism,[6] but clearly his conversion was more an act of convenience which removed the obstacle of Judaism from an appointment to the Court Theatre in Vienna, and it is treated as such in the film. Russell, on the other hand, converted out of sincerity—finding in the religion a "rock" in an unstable universe. Although no longer a practicing Catholic, his mystical inclinations are still present, and one suspects that Mahler's explanations to his daughters, Putzi and Glucki, concerning God and the nature of the universe, which were not found in the shooting script, come as much from Russell as from any account of Mahler's beliefs.

Given these parallels, one can easily understand why Russell elects to stress his own personal response to Mahler and to define the man's inner life through his music rather than through historical facts of his life and times. Pointing out violations of literal truth in the film can be interesting and perhaps even necessary, but ultimately such observations have little to do with the film as Russell conceived it, and should not be part of the criteria for judging it.

Metaphor is the key to *Mahler*, and Russell underscores this concept both visually and verbally in the opening moments of the film. Mahler's dream, edited to the first movement of *Symphony #3*, is actually an allegorical ballet in which the figure of a struggling woman, after failing to break through the confines of a chrysalis, crawls slowly across a barren landscape to caress a rock shaped much like the composer's face. For those who know Mahler's music beyond a fleeting acquaintance, the rock image becomes a visual pun linked to the original title of the symphony's first movement, "What the Rocks Tell Me", but on a more serious level, the dream is an accurate representation of the emotional relationship between Mahler and his wife. Mahler (Robert Powell) awakens ("I slept like a log. (pause) No, like a rock.") and, in a dialogue with his wife, offers a verbal explanation of the images from the dream and their relationship to his music. Throughout the film, Russell employs this method of explaining in verbal terms what he has just presented in a visual sequence through the matching of image and music, perhaps as a concession to those in his audience totally unfamiliar with the composer's music. This strange shifting from subtle allusion to obvious verbal explanation, perhaps as a sop to the general audience, and the over-emphasis on spoof raise a number of questions about the exact nature of Russell's response to the composer. As Derek Elley has noted: "in *Mahler* he [Russell] sometimes appears uncertain whether to go all-out (as in the Strauss piece) or make a more deeply-felt (but honest) appraisal (as with Delius)".[7]

In any event, after the initial dialogue, the train stops at a station, and Alma (Georgina Hale) flits out for a fashion magazine. Enter Krenek, an intrepid journalist, who pesters Mahler with a series of questions and interprets the answers only on the lowest, most literal level. Finally, the impatient Mahler spits out words which interestingly enough Russell himself uttered at an awkward moment in an interview with Gordon Gow,[8] and which could easily be used as an epigraph for the entire film: "I was speaking metaphorically."

According to Russell, Mahler's music dictated the content and the musical shape of the film, but the concern with achieving metaphorical truth determined both the narrative frame and the nature of the characters. The film's structure offers little to a passive viewer concerned primarily with the story line; the framework of the film is a last train ride from Paris to Vienna in 1911, a trip which in her memoirs Alma remembers as being like the last journey of a dying king,[9] but which here becomes a pilgrimage to self-discovery which ends paradoxically in both defeat and triumph. Mahler the man will die at the moment he most wants to live, but Mahler the artist will live through his music. The ending, however, is far more ambiguous than this description suggests. One can't help feeling that the final joke is on poor old Gustav, who has just told Alma that "as long as my music lasts (pause) our love will last". This, of course, is the same Alma who, after Mahler's death, will go through a string of lovers and three husbands (including Walter Gropius and Franz Werfel) before her own death in 1964.

Other similar ironies abound throughout the film. The African princess, who within the metaphorical dimensions of the film serves as an avatar of death, toys with Mahler in a peculiarly Russellian manner. The bemused composer thinks that at long last he has found someone who understands his quest for "the harmony of the universe".

> Princess: It's a great privilege to meet someone who knows what it's all about.
>
> Mahler: The music of the spheres you mean.
>
> Princess: No, I mean death.

This deflating of the composer's accomplishments continues with the appearance of the doctor who examines him on the train. Mahler claims that he is unable to express in words the answers to the metaphysical questions posed by the doctor. He has written about death, resurrection, and the spirit of creation in his music; only none of the meaning that he has found there can ever be known to the tone deaf doctor.

Mahler is also harassed by Max, the officer in love with Alma, who, like Chiluvsky in *The Music Lovers*, is a symbolic character embodying a number of men, including Walter Gropius. For Mahler, Max is more than a mere threat to his marriage; he is the very embodiment of betrayal. The hostile aural/visual associations of military band music and soldiers which began in the composer's childhood return throughout the film and finally culminate in Mahler's death fantasy—a vision of Alma's treacherous violation of trust in which she, Max, and future lovers dressed in SS uniforms carry off a casket containing the still-living composer to a crematorium. This fantasy sequence, which attempts to depict the emotional reality of Mahler's fears that his wife would leave him in a manner appropriate to a post-Auschwitz audience, uses methods that Russell employs again in the flamboyant, but much less successful, silent movie version of Mahler's conversion to Catholicism. Here Russell seeks to synthesize the trappings of Norse myth, images from Fritz Lang's *Siegfried*, Wagner's "Ride of the Valkyries", and Nazi symbolism to delineate his own reaction as an artist to what he believes was Mahler's self-betrayal for financial reward and social prestige.

Even though much of the film derives from Russell's responses to Mahler's music, many of the visual images still have their origins in the facts of Mahler's life reinterpreted so that they function within the film's unique structure. A remark in Alma's memoirs in which she describes her growing sense of inferiority in her husband's presence, "I felt I was nothing but his shadow", is taken over by Russell and acted out to Mahler's music.[10] In the film, Alma appears dressed as a shadow behind her husband as admirers crowd around and brush her aside. Also, Alma's quieting of cattle, shepherds, children, church bells, and brass bands while Mahler composes in his secluded hut has a basis in fact. In 1896, while he was finishing his Third Symphony at Steinbach, his sister Justi and a friend had to resort to similar tactics to preserve silence. In the film, the cross-cutting, the symbolic clothing to reflect the innocence of their relationship,[11] the swirling, careening camera, and masterful editing of the images to the music work together to produce one of the film's best moments. Although not entirely accurate on a literal level, this sequence, like so many others in Russell's films, reflects accurate psychological and emotional dimensions of the characters.

Within the outer framework of the train journey then, Russell reveals the emotional lives of Alma and Gustav and his responses to them through flashbacks, dreams, his own fantasies, and those of his characters. This complex pattern of devices is grouped with total disregard for chronological designation and conventional form. At one point, for instance, in the middle of Alma's flashback of the "burial" of her talent through the literal burial of her early songs, there is a long reverie by Mahler depicting Russell's rather unique interpretation of Hugo Wolf's insanity as the result of strain from failure of recognition, rather than syphilis. This and other strange configurations of sequences, according to Russell, are part of a Rondo form derived from Mahler's total musical output.

> Rondo form is ABACADAE etc. In this case A, the recurring theme, is love—the love of Mahler for his wife—B, C, D, E, etc. are all variations on the theme of death including the death of innocence, responsibility, aspiration, trust, understanding, etc. Some of the death themes are also connected with the main theme and one of these is developed at some length. It is probably the most important of all—the death of love.[12]

Interesting as this explanation is in providing a rationale for the film's dense texture and subtle organization of recurring visual motifs, it does not guarantee the organic unity of the film. Unlike *The Music Lovers*, which contains nothing gratuitous, *Mahler* is, in the final analysis, a fragmented film of brilliant sequences.

Perhaps this generalization can be best supported by examining Russell's working script of *Mahler*. The overall conception of the film as a journey remains, but in many ways, this script is less metaphorical than the final version and more conventionally structured. The flashbacks, for instance, contrast and balance each other in a somewhat obvious pattern of variations.

During the actual filming process, Russell frequently revises his script according to the needs of the shooting or from sudden bursts of intuition, but with *Mahler*, it seems that he frequently embellished or exaggerated an individual sequence without his usual consideration for its role within the film's entire framework. As a result, there is an uncomfortable mixture of styles and attitudes rather than the successful synthesis of seemingly divergent or even contradictory aspects he so masterfully achieved in *The Devils*.

This does not mean, however, that all of Russell's reworkings in *Mahler* were to ill purpose. The real Gustav as a child of eleven, for instance, while boarding with the Grunfeld family in Prague, witnessed "a brutal sexual encounter between the chambermaid and the son of the house".[13] The incident was a traumatic experience, and for Kurt Balukopf, "some of the difficulties in uniting the sexual and the emotional aspects of love making may be traced back to this incident, as may the strengthening of his ties with his mother, and his ideals of purity and renunciation".[14] In Russell's first treatment, Gustav, on the way home from school one day, witnesses a rather touching moment of love-making between a woman and her drum major husband. The episode, however, conveys none of the terror and horror that suggests the linking of passion and pain in Gustav's mind. In the final script, Gustav sees his father forcing himself upon the family's servant girl, and while certainly not literally accurate, this depiction does much to suggest the psychological trauma that the boy Mahler endured, and the latent Oedipal fixation which some critics find embellished in the Eighth Symphony.[15]

Some of the visuals only briefly described in the early script are also altered for the better in the film itself, but perhaps the most intriguing aspect of Russell's attempts to match visuals to music is the way in which they frequently hint at certain psychological underpinnings of the composer—or as Derek Elley phrases it, "the claustrophobia of his many complexes".[16] Many, including the image of the nearly demonic, rearing white stallion whose appearance jolts the viewer's vision just as the accompanying eerie notes from the third movement of the Third Symphony jolt his hearing, suggest the fear of defeat, death and/or madness.

Finally, Russell's movement from some of the more conventional episodes and characters of the early script to the symbolic representations of the film itself certainly intensifies the metaphorical dimensions of the film. In the first treatment, there is no metaphorical dimension to the Princess who exchanges compartments with Mahler on the train; she is simply a somewhat foolish bohemian blue-stocking. Neither is Max a soldier who embodies all of Alma's real and/or projected admirers; he is clearly only Gropius, and Mahler is even capable of defending himself by attacking Bauhaus architecture as "crude, obvious and square". Also, in the pre-production script, a General von Muller shares Mahler's compartment for a brief time and serves as the catalyst for a silly fantasy dealing with Mahler as a soldier making love to a woman who embodies the spirit of Nationalism and military glamor.

This last episode derives from attitudes that Russell first explored in his abandoned treatment of *Music Music Music*, and the anachronistic use of a gas mask on Mahler, the soldier (?), as he wanders through no-man's land is simply a reworking of a scene in which John Fairfax, the protagonist of *Music Music Music*, fantasizes a similar situation. This preoccupation with making a statement about the artist's allegiance to his country, to his conscience, or to humanity, however, is not abandoned in *Mahler* simply because General von Muller and this bizarre fantasy are eliminated. In their stead, Russell, again at the expense of unity of tone and style, radically revised the fantasy sequences in which Mahler imagines himself dead and in which he confronts Cosima Wagner. This latter sequence, which is conceived in silent film form, might be compared to the *1812 Overture* section of *The Music Lovers*, but unlike its predecessor, the sequence from *Mahler* is cinematically dull, infused with in-jokes, and unrewarding in terms of the matching of music, song, and images.

In his own notes on the film, however, Russell defends his depiction of these episodes:

> Mahler also betrayed himself when he changed his religion ostensibly for social and financial reasons. Cosima Wagner ruled the musical world of Austria and to "get to the top" in his bread and butter job as a conductor, Mahler simply had to renounce his Judaism and embrace a religion acceptable to her. In a sense this was almost like Siegfried's courtship of Brunhilda—only Mahler was no Aryan like Wagner's hero, so he had to become one. As any convert knows there is an awful lot of mystery to go through before Baptism. Wagner created a religion of his own based on the mythical claptrap of old Norse legends, which his famous opera cycle the Ring is all about, coupled with his manic

> anti-semitism as propounded in his opera Parsifal—one of the philosophical foundations on which Hitler's Nazi Germany was built.
>
> Bearing all this in mind there was no way to treat Mahler's "conversion" in terms other than those I used in the film—if the implications as they appear to me were to be realized.
>
> In yet another fantasy sequence Mahler appears to be cremated by S.S. Men. When I first planned this, his pall bearers were not conceived as being anything other than the usual mourners, albeit military ones. But in depicting the nightmare in which the dead Mahler sees his wife desecrating his memory with her lovers of the future (the most prominent being Max who has already been established in the film as the symbolic threat to love—the military man) it becomes inevitable; put an Austrian officer of 1900 into a uniform of mourning and you have an S.S. Man. Take a Jew pretending not to be a Jew, project him a few years into the future and you have Mahler—or someone like him—being carried off to the crematorium—alive.[17]

Again, Russell suggests that the results, like the subjects of his films, are inevitable, but here one can seriously question the logic of his argument. Why, for instance, does an Austrian officer of 1900 in a uniform of mourning become an SS Man? Perhaps the answer rests with Russell wanting to deal with the theme of the artist's allegiance to himself and to the demands of nationalism—a theme that he treats in *The Dance of the Seven Veils* and even in *Savage Messiah*, where he ignores Gaudier-Brzeska's response to World War I and incorporates some of his own attitudes.

In any event, too much of *Mahler* belongs in other films. One of the projects, for instance, that Russell devised between the shooting of *Savage Messiah* and *Mahler* was a plan to adapt an Isaac Babel story for the BBC.[18] Although this particular film was never made, Russell has made film adaptations of some of Babel's stories and, unfortunately, they are found in *Mahler*. The young Mahler's encounter with his father over the failure to win a scholarship is taken from "The Story of My Dovecot", and all the other experiences of the composer's youth—the dialogue at the dinner table, the encounter with Sladky, the flight to the privy, and even the character of old Nick—are taken from Babel's autobiographical tale "The Awakening".[19] As a result, aside from having an uneasy response at seeing old Nick sitting on a tombstone in Mahler's death fantasy, one must call into doubt Russell's own comment that *Mahler* "is simply about some of the things I feel when I think of Mahler's life and listen to his music".[20]

Although Russell used material from Isaac Babel in his film, it is interesting to note that he did not include the famous meeting between Freud and Mahler. It was during this meeting, according to Ernest Jones, that Mahler supposedly claimed that his music failed to reach the highest order of art because the noblest passages, which had been inspired by the expression of tragic feeling or profound emotions, were constantly interrupted by frivolous or banal melodies. Mahler himself then traced this back to a childhood incident in which he witnessed an especially painful quarrel between his parents and while rushing away encountered a hurdy-gurdy man grinding out "Ach, du lieber Augustin", a trivial popular melody. "In Mahler's opinion the conjunction of high tragedy and light amusement was from then on inextricably fixed in his mind, and the one mood inevitably brought the other with it."[21]

If this unfortunate conjunction kept Mahler from reaching art of the highest order, it is an affliction occasionally shared by Russell himself, and perhaps to no worse effect than in this very film. Russell's undercutting of the seriousness of his subject matter is not the issue, for all too often this device has simply been misunderstood. Like medieval mystery plays, his films mingle humor, horror, earthy details and lyricism, and for instance, in *The Devils*, the humor and satire are fittingly appropriate to the period's "dance of death" atmosphere. Instead, the excessiveness that detracts from some of Russell's films is the penchant for the in-joke. A few in-jokes for the initiated can be fun, but too much of *Mahler* is a collection of in-jokes, borrowings from his own previous films, and pastiches of other films.

The in-jokes are perhaps too numerous to mention, but they range from verbal references to *The Music Lovers* to a quick close-up of Oliver Reed as a train conductor. The borrowings include images, such as young Mahler's ride on the white stallion taken over from *Elgar*; and they include locations, such as the lake setting of Gustav's hut already used in *Dante's Inferno* and the "Cave of the Dragon of the Old Gods" for the silent film rendering of Mahler's conversion taken over from the Zarathustra sequence of *The Dance of the Seven Veils*. It is the excessive number of parodies of other films, however, which finally become too obvious and too distracting. We have Mahler lying in his coffin à la David Gray in *Vampyr*, slaying a dragon (in this case a pig) in the fashion of Siegfried from Lang's *Die Nibelungen*, watching a railway scene caricatured from *Death in Venice*, imitating Al Jolson's famous "Mammy" pose from *The Jazz Singer*, and smoking a cigar as Groucho with the two other Marx-Mahler brothers. In *The Dance of the Seven Veils*, the numerous pastiches of Von Stroheim, Disney, and Busby Berkeley succeeded on a variety of levels because of the comic strip style of the film, but in *Mahler*, they are never integrated beyond the level of the momentary joke.

Mahler then is a mixed bag. It lacks the unity of Russell's best films and is seriously flawed by the director's over-indulgence in the in-joke and pastiche for the sake of a quick laugh. It does, however, contain a rich, dense texture, some visually stunning sequences, further advances in the matching of music and image, and most significantly, a continuation of experimental methods in adapting literary material to biopic form.

NOTES

[1]Cited in John Walker, "Ken Russell's New Enigma", *Observer,* 8 September 1974, Magazine Section, p. 55.

[2]Ken Russell, "Discussion Between Ken Russell, Alexander Walker, and George Melly", *Film Night—Confrontation,* BBC telecast on 28 February 1971.

[3]John Baxter, *An Appalling Talent/Ken Russell* (London: Michael Joseph, 1973), p. 182.

[4]Derek Elley, "Mahler", *Films and Filming,* May 1974, p. 41.

[5]Kurt Blaukopf, *Gustav Mahler* (New York: Praeger, 1973), p. 104.

[6]Alma Mahler, *Gustav Mahler: Memories and Letters,* ed. Donald Mitchell (New York: Viking, 1969), p. 48.

[7]Elley, p. 42.

[8]Gordon Gow, "Shock Treatment", *Films and Filming,* July 1970, p. 10.

[9]Alma Mahler, p. 199.

[10]*Ibid.,* p. 75.

[11]Shirley Russell, "Costume Fantasia", *Mahler Brochure* (London: Sackville Publishing, 1974).

[12]Ken Russell, "Mahler the Man", *Mahler Brochure* (London: Sackville Publishing, 1974).

[13]Blaukopf, p. 24.

[14]*Ibid.*

[15]See Elley, p. 42.

[16]*Ibid.*

[17]Ken Russell, "Mahler the Man".

[18]Jan Dawson, "Other Channel", *Sight and Sound* 41 (Autumn 1972), pp. 204–5.

[19]See Isaac Babel, *Collected Stories* (Harmondsworth, England: Penguin, 1961). Hollis Alpert so misconstrues these sequences that he claims "The scenes of Mahler's early family life . . . might have been written by Joseph Goebbels, so anti-Semitic is their net effect." See Hollis Alpert, "The Murder of Mahler", *Saturday Review,* 8 February 1975, p. 39.

Family group – *Mahler*

"The creator and his muse" – as Mahler composes in the seclusion of his hut Alma removes baby from carshot – *Mahler*

Second subject, first movement, Sixth Symphony – *Mahler*

The conversion of Gustav Mahler (Robert Powell) to the faith of Wagner – *Mahler*

Alma (Georgina Hale) and her lovers mock Mahler's music – *Mahler*

Ken Russell walking up to Valhalla – *Mahler*

The deaf, dumb and blind Tommy (Roger Daltrey) stands inside the Acid Queen ready to receive the drug injections – *Tommy* (Hemdale)

Nora (Ann-Margret) and little Tommy (Barry Winch) leaves Bernie's Holiday Camp with Frank (Oliver Reed) – *Tommy* (Hemdale)

Reflected in the mirror; Frank (Oliver Reed); Tommy (Roger Daltrey) and Nora (Ann-Margret) – *Tommy* (Hemdale)

Ann-Margret as Nora Walker watches the good life on TV and sings "The Day it Rained Champagne" – *Tommy* (Gomez)

Pete Townshend, Keith Moon and John Entwhistle in the Pinball Wizard number from *Tommy* (Hemdale)

Cousin Kevin (Paul Nicholas) tries to "iron out" Tommy's (Roger Daltrey) problems, during his sadistic tormenting of the deaf, dumb and blind boy – *Tommy* (Gomez)

Roger Daltrey as Tommy after he has won the Pinball Championships – *Tommy* (Gomez)

The Pinball Wizard (Elton John) competes against Tommy for the World Championship title – *Tommy* (Hemdale)

Shirley and Ken Russell on "Tommy" location with Hell's Angels.

About to "start the rain". Ken Russell on the set of *Tommy* (Gomez)

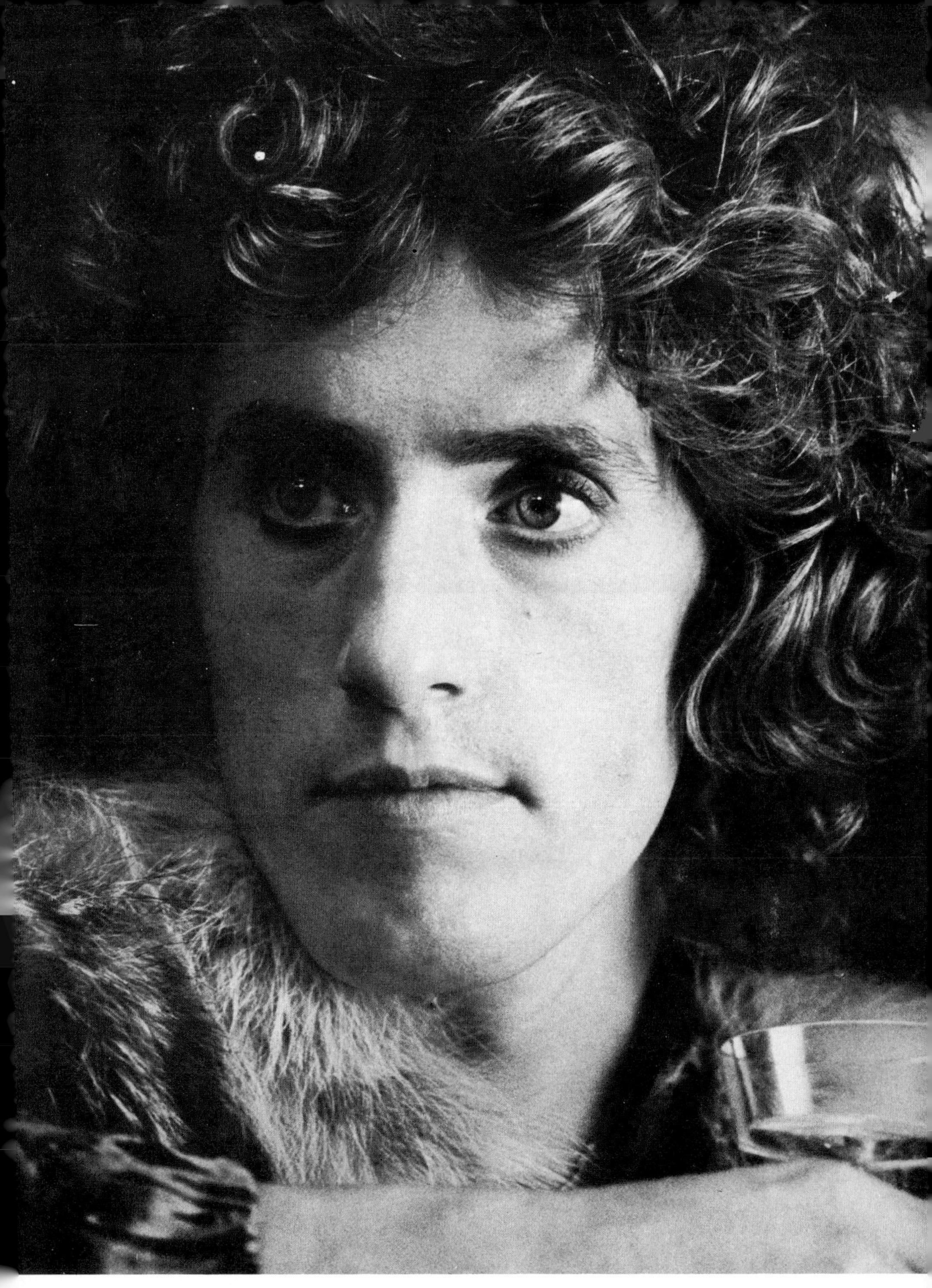

Roger Daltrey as Franz Liszt in *Lisztomania*

Cuckold gets his come-uppance in *Lisztomania*

Shades of Fairbanks as Liszt escaped husband's wrath – *Lisztomania*

Hungarian Rhapsody – *Lisztomania*

Herr Liszt you are on in five minutes – *Lisztomania*

Chaplin fantasy – Dream of Love from *Lisztomania*

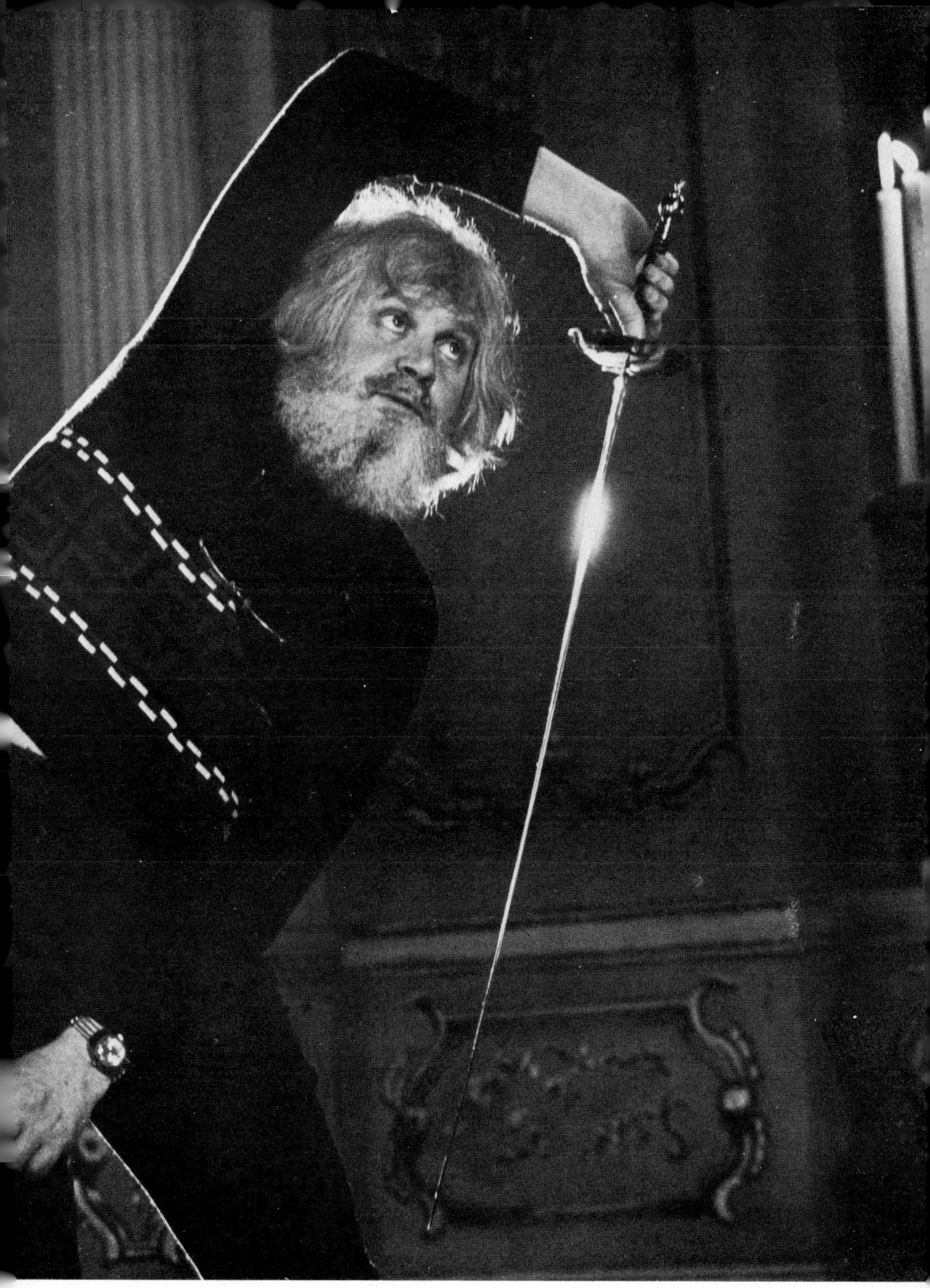

Ken Russell conducts a duel – *Lisztomania*

[20]Ken Russell, "Mahler the Man". In private correspondence with the author, Russell reiterates this position and defends his use of the Babel material. "The film is about things that come to mind when I think of Mahler. Isaac Babel's childhood is one of them—I'm sure it's a lot closer to Mahler than anything I could have dreamed up—they seem uncannily similar."

[21]Donald Mitchell, "Introduction", to Alma Mahler, *Gustav Mahler*, p. xiii.

Ringo Starr as Pope in *Lisztomania*

10

Tommy and *Lisztomania*

The Beat Goes On

Sickness will surely take the mind
Where minds can't usually go.
Come on the amazing journey
And learn all you should know.

Tommy[1]

Anyone familiar with the work of Ken Russell must have registered mild surprise when it was announced that, upon the completion of *Mahler*, Russell would make a film version of The Who's *Tommy*, starring Roger Daltrey, Oliver Reed, Ann-Margret, Tina Turner, Jack Nicholson, Elton John, and Eric Clapton. What, after all, did the foremost director of biography films have to do with a rock opera about a deaf, dumb, and blind boy who becomes the world's champion pinball player? Indeed, Russell had claimed that he would never make another musical after his unfortunate experience filming *The Boy Friend*, and *Mahler* was only the first of six films on composers contracted for Goodtimes Enterprises. Why then *Tommy*?

The publicity releases for the film claim that Russell directed it because he thinks *Tommy* is the best opera written since World War II, but many of those familiar with the state of the British film industry replied that Russell needed a commercial success at this point in his career, and *Tommy* certainly has become that. Cynical detractors, who mistakenly think Russell reduces literary masterpieces to visual masterplots and popularizes the biographies of artists, suggested that he was simply seeking a new, appropriately low level

—popularizing the already popular. Although none of these responses really explains anything about the motivations which probably prompted Russell to agree to The Who's request that he direct the film version of their rock opera, one can put little stock in newspaper accounts and supposed comments from the director that he knew he would have to make a film version of *Tommy* when he first heard the album.[2] Contrary to this report, Russell, in an interview with David Sterritt of *The Christian Science Monitor*, states that he didn't like the original rock music and still doesn't. "But what it is about, I find very exciting. . . . It's about a modern messiah, a possible messiah, who might have been a messiah but was totally exploited and commercialized."[3]

Variations on this theme are found in a number of Russell's films, but this concern especially dominated the numerous schemes that Russell attempted to bring to fruition after finishing *Savage Messiah*, and perhaps part of the answer to the question why *Tommy* rests with these aborted projects.

First of all, there were plans outside the realm of filmmaking. Russell was scheduled to direct Peter Maxwell Davies' *Taverner*, an opera biography of a little known sixteenth century composer and mystic, John Taverner, but he finally declined to do so after hearing tapes of a piano and vocal score. Next was an idea, suggested by his wife Shirley, for a stage production about racial conflict in America using elements of opera, ballet, mime, and the musical.[4] In the meantime, an adaptation of George Neveux's *Juliette ou la Clé des Songes* was tentatively listed as Russell's next film project. Little by little, however, the Neveux adaptation and Shirley's scheme merged together, and finally Russell wrote what must surely be his most bizarre script. *The Angels* combines, in kaleidoscopic fashion, episodes inspired by the Neveux play, large chunks of material about racial problems, outrageous satire on organized religion and established forms of government, and cryptic autobiographical references. All these concerns are contained within the framework of film director Michael Mann's journey to a film festival in an unnamed East European country. Aside from merely a physical journey, however, Mann's pilgrimage becomes a mental excursion into the nature of the self and the problems of the artist in the modern world; from this, the film script emerges as a Kafkaesque nightmare, sprinkled with imitations of Fellini's *8½*, filtered through Russell's own unique style and vision. Some sequences are extraordinary, but with each successive reading of the work, it becomes only too clear that its center cannot hold.

One of the most notable sequences in the script deals with the religious cult worship which springs up after the supposed death of Mann's big star—Poppy Day. Poppy's shrine, a satirical jibe at

Lourdes, contains a life-size statue of the pop star to which lines of cripples mutter prayers. At the very end of the script, Poppy, who has been hiding out in Spain, returns to the shrine.

> Poppy descends by rope from a helicopter. She lands by her statue. She is dressed identically. She speaks but her voice cannot be heard over the din from the helicopter. She seems to be pleading. A disillusioned Pilgrim—a young robed man with beard and matted hair throws a stone at her. Others follow suit. Angy, who at first dropped to her knees, now runs to protect her but is hit by a stone. People are running everywhere. Sammy is knocked down and trampled to death.[5]

After MGM turned down this script, in part because they couldn't understand it, Russell began work on *Music Music Music*, which he enthusiastically described to Guy Flatley in an interview while in New York in September 1972 to promote *Savage Messiah.*

> The movie will be about the things you have to do for money, from writing music for mad dukes to writing commercials for canned lamb. The artist has always been at the mercy of the commercial, or of somebody who will butcher his work.[6]

This new film then was to carry over some of the same concerns manifested in *The Angels* through the adventures of John Fairfax, the composer of a religious rock opera entitled *Jesus on Venus*—"something that would make *Jesus Christ Superstar* look as old fashioned as a Victorian performance of Handel's *Messiah* among the cast-iron pillars and potted palms of the Crystal Palace".[7] Although the opera is exciting and spectacular, the essence of art, "humanity, love, truth, faith—call it what you will", is missing, perhaps in part because the composer finds it necessary to supplement his income by doing the music for TV commercials. However, after an incident in which a child spews up canned lamb, Fairfax grabs the child and flees from the studio only to be knocked over as he gets outside. When he gets up, he's in the past talking to Johann Sebastian Bach himself. Like Mann in *The Angels*, Fairfax must probe into the nature of the self and examine his role as an artist in the modern world, and he does so as the result of a metaphorical tour through a history of music which includes the trials and tribulations of Bach and Beethoven and the perversion of established compositions of the past by Hollywood hacks, like Dimitri Tiomkin. The upshot of this exploration is Fairfax's abandonment of the pop religious musical and a new commitment to the writing of a requiem in which life, death, and resurrection are presented through the songs and street games of school children. John Taverner wrote such a work, and Russell planned to use excerpts from it to end the film.

After Russell himself scrapped *Music Music Music*, plans were made for *Gargantua*, a screen adaptation of the Rabelais classic to be financed by an Italian production company. The first section of this proposed film revolved around the giant's story presented as a theatrical production, but the emphasis was clearly on a merging of various art forms, including song, dance, drama, farce, acrobatics, and burlesque. The remainder of the film, in which the "real" Gargantua appears, contains numerous, often uncomfortably blatant, examples of religious and political satire which Russell culled from the scripts of *The Angels* and *Music Music Music*. Unfortunately, however, the Italians backed out just before the production was about to begin.

This brief list of Russell's aborted projects is not meant to intimate that the director accepted *Tommy* out of desperation; rather it should suggest that this project was especially welcome because so much of the material that had been scrapped over the past months could be accommodated in *Tommy*, without the type of forcing that occurred in *Mahler*.

Tommy is yet another work depicting an episodic passage to self-discovery. According to Russell, the film is structured as "an evolutionary journey" in which the deaf, dumb, and blind protagonist undergoes "a kind of pilgrim's progress" through the horrors of the modern age. The shooting script begins with Tommy's mother and father high atop a mountain at the moment of his conception and closes with an epilogue on the same mountain top years later as Tommy, in "affirmation of Man's eternal divinity", reaches out "as if to embrace the life giving sun".[8]

The climactic scene of the rock opera as conceived by The Who, the revolt of the converts at Tommy's Holiday Camp, bears a remarkable similarity to the denouement of Russell's *The Angels*. Tommy becomes yet another space-age Messiah whose followers become disillusioned with him and his messsage, and the final section of the opera, as Russell interprets it, harkens back to his own abandoned script.

> They [the converts] feel they've been cheated, sold out, betrayed—they overturn the pin tables, smash the glass and set fire to them. As they did before—in the "Sally Simpson" number—they storm up to touch the new Messiah not reverently this time but to batter him. Not least in the forefront of the attack are the Blind. . . . Accordingly they belabour him with their sticks. Mister Normal "puts the boot in", the Drunk breaks his bottle over Tommy's head. . . . Frank and Nora do their best to protect Tommy, but the odds are hopeless and they are knocked down and trampled.[9]

Also, the visuals which accompany the Preacher's (Eric Clapton) rendition of "Eyesight to the Blind" draw heavily from Russell's conception of Poppy Day's shrine from *The Angels*. Only here the life-size plaster statue is of Marilyn Monroe, "one of the great lay saints of the 20th century".

Russell even managed to manipulate some of the new material added to the rock opera in order to express his attitude towards the realm of commercial advertising, a major concern in the scripts of both *The Angels* and *Music Music Music*, where he savagely attacked immoral commercials which, without our conscious recognition, shape the images that we form of ourselves. In the shooting script of *Tommy*, Tommy's mother, on the verge of a nervous breakdown, sings "Today It Rained Champagne" while a TV set blares out ads for baked beans, detergents, and chocolates. Finally at the end of the song, she fantasizes that the TV screen splinters into a thousand pieces and a flow of baked beans, face creams, detergents, and chocolates engulfs her bedroom, "like an obscene stream of lava", while the lush music score degenerates into fragments of Rachmaninoff, Tchaikovsky, and Liberace played against each other. In the final film, the musical parody is eliminated, and the visuals emphasize Nora's perverse, almost sexual, ecstasy as she rolls over in the mush and fondles the phallic-like cushions.

Finally, just as the opening of the *Gargantua* project attempted to fuse together various art forms, *Tommy* dispenses with dialogue throughout the film and merges song, music, mime, dance, and visual images. More than that, however, the *Gargantua* treatment also provides key images which reappear with great success in *Tommy*. The most notable is Russell's imaginative idea of putting the Pinball Wizard (Elton John) on stilts and having him dragged from the auditorium so that only his huge shoes show. It should also be added that some of *Lisztomania*, Russell's latest film, comes directly from the proposed screen treatment of *Gargantua*. Liszt's (Roger Daltrey) fantasy of his giant erected penis, for instance, is derived from a song and dance number in which nursemaids decorate Gargantua's "codpiece" with flowers as his penis gradually "rises to the height of a maypole when they decorate it with ribbons and dance gaily around it, singing its praises".[10]

Once committed to the making of *Tommy*, Russell worked for a period of six months with Peter Townshend, composer of most of the songs from the rock opera and musical director of the film. Together they made slight, but often necessary, alterations to the original lyrics and created six new songs to assist in the transformation of the work to film form. The 66-page shooting script reveals Russell's remarkable success as the adaptor-creator who walks a tightrope between his own personal vision and the vital concerns of the work from which the film is made. Although he changed the order of some of the songs, slightly altered the words of others, and obviously instigated the addition of the new ones, Russell still claims that he has remained faithful to the rock opera as conceived by The Who. The problem with the original work, as Russell sees it, rests with the development of the narrative. "It simply jumps into the middle of things and even The Who recognize this as a weakness."[11] As a result, two of the new pieces, an instrumental entitled "Prologue 1945" and "Bernie's Holiday Camp" supply the basis for a functional, if somewhat cliché-ridden, background. Group-Captain Walker has an idyllic leave with his wife Nora just before his plane is shot down over Germany. Some months later, on V-E Day, Nora gives birth to Tommy. Six years later, at Bernie's Holiday Camp, she meets Frank Hobbs, "your friendly greencoat", falls in love, and later marries him. Captain Walker, a cured amnesia victim, finally returns home only to find Frank and Nora in bed. In the ensuing turmoil, Walker is killed before the horrified Tommy, who through the shock of perception, is struck deaf, dumb, and blind. Tommy's condition then becomes a perfect metaphorical representation of man's self-imposed limitations. He must journey through the dark traumas of an illusory selfhood, which must be destroyed before he can become "totally aware, totally free, totally in command of all his faculties".[12]

Tommy, perhaps more than any other of his film adaptations, also allowed Russell to be totally free in creating visuals from his own personal vision to match the songs and music from the original source, and this is the greatest strength of the film—especially in the first hour. The personal romanticism of the mountain top scenes and the almost surreal images of the half-naked girls in gas masks provide a striking illustration in the opening sequence of the blend of literal and metaphorical images that assault the viewer throughout this unique "musical", which consists entirely of production numbers. "Bernie's Holiday Camp", although one of the less heralded moments in the film, stands as a superb example of Russell's characteristic fusion of image and sound. The entire sequence is carefully, almost geometrically structured, and the constantly moving camera, which weaves through the carefully planned back-and-forth movements of the holiday campers as Frank leads Nora and Tommy to their cabin, is cinema choreography at its best. The same might also be said for "Christmas" and the more spectacular "Acid Queen" and "Pinball Wizard" sequences, but after such grand moments, the viewer might feel somewhat disappointed with the conventional rear screen effects which accompany some of "I'm Free" and with the surprisingly awkward choreography of much of the "We're Not Gonna Take It" number.

Tommy has been praised in almost all critical quarters, perhaps because most popular reviewers felt that Russell's method of overstatement was especially appropriate to the subject matter. This may be true, but as in so many of his other films, subtle visual patterns abound throughout the film and contribute to its rich, dense texture. Images of water, shattered glass, the sun, pinballs, airplanes, crosses, earrings, and mirrors, for instance, provide the kind of visual unity which is as much a part of Russell's method as is overstatement.

More than anything else, however, Russell himself sees *Tommy* as "the one thing I've done that satisfies me aesthetically",[13] and he even goes so far as to suggest that the film "is a culmination of much in *my* work".[14] Certainly, it has been his most sustained effort, to date, to achieve a synthesis of the arts—the dream also held by Alexander Scriabin, one of the director's acknowledged influences. There is every indication, however, that Russell will continue his experimentation in this direction in some future project—perhaps his long planned biopic of Ralph Vaughan Williams, in which he may dispense with narration and dialogue altogether and depend solely on the marriage of his images and the composer's symphonic and choral works to provide characterization, narrative line, and emotional impact.

Before continuing in this direction, however, Russell has paused to present his attitudes towards life and art to the newly acquired young audience (between 17 and 25 years of age) which became acquainted with his work through *Tommy*. While shooting *Tommy*, Russell claimed that his encounters with various sub-culture groups in England caused him to reconsider his responses and responsibilities to this young rather different type of audience. Although often considered a popularizer by most American and British film critics, Russell stated that he had never consciously seen himself in this role until now. With *Lisztomania* (1975), he was consciously aiming at a marriage of "the popular and the classical"—a union which be believes was successfully achieved by the late Russian composer Dimitri Shostakovitch.[15]

Lisztomania was conceived as a rock musical fantasy on the life of Franz Liszt, but if the rock lyrics and Rick Wakeman's arrangements of Liszt's music communicate Russell's message to a youthful audience, the film's dismissal of a conventional narrative structure, almost complete excursion into fantasy, and constant allusions to and parodies of other movies make it rough going for many of the very members of the audience that the film seeks to attract. Most of the young people who came to see *Tommy* already knew the narrative development (such as it was) from having heard the rock opera on record. As such, they could follow Russell's visual delineation of the fantasies of the deaf, dumb, and blind protagonist. With *Lisztomania*, the necessary biographical background of Liszt's life and elementary knowledge of the world of 19th century music were frequently unknown to many of these young people. Certainly most members of the audience, however, no matter what age, recognized the parodies of Chaplin's *The Gold Rush, The Perils of Pauline, The Exorcist,* and the Frankenstein and Dracula films, but probably the more subtle, possible allusions to such films as *Potemkin* and *A Matter of Life and Death* escaped most viewers, who also probably failed to recognize that the entire "underlying conception" and "unifying style" of the film are "built on parodies of old movie genres".[16] Without stretching the point too far, even the controversial 10-foot long penis scene looks as if it had been staged by a berserk Busby Berkeley hard at work on a porno flick.

Lisztomania, however, is not pure escapist entertainment, like *The Boy Friend.* In the film, Russell offers a serious statement about the role of the artist in today's world, a dominant theme of many of his biopics, in a humorous, cartoon-like, pop art method of presentation. Of course, a similar satiric, comic-book style had been previously used by Russell in *The Dance of the Seven Veils,* a far funnier and far more effective film in revealing the dangers of an artist selling out to commercialism and/or becoming enmeshed in the quagmire of irresponsible political beliefs; both of which, in turn, reflect a kind of moral bankruptcy. The one-dimensional, vicious portrait of Richard Strauss in this film seems entirely appropriate given Russell's vision of the composer as a bombastiloquent, pompous megalomaniac who could have "prevented a lot of suffering", but with Liszt, such is not the case. Even in this comic-book version of Liszt's life, the protagonist emerges as a figure about whom the director himself has ambivalent feelings. The first half of the film presents Liszt as an artist who sells out to the forces of commercialism. The image of Liszt as the world's first pop star is best conveyed in the concert sequence, during which, complete with Liberace candelabrum, he plays "Chopsticks" to pacify his screaming, young admirers. More than that, the sequence also depicts the clash between the world of the artist's music and his personal faults. Women from Liszt's past life, including one who pleads with him to acknowledge that he is the father of her child, attempt to gain his attention as he bangs away at one of his Hungarian Rhapsodies. Much later in the film, however, Liszt emerges as the sympathetic hero who embodies, in somewhat simplistic fashion, many of Russell's own attitudes about the power and significance of art.

The rock-cartoon format of the film unfortunately does not really allow for this major shift of attitude, and nothing in Roger Daltrey's performance suggests any subtle psychological reason for such a change in Liszt's response to his music. Russell, however, is clearly not interested in characterization here, and it is enough for him that, by the end of the film, Liszt epitomises the artist who has journeyed to self-discovery. Liszt, who had once put his faith in the whims of popularity and then in the Church, must come to the realization that he must place his faith in himself and in the power of his music. As such, the dramatic, thematic, and technical highpoint of the film is the confrontation between Wagner (Paul Nicholas) and Liszt—during which Liszt "exorcizes" Wagner's demon by sending bursts of fire from the piano as he plays his terrifying "Dance of Death".

The conflict between Wagner and Liszt is at the core of the second half of the film and is most obviously stated in the contrasting lyrics of the songs that both composers sing. For Russell, Wagner, like Strauss, was a megalomaniacal, fascist composer whose musical output was a total glorification of the Master Race—as the lyrics of "Excelsior Song" make clear.

> The new Messiah
> His day has come.
> We'll drive the beast from our land.
> He will restore Teutonic Godhead
> The hour of the Aryan soon will come.

The legacy of Wagner is the Frankenstein/Hitler monster created out of his music and philosophy, and the Nazi imagery, which Russell had already used in *Dance of the Seven Veils* and *Mahler* to suggest "the abuses of art", reaches its most extreme manifestation in the last third of *Lisztomania*. "The Nazi scenes", as Stephen Farber aptly notes, "are not meant to be taken literally; they express Russell's worst fears of what can happen when art is perverted by show business and political fanaticism."[17]

It is this symbolic monster with his machine-gun guitar that is finally destroyed by Liszt's "angelic music" generated by his organ-like rocketship. As the ship returns to the heavens after destroying the Frankenstein/Hitler creature in the war-torn streets of Berlin, Liszt sings "Peace at Last", a song which clearly answers the lyrics of Wagner's perverted superman hymn.

> Now Love, sweet Love
> Oh now that Love has won
> Oh now that Love has won
> Now Love, our Love
> Our Love has ended war
> He'll torture man no more
> Your words give meaning to my song
> Our Love created harmony
> With Faith, we'll guide the universe
> Through infinity
> At last, at last, I'll give him

Peace at last
Forgive him for the past
Peace at last.

Thus, *Lisztomania* ends with one of Russell's most optimistic endings. As Stephen Farber again wisely observes, " . . . there is something irresistibly romantic in Russell's concern for the artist's integrity. In a world where everything has been debased and devalued, Russell still envisions art as the central creative act that brings order to a chaotic universe. The fact that most of his films examine the artist's betrayal of his vocation cannot obscure Russell's belief in the moral importance of art."[18]

NOTES

[1]The Who, "Amazing Journey", *Tommy*.

[2]See William Hall, "What the Blazes is Ken Russell Up to Now? A Rock Opera", *New York Times*, 23 June 1974, Arts and Leisure Section, p. 29, cols. 5–8.

[3]David Sterritt, "Whole Film is 'One Flash' In His Mind", *The Christian Science Monitor*, 2 June 1975, p. 27, cols. 1–4.

[4]John Baxter, *An Appalling Talent*, p. 57.

[5]Ken Russell, *The Angels* (unpublished first draft, July 1972), TS, p. 74.

[6]Guy Flatley, "I'm Surprised My Films Shock People", *New York Times*, 15 October 1972, Arts and Leisure Section, p. 15, cols. 1–5.

[7]Ken Russell, *Music Music Music* (unpublished screen treatment, August 1972), TS, p. 1.

[8]Discussion between Russell and the author on June 19, 1974.

[9]Ken Russell, *Tommy* (unpublished shooting script, April 1974), TS, p. 64.

[10]Ken Russell, *Gargantua* (unpublished screen treatment, January 1973), TS, p. 4

[11]Discussion with Russell on June 19, 1974.

[12]Ken Russell, *Tommy*, TS, p. 43.

[13]Sterritt, "Whole Film is 'One Flash' In His Mind", p. 27.

[14]Private correspondence with Russell.

[15]Discussion with Russell on June 19, 1974.

[16]Stephen Farber, "Russellmania", *Film Comment*, 11, No. 6 (November–December 1975), p. 44.

[17]*Ibid.*, p. 46.

[18]*Ibid.*

11

Conclusions

Ken Russell's methods of adaptation and his extravagant style of filmmaking have been grossly misunderstood, but the usual naive pronouncements of film critics can no longer be considered justified. Ken Russell is not a "compulsive Hollywoodizer" who distorts facts in order to outrage audiences for the sake of pure sensationalism.[1] He does not "murder" his subjects, and his films are not examples of "bad art".[2] He is not motivated by sadism or "egoistic frenzy".[3] He is not driven by cruelty or insanity to embrace excessiveness,[4] and his films are neither "degenerate" nor "despicable".[5] True, they do cultivate a baroque vulgarity, and they are frequently punctuated with bizarre humor which manifests itself in "camp" images, but even to describe his films as notable illustrations of "kitsch" is to do them a serious injustice.

Russell's major films owe little to Hollywood biopics or to the tradition of carefully reconstructed historical films. Therefore, his rendering of historical inaccuracies must not be judged by standards applicable to either kind of film. His films deal with biography and history in a different manner, and in a style appropriate to the excess and extravagance of the subject matter he willfully chooses.

A lengthy study of the sources and films of Ken Russell supports George Bluestone's contention that the serious film adaptor is a creator in his own right who uses literary sources as raw material to evolve new artistic entities. More than that, however, Russell's works also show that a filmmaker can develop a unique style of adaptation which may be of major importance in defining his characteristics as a film artist.

All of Russell's films are adaptations in one form or another, but his attitudes toward and methods of adapting material for his films have changed considerably from the early, rigid BBC portraits—so restricted in format—to the experimental, metaphorical explorations found in *Mahler* and *Lisztomania.* Russell's earliest efforts at biopics were rooted in the pursuit of factual truth, and only with the grudging consent of his superiors at the BBC was he able to experiment with matching music to images, with using actors in documentary-portraits, and with offering metaphorical interpretations in place of humdrum visual catalogues of facts. Russell, however, did not stress dramatization as an alternative to the traditional BBC documentary format; he created an entirely new approach to depicting the lives of his protagonists. His tripartite structure is a major contribution to the genre of biographical films, and all of his major films (even those, like *Women in Love* and *The Boy Friend*, outside the area of biography) are a variation on this method.

The tripartite structure incorporates the "facts" (be they historical or supplied by a novel, play, or rock opera), the legendary image or self-imposed view that historical personages or fictional characters have of themselves, and finally Russell's own attitude or, in some cases, his responses. Suggested in *Bartók* (1964), this approach first clearly manifested itself in *The Debussy Film* (1965) and then came to fruition in *Isadora Duncan* (1966). The major emphases within his tripartite structure often shifted from film to film, depending on the specific nature of the subject matter. *Song of Summer* (1968), for instance, stressed the "facts" and the character of Delius as Fenby remembered him. Most of the other major Russell films of the mid and late sixties—*Isadora Duncan* (1966), *Dante's Inferno* (1967), and *Women in Love* (1969)—maintained a balance of the three perspectives which comprise his unique structure. In *The Dance of the Seven Veils* (1970), however, Russell expanded his own personal response to Richard Strauss so much so that the areas of fact (aside from Strauss's letters providing most of the dialogue) and legend were reduced to a minimum. The emphasis on personal vision continued in *The Music Lovers* (1970), but history, legend and Russell's visual interpretations merged in such a complex manner that the specific components of his tripartite structure were no longer readily discernible. In *The Devils* (1971), *The Boy Friend* (1971), *Savage Messiah* (1972) and *Tommy* (1975) Russell returned to a more balanced presentation of the tripartite structure; but *Mahler* (1974), another composer biopic, again stressed his personal response, especially in the long sequences depicting subjective interpretations of the music. Finally, *Lisztomania* (1975) was almost entirely a rock musical fantasy which presented, in cartoon fashion, Russell's own views on art for the youthful audience which became familiar with his name through *Tommy*.

When dealing with the lives of composers, Russell allows himself a special freedom of handling. When dealing with specific biographies which employ conventional or inconsequential structures (Catherine Drinker Bowen's *Beloved Friend* and H. S. Ede's *Savage Messiah*), he uses the written account only in order to shape his own meaningful pattern of organization. When dealing with complexly structured works of significant artistic accomplishment (Lawrence's *Women in Love* and Huxley's *The Devils*), he respects the artist's methods and seeks to find appropriate visual equivalents to suggest the techniques employed by the writer—e.g. counterpointing in *Women in Love*, and allusion and anachronism in *The Devils*.

More often than not, the excessiveness and frenzy of Russell's films are derived from his original sources, and he often wisely selects material especially appropriate to his unique style of filmmaking. Subtlety does exist in his films—in the complexity of his allusions, the effectiveness of his *mise-en-scène*, the richness of his visual patterning, and the mastery of his matching images to music—but it is his shock editing, his obsessive camera movements, his penchant for theatricality and overblown performances, and his extraordinary, phantasmagoric images which overwhelm his audiences. For Russell, the art of gentle persuasion is lost in this present age; audiences have become complacent and therefore must be assaulted and jolted into awareness, or into sharing emotions of ecstasy or outrage about a particular subject.

To some extent, Russell's methods can be compared to those of D. H. Lawrence, another experimental artist too often dismissed as excessive and extravagant. Lawrence uncompromisingly, intemperately, and compulsively assaulted his readers in an attempt to alter their responses. He over-emphasized the power of the body and the "blood" because he claimed that this aspect had been denied by twentieth century man's over-dependence on abstract reasoning. His purpose, however, was not to tip the scale in favor of the flesh at the expense of the spirit. Instead, he used extremes to compensate for man's dominant preoccupations and to aid in the development of the total self. Russell's methods of assaulting his audience are not really dissimilar. He, too, goes to extremes to bring his audience to his position, which frequently rests somewhere between their conventional pieties or indifference and the presentation on the screen.

Given this context, perhaps the death scene of Grandier in *The Devils* becomes the quintessential Russell sequence. The skin on Grandier's face blisters and pops before the viewer's eyes as the flames consume him, but in his last moments, he looks out at the inhabitants of Loudun and at the audience of the film and cries out, "Don't look at me. Look at your city." It is a deep, strong, overpowering voice, but one which, like Russell's, cannot be denied or ignored.

Ken Russell possesses a remarkable visual flair, a trait uncommon among British filmmakers; as in the past, he continues to experiment with film as a fusion of various art forms at a time when most film critics are praising what could be called "pure film"; and finally he has changed and continues to change the ways of making and of viewing biographical films. When seen from this perspective, Ken Russell emerges as the most significant filmmaker presently working in Great Britain.

NOTES

[1]Pauline Kael, "Hyperbole and Narcissus", *New Yorker*, 18 November 1972, p. 228.

[2]Hollis Alpert, "The Murder of Mahler", *Saturday Review*, 8 February 1975, p. 39.

[3]*Ibid.*

[4]Paul Zimmerman, cited in "*The Devils*", *Filmfacts*, 14 (1971), p. 339.

[5]Charles Champlin, *Ibid.*, p. 340.

Filmography

This filmography is an expanded and corrected version of the filmography which appears in John Baxter's *An Appalling Talent/Ken Russell*. Additional information concerning the TV films has been added when known, but no attempt has been made to list Russell's TV commercials.

AMATEUR FILMS

Peepshow. 1956.
Knights on Bikes (unfinished). 1956.
Amelia and the Angel. 1957.
Lourdes. 1958.

FILMS FOR TELEVISION

Poet's London (with John Betjeman). Monitor. Telecast 1 March 1959.
Gordon Jacob. Monitor. Telecast 29 March 1959.
Guitar Craze. Monitor. Telecast 7 June 1959. Repeated 24 July 1960.
Variations on a Mechanical Theme (Mechanical musical instruments). Monitor. Telecast 27 September 1959.
McBryde and Colquhoun: Two Scottish Painters. Monitor. Telecast 25 October 1959. McBryde section only repeated 8 May 1966.
Portrait of a Goon (Spike Milligan). Monitor. Telecast 16 December 1959.
Marie Rambert Remembers (Ballet Rambert). Monitor. Telecast 17 January 1960.
Architecture of Entertainment (John Betjeman). Monitor. Telecast 28 February 1960. Repeated 15 December 1964.
Cranks at Work (John Cranko). Monitor. Telecast 24 April 1960.
The Miners' Picnic (Brass Bands). Monitor. Telecast 3 July 1960.
Shelagh Delaney's Salford. Monitor. Telecast 25 September 1960.

A House in Bayswater. Produced for the BBC Film Department. Telecast 14 December 1960. Repeated 25 June 1968.

The Light Fantastic (Dancing in England). Monitor. Telecast 18 December 1960.

Old Battersea House (Pre-Raphaelite museum). Monitor. Telecast 4 June 1961.

Portrait of a Soviet Composer (Sergei Prokofiev). Monitor. Telecast 18 June 1961. Repeated 6 August 1962.

London Moods. Monitor. Telecast 5 November 1961.

Antonio Gaudi. Monitor. Telecast 3 December 1961.

Pop Goes the Easel (Pop artists). Monitor. Telecast 25 March 1962.

Preservation Man (Bruce Lacey). Monitor. Telecast 20 May 1962.

Mr. Chesher's Traction Engines. Monitor. Telecast 1 July 1962.

Lotte Lenya Sings Kurt Weill (co-director Humphrey Burton). Monitor. Telecast 10 September 1962. Repeated 19 August 1964.

Elgar. Monitor. Telecast 11 November 1962. Repeated 16 May 1963, 26 June 1966, 16 July 1968.

Watch the Birdie (David Hurn). Monitor. Telecast 9 June 1963. Repeated 15 July 1964.

Lonely Shore. Monitor. Telecast 14 January 1964.

Bartók. Monitor. Telecast 24 May 1964. Repeated 9 July 1968.

The Dotty World of James Lloyd. Monitor. Telecast 5 July 1964. Repeated 2 July 1968.

Diary of a Nobody. Produced by John McGrath for BBC 2. Adapted from the book by George and Weedon Grossmith. With: Bryan Pringle and Murray Melvin. Telecast 12 December 1964.

The Debussy Film. Monitor. Co-scripted by Russell and Melvyn Bragg. With: Oliver Reed and Vladek Sheybal. Telecast 18 May 1965. Repeated 12 June 1966.

Always on Sunday (Henri Rousseau). Monitor. Co-scripted by Russell and Melvyn Bragg. Narrated by Oliver Reed. Telecast 29 June 1965. Repeated 2 July 1968, 1 June 1969.

Don't Shoot the Composer (Georges Delerue). Omnibus. Telecast 29 January 1966.

Isadora Duncan, The Biggest Dancer in the World. Omnibus. Director of Photography: Dick Bush. With: Vivien Pickles, Iza Teller, and Murray Melvin. Telecast 22 September 1966. Repeated 26 March 1967, 19 March 1969.

Dante's Inferno (Rossetti). Omnibus. With: Oliver Reed, Judith Paris, Christopher Logue, Andrew Faulds, Gala Mitchell, and Iza Teller. Telecast 22 December 1967.

Song of Summer (Delius). Omnibus. Director of Photography: Dick Bush. With: Max Adrian, Christopher Gable, Maureen Pryor, and David Collings. Telecast 15 September 1968.

The Dance of the Seven Veils: A Comic Strip in Seven Episodes on the Life of Richard Strauss. Omnibus. With: Christopher Gable, Judith Paris, and Vladek Sheybal. Telecast 15 February 1970.

FEATURES

French Dressing. ABPC. 1963. Producer: Kenneth Harper. Associate Producer: Andrew Mitchell. Director: Ken Russell. Screenplay: Peter Myers, Ronald Cass and Peter Brett. Costume design: Shirley Russell. Original story: Peter Myers and Ronald Cass. Photography: Ken Higgins. Editor: Jack Slade. Art direction: Jack Stephens. Music: Georges Delerue. With: James Booth (Jim), Roy Kinnear (Henry), Marisa Mell (Francoise Fayol), Alita Naughton (Judy), Bryan Pringle (The Mayor), Robert Robinson (Himself), Norman Pitt (Westbourne Mayor), Henry McCarthy (Bridgmouth Mayor), Sandor Eles (Vladek).

Billion Dollar Brain. United Artists. 1967. Executive Producer: André de Toth. Producer: Harry Saltzman. Director: Ken Russell. Screenplay: John McGrath from Len Deighton novel. Photography: Billy Williams. Editor: Alan Osbiston. Production Designer: Syd Cain. Art Direction: Bert Davey. Music: Richard Rodney Bennett. Production Manager: Eva Monley. Camera Operator: David Harcourt. Sound Mixer: John Mitchell. First Assistant Director: Jack Causey. Second Assistant Director: Jim Brennan. Continuity: Angela Martelli. Costume Designer: Shirley Russell. Make-Up: Freddie Williamson, Benny Royston. Hairdresser: Joan Smallwood. Wardrobe Supervisor: John Brady. Wardrobe Mistress: Maggie Lewin. With: Michael Caine (Harry Palmer), Karl Malden (Leon Newbegin), Françoise Dorleac (Anya), Oscar Homolka (Colonel Stok), Ed Begley (General Midwinter), Guy Doleman (Colonel Ross), Vladek Sheybal (Dr. Eiwort), Milo Sperber (Basil), Mark Elwes (Birkinshaw), Stanley Caine (GPO Delivery Boy).

Women in Love. United Artists. 1969. Producers: Larry Kramer and Martin Rosen. Associate Producer: Roy Baird. Production Controller: Harry Benn. Director: Ken Russell. Screenplay: Larry Kramer from the D. H. Lawrence novel. Photography: Billy Williams. Editor: Michael Bradsell. Set Designer: Luciana Arrighi. Costume Designer: Shirley Russell. Music: Georges Delerue. Unit Manager: Neville C. Thompson. Camera Operator: David Harcourt. Assistant Director: Jonathan Benson. Continuity: Angela Allen. Choreographer: Terry Gilbert. Sound Recordist: Brian Simmons. Dubbing Editor: Terry Rawlings. Dubbing Mixer: Maurice Askew. Assistant Cameraman: Stephen Claydon. Location Manager: Lee Bolon. With: Alan Bates (Rupert Birkin), Oliver Reed (Gerald Crich), Glenda Jackson (Gudrun Brangwen), Jennie Linden (Ursula Brangwen), Eleanor Bron (Hermione Roddice), Alan Webb (Mr. Crich), Vladek Sheybal (Loerke), Catherine Wilmer (Mrs. Crich), Sarah Nicholls (Winifred Crich), Sharon Gurney (Laura Crich), Christopher Gable (Tibby Lupton), Michael Gough (Mr. Brangwen), Norma Shebeare (Mrs. Brangwen), Nike Arrighi (Contessa), James Laurenson (Minister), Michael Graham Cox (Palmer), Richard Heffer (Loerke's friend), Michael Garratt (Maestro).

The Music Lovers. United Artists. 1970. Executive Producer: Roy Baird. Director: Ken Russell. Screenplay: Melvyn Bragg from *Beloved Friend* by Catherine Drinker Bowen and Barbara von Meck. Photography: Douglas Slocombe. Editor: Michael Bradsell. Art Direction: Michael Knight. Production Designer: Natasha Kroll. Set Decoration: Ian Whittaker. Music: Tchaikovsky, conducted by André Previn. Solo pianist: Raphael Orozco. Solo soprano: April Cantelo. Choreographer: Terry Gilbert. Costume Designer: Shirley Russell. Sound Editor: Terry Rawlings. Sound Recordist: Derek Ball, Maurice Askew. Production Manager: Neville C. Thompson. Assistant Director: Jonathan Benson. Musical Advisers: Michael Moores, Elizabeth Corden. With: Richard Chamberlain (Peter Tchaikovsky), Glenda Jackson (Antonina Milyukova), Max Adrian (Nicholas Rubenstein), Christopher Gable (Count Anton Chiluvsky), Izabella Telezynska ("Iza Teller") (Madame von Meck), Kenneth Colley (Modeste Tchaikovsky), Sabina Maydells (Sasha Tchaikovsky), Maureen Pryor (Antonina's Mother), Bruce Robinson (Alexei), Andrew Faulds (Davidov), Ben Aris (Young Lieutenant), Joanne Brown (Olga Bredska), Imogen Clair (Lady in White), John and Dennis Myers (Von Meck twins), Xavier Russell (Koyola), James Russell (Bobyek), Victoria Russell (Tatiana), Alexander Russell (Mme. von Meck's Grandson), Alex Jawdokimov (Dmitri Shubelov), Clive Cazes (Doctor), Graham Armitage (Prince Balukin), Ernest Bale (Head Waiter), Consuela Chapman (Tchaikovsky's mother), Alex Brewer (Young Tchaikovsky). Georgina Parkinson, Alain Dubreuil, Peter White, Maggie Maxwell (Dancers in *Swan Lake*).

The Devils. Warner Brothers. 1971. Producers: Robert H. Solo and Ken Russell. Associate Producer: Roy Baird. Director: Ken Russell. Screenplay: Ken Russell from *The Devils* by John Whiting and *The Devils of Loudun* by Aldous Huxley. Photography: David Watkin. Editor: Michael Bradsell. Set Designer: Derek Jarman. Art Direction: Robert Cartwright. Costume Designer: Shirley Russell. Choreographer: Terry Gilbert. Music: Peter Maxwell Davies. Period Music Arranged and Conducted by David Munrow. Unit Manager: Graham Ford. Set Dresser: Ian Whittaker. Production Manager: Neville C. Thompson. Chief Make-Up: Charles Parker. Chief Hairdresser: Ramon Gow. Assistant Director: Ted Morley. With: Vanessa Redgrave (Sister Jeanne), Oliver Reed (Father Urbain Grandier), Dudley Sutton (Baron de Laubardemont), Max Adrian (Ibert), Gemma Jones (Madelyn de Brou), Murray Melvin (Mignon), Michael Gothard (Barré), Georgina Hale (Philippe), Brian Murphy (Adam), Christopher Logue (Richelieu), Graham Armitage (Louis XIII), John Woodvine (Trincant), Andrew Faulds (Rangier), Kenneth Colley (Legrand), Judith Paris (Sister Judith), Catherine Wilmer (Sister Catherine), Iza Teller (Sister Iza).

The Boy Friend. EMI–MGM. 1971. Producer and Director: Ken Russell. Associate Producer: Harry Benn. Screenplay: Ken Russell from Sandy Wilson's musical play. Production Associate: Justin de Villeneuve. Photography: David Watkin. Design Consultant: Tony Walton. Art Director: Simon Holland. Editor: Michael Bradsell. Costume Designer: Shirley Russell. Musical Director: Peter Maxwell Davies. Production Manager: Neville C. Thompson. Music Associate: Peter Greenwell. Choreography: Christopher Gable, Gillian Gregory, Terry Gilbert, and members of the cast. Assistant Director: Graham Ford. Camera Operator: Alan McCabe. Sound Recordist: Brian Simmons. Wardrobe Supervisor: John Brady. Chief Make-Up: Freddie Williamson. Chief Hairdresser: Barbara Ritchie. Property Master: George Ball. With: Twiggy (Polly Browne), Christopher Gable (Tony Brockhurst), Barbara Windsor (Hortense), Moyra Fraser (Madame Dubonnet/Mrs. Parkhill), Bryan Pringle (Percival Browne/Mr. Percy Parkhill), Max Adrian (Lord Brockhurst/Max Mandeville), Catherine Wilmer (Lady Brockhurst/Catherine), Vladek Sheybal (DeThrill), Ann Jameson (Mrs. Peter), Peter Greenwell (The Pianist), Antonia Ellis (Maisie), Caryl Little (Dulcie), Georgina Hale (Fay), Sally Bryant (Nancy), Tommy Tune (Tommy), Murray Melvin (Alphonse), Graham Armitage (Michael), Brian Murphy (Peter), Glenda Jackson (Rita).

Savage Messiah. MGM–EMI. 1972. Producer and Director: Ken Russell. Associate Producer: Harry Benn. Production Associates: John and Benny Lee. Production Manager: Neville C. Thompson. Screenplay: Christopher Logue from the book by H. S. Ede. Photography: Dick Bush. Editor: Michael Bradsell. Production Designer: Derek Jarman. Costume Designer: Shirley Russell. Set Decoration: Ian Whittaker. Art Direction: George Lack. Music: Michael Garratt. Song: "Two Fleas" by Dorothy Tutin, sung by Dorothy Tutin. Sound Editor: Stuart Baird. Sound Recording: Robin Gregory. With: Dorothy Tutin (Sophie Brzeska), Scott Antony (Henri Gaudier), Helen Mirren ("Gosh" Smith-Boyle), Lindsay Kemp (Angus Corky), Michael Gough (M. Gaudier), John Justin (Lionel Shaw), Aubrey Richards (Mayor), Peter Vaughan (Museum Attendant), Ben Aris (Thomas Buff), Eleanor Fazan (Mme Gaudier), Otto Diamant (Mr. Saltzman), Susanna East (Pippa), Maggy Maxwell (Tart), Imogen Claire (Mavis Coldstream), Judith Paris (Kate), Robert Lang (Major Boyle).

Mahler. Goodtimes Enterprises. 1974. Producer: Roy Baird. Executive Producers: David Puttnam and Sanford Lieberson. Director: Ken Russell. Screenplay: Ken Russell. Director of Photography: Dick Bush. Production Supervisor: John Comfort. Assistant Director: Michael Gowans. Location Manager: Richard Green. Producer's Assistant: Brenda Dale. Choreographer: Gillian Gregory. Camera Operator: Eddie Collins. Costume Designer: Shirley Russell. Art Director: Ian Whittaker. Associate Art Director: Roger Christian. Film Editor: Michael Bradsell. Assistant Editor: Stuart Baird. Sound Recordist: Ian Bruce. Continuity: Kay Mander. Make-Up: Peter Robb-King. Camera Assistant: Malcolm Vinson. Sound Assistant: Charles McFadden. Production Assistant: Clinton Cavers. Special

Effects: John Richardson. Mahler Symphonies conducted by Bernard Haitink and played by the Concertgebouw Orchestra, Amsterdam. Music Co-ordinator: John Forsythe. "In Stormy Weather", sung by Carol Mudie and performed by The National Philharmonia Orchestra. "Sunset", arranged by Michael Moores. "Alma's Song": words by William Blake, music by Dana Gillespie, and sung by Carol Mudie. With: Robert Powell (Gustav Mahler), Georgina Hale (Alma Mahler), Richard Morant (Max), Lee Montague (Bernhard Mahler), Rosalie Crutchley (Marie Mahler), Benny Lee (Uncle Arnold), Miriam Karlin (Aunt Rosa), Angela Down (Justine), David Collings (Hugo Wolf), Ronald Pickup (Nick), Antonia Ellis (Cosima Wagner), Dana Gillespie (Anna Von Mildenburg), Elaine Delmar (Princess), Michael Southgate (Alois Mahler), Gary Rich (Young Mahler), Peter Eyre (Otto), Sarah McLellan (Putzi), Claire McLellan (Glucki), George Coulouris (Doctor Roth), Arnold Yarrow (Grandfather), David Trevina (Doctor Richter), Otto Diamant (Professor Sladky), Ken Colley (Krenek), Andrew Faulds (Doctor on the train).

Tommy. Columbia. 1975. Producers: Robert Stigwood and Ken Russell. Executive Producers: Beryl Vertue and Christopher Stamp. Director: Ken Russell. Screenplay: Ken Russell. Associate Producer: Harry Benn. Production Manager: John Comfort. Director of Photography: Dick Bush. Camera Operator: Ronnie Taylor. Art Director: John Clark. Editor: Stuart Baird. Assistant Directors: Peter Cotton and Jonathan Benson. Musical Director: Peter Townshend. Continuity: Kay Mander. Sound Mixer: Ian Bruce. Costume Designer: Shirley Russell. Wardrobe Master: Richard Pointing. Wardrobe Mistress: Gillian Dodds. Chief Make-Up: George Blackler and Peter Robb-King. Chief Hairdresser: Joyce James. Location Manager: Lee Bolan. Set Dresser: Ian Whittaker. Choreographer: Gillian Gregory. Special Effects: John Richardson. With: Oliver Reed (Frank Hobbs), Ann-Margret (Nora Walker), Roger Daltrey (Tommy), Elton John (Pinball Wizard), Eric Clapton (Preacher), Keith Moon (Uncle Ernie), Jack Nicholson (Specialist), Robert Powell (Group-Captain Walker), Paul Nicholas (Cousin Kevin), Tina Turner (Acid Queen), Barry Winch (Young Tommy), Victoria Russell (Sally Simpson), Ben Aris (Reverend Simpson), Mary Holland (Mrs. Simpson), Jennifer Baker (1st Nurse), Susan Baker (2nd Nurse), Juliet King and Gillian King (Handmaidens to Acid Queen), Imogen Claire (Nurse), and The Who—Peter Townshend, Roger Daltrey, John Entwistle and Keith Moon.

Lisztomania. Goodtimes Enterprises. 1975. Producer: Roy Baird. Co-Producer: David Puttnam. Director/Writer: Ken Russell. Executive Producer: Sanford Lieberson. Production Manager: Peter Price. Production Secretary: Jean Hall. Assistant Director: Jonathan Benson. Continuity: Ann Skinner. Director of Photography: Peter Suschitzky. Operator: John Harris. Sound: Ian Bruce. Accountant: Paul Cadiou. Art Director: Philip Harrison. Special Effects: Colin Chilvers. Costumes Shirley Russell. Wardrobe: Richard Pointing. Make-Up: Wally

Schneiderman. Hair: Colin Jameson. Editor: Stuart Baird. Stills: Graham Attwood. Musical Arranger: Rick Wakeman. Music Co-ordinator: John Forsyth. With: Roger Daltrey (Franz Liszt), Sara Kestelman (Princess Carolyn), Paul Nicholas (Richard Wagner), Fiona Lewis (Countess Marie), Veronica Quilligan (Cosima), Nell Campbell (Olga), Andrew Reilly (Hans von Bulow), Ringo Starr (Pope), John Justin (Count d'Agoult), Anulka Dziubinska (Lola Montez), Imogen Claire (George Sand), Peter Brayham (first body-guard), David English (Captain), Rikki Howard (Countess), Felicity Devonshire (Governess), Aubrey Morris (Manager of the Opera House), Oliver Reed (Princess Carolyn's servant), Ken Colley (Chopin), Ken Parry (Rossini), Otto Diamant (Mendelssohn), Murray Melvin (Berlioz), Andrew Faulds (Lévi-Strauss), Georgina Hale (actress), Iza Teller (millionairess), and Rick Wakeman (Wagner's Superman).

Bibliography

WORKS CITED

Alpert, Hollis. *The Murder of Mahler*, Saturday Review, 8 February 1975, p. 39.

Anon. *The Boy Friend*, Filmfacts, 14 (1971), 469–72.

The Devils, Filmfacts, 14 (1971), 338–41.

Director in a Caftan, Time, 13 September 1973, p. 53.

For Herman Roucher, Family Weekly, 29 July 1973, p. 2.

Many Stories in One, MGM Pressbook for Savage Messiah. Metro-Goldwyn-Mayer, Inc., 1972, n. pag.

The Music Lovers, Filmfacts, 14 (1971), 146–9.

Savage Messiah, Filmfacts, 15 (1972), 578–82.

What's New at the Movies? New York Times, 26 November 1972. Arts and Leisure Section, p. 20, cols, 2–5.

Arnold, Gary. *Music Lovers*, Washington Post, 25 February 1971, Section C, p. 14, cols. 1–2.

Babel, Isaac. *Collected Stories*, Harmondsworth, England: Penguin, 1961.

Battestin, Martin C. *Osborne's Tom Jones: Adapting a Classic*, Man and the Movies. Ed. W. R. Robinson. Baltimore: Penguin Books, 1969, pp. 31–45.

Baxter, John. *An Appalling Talent/Ken Russell.* London: Michael Joseph, 1973.

An Appalling Talent/Ken Russell, unpublished first draft, TS.

Bazin, André. *What is Cinema?* Berkeley: Univ. of California Press, 1967

Bertocci, Angelo P. *Symbolism in Women in Love.* A D. H. Lawrence Miscellany. Ed. Harry T. Moore. Carbondale Ill. Southern Illinois Univ. Press, 1959, pp. 83–102.

Bertolucci, Bernardo. *Last Tango in Paris,* New York: Dell, 1973.
Bihalji-Merin, Otto. *Great Masks,* New York: Abrams, c. 1971.
Blaukopf, Kurt. *Gustav Mahler,* New York: Praeger, 1973; London: A. Lane, 1973.
Bluestone, George. *Novels into Film,* Berkeley: Univ. of California Press, 1961.
Blumenthal, J. *Macbeth into Throne of Blood,* Sight and Sound, 34 (1965), 190–5.
Bowen, Catherine Drinker and Barbara von Meck, *Beloved Friend: The Story of Tchaikovsky and Nadejda von Meck,* New York: Random House, 1937.
Bowen, Catherine Drinker. *Biography: The Craft and the Calling,* Boston: Little, Brown and Co., 1969.
Bowers, Faubion. *Scriabin,* Vol. I. Tokyo: Kondansha International Ltd., 1969.
Bragg, Melvyn. Correspondence with Joseph A. Gomez, December 2, 1973.
Braudy, Leo. *Jean Renoir: The World of His Films,* Garden City, N.Y.: Doubleday, 1972.
Briggs, John. *The Collector's Tchaikovsky and the Five,* Philadelphia: J. B. Lippincott, 1959.
Brodzky, Horace. *Henri Gaudier-Brzeska 1891–1915,* London: Faber and Faber, 1933.
Bruxner, David. *Russell's Rossetti,* Manchester Guardian, 26 November 1966, p. 7. cols. 1–3.
Buckley, Peter. *Savage Saviour,* Films and Filming, October 1972, pp. 13–16.
Byron, Lord. *The Selected Poetry of Lord Byron,* Ed. Leslie Marchand. New York: Random House, c. 1951.

Cocteau, Jean. *Three Screenplays: L'Eternal Retour, Orphée, La Belle et la Bête,* New York: Grossman, 1972.
Cohen, J. M. *The Devil and His Works,* Spectator, 3 October 1952, p. 440.
Combs, Richard. *Women in Love,* Monthly Film Bulletin, 36 (December 1969), 263–4.

Dawson, Jan. *Other Channel,* Sight and Sound, 41 (Autumn 1972), 204–5.
Deighton, Len. *The Billion Dollar Brain,* New York: Berkley Medallion G. P. Putnam, 1973; London: Jonathan Cape, 1966.
Dempsey, Michael. *Savage Messiah,* Film Heritage, 9 (Winter 1973–4), 9–16.
The World of Ken Russell, Film Quarterly, 25 (Spring 1972), 13–25.
Didion, Joan. *Hollywood: Having Fun,* New York Review of Books, 22 March 1973, pp. 15–18.
Doughty, Oswald. *Dante Gabriel Rossetti: A Victorian Romantic,* New Haven: Yale Univ. Press, 1949; London: O.U.P., 1960.
Durgnat, Raymond. *An Evening with Meyer and Masoch: Aspects of Vixen and Venus in Furs,* Film Comment, 9 (January–February 1973), 52–61.

Ede, H. S. *Savage Messiah,* 1931; rpt. New York: Avon, 1972; London: Gordon Fraser, 1971.

Eidsvik, Charles. *Demonstrating Film Influence,* Literature/Film Quarterly, 1 (1973), 113–21.

Soft Edges: The Art of Literature, the Medium of Film, Literature/Film Quarterly, 2 (1974), 16–21.

Eisenstein, Sergei. *Film Form,* New York: Harcourt, Brace and World, c. 1949.

Elley, Derek. *Mahler,* Films and Filming, May 1974, pp. 41–3.

Ellmann, Richard. *Golden Codgers: Biographical Speculations,* New York: Oxford Univ. Press, 1973.

Evans, Edwin. *Tchaikovsky,* New York: Dent and E. P. Dutton, 1935.

Farber, Stephen. *The Devils Finds an Advocate,* New York Times, 15 August 1971, Arts and Leisure Section, p. 1, col. 6 and p. 9, cols. 1–2.

Russellmania, Film Comment, 11 (November–December 1975), 39–46.

Fenby, Eric. *Delius as I knew Him,* London: Icon Books, 1966.

Flatley, Guy. *I'm Surprised My Films Shock People,* New York Times, 15 October 1972, Arts and Leisure Section, p. 15, cols. 1–5.

Ford, George. *Double Measure: A Study of the Novels and Stories of D. H. Lawrence,* New York: Holt, Rinehart and Winston, 1965.

Fox, Terry Curtis. *Conversations with Ken Russell,* Oui, June 1973, pp. 63–4 and 102–8.

Fremantle, Anne. *Faith Ruptured,* Saturday Review, 22 November 1952, p. 15.

Gaunt, William. *The Pre-Raphaelite Tragedy,* New York: Harcourt, Brace and Co., 1942.

Giannetti, Louis D. *Understanding Movies,* Englewood Cliffs, N.J.: Prentice Hall, 1972.

Gilson, René. *Jean Cocteau,* New York: Crown Publishers, 1969.

Gordon, David J. *Women in Love and the Lawrencean Aesthetic,* Twentieth Century Interpretations of Women in Love, Ed. Stephen J. Miko. Englewood Cliffs, N.J.: Prentice-Hall, 1969, pp. 50–60.

Gow, Gordon. *Shock Treatment,* Films and Filming, July 1970, pp. 8–12.

Hall, William. *What the Blazes is Ken Russell Up to Now? A Rock Opera,* New York Times, 23 June 1974. Arts and Leisure Section, p. 13, cols. 1–6 and p. 29, cols. 4–8.

Henderson, Philip. *William Morris: His Life, Work, and Friends,* New York: McGraw Hill, 1967.

Henderson, Robert M. *D. W. Griffith: The Years at Biograph,* New York: Farrar, Straus and Giroux, 1970.

Houston, Penelope. *The Contemporary Cinema,* Harmondsworth, England: Penguin, 1964.

Hughes, Robert. *Erratic Bust,* Time, 22 November 1972, pp. 98–9.

Huxley, Aldous. *Ape and Essence,* New York: Harper, 1948.

The Devils of Loudun, 1953; rpt. New York: Harper and Row, 1971; London: Chatto and Windus, 1970.

The Doors of Perception, New York: Harper, 1954; London: Chatto and Windus, 1968.

Grey Eminence, New York: Harper, 1941; London: Chatto and Windus, 1941.

Letters of Aldous Huxley, Ed. Grover Smith. New York: Harper and Row, 1969; London: Chatto and Windus, 1969.

The Perennial Philosophy, New York: Harper, 1945; London: Chatto and Windus, 1969.

Variations on a Philosopher, Great Short Works of Aldous Huxley, Ed. Bernard Bergonzi. New York: Harper and Row, 1969. pp. 381–479.

Kael, Pauline. *Genius,* New Yorker, 30 January 1971, pp. 76–9 [rev. of *The Music Lovers*].

Hyperbole and Narcissus, New Yorker, 18 November 1972, pp. 225–32 [rev. of *Savage Messiah*].

Lust for 'Art', New Yorker, 28 March 1970, pp. 97–101 [rev. of *Women in Love*].

Pleasing and Punishing, New Yorker, 8 January 1972, pp. 74–8 [rev. of *The Boy Friend*].

Kolker, Robert Philip. *Ken Russell's Biopics: Grander and Gaudier,* Film Comment, 9 (May–June 1973), 42–5.

Langley, Lee. *Ken Russell: A Director Who Demands the Right to be Outrageous,* Show, October 1971, pp. 34–8.

Lawrence, D. H. *Women in Love,* 1920; rpt. New York: Viking, 1961; London: Heinemann, 1954.

Leahy, James. *The Cinema of Joseph Losey,* London: A. Zwemmer Limited, 1967.

Lellis, George. *Recent Richardson—Cashing the Blank Cheque,* Sight and Sound, 38 (1969), 130–3.

Linden, George W. *Reflections on the Screen,* Belmont, Calif.: Wadsworth, 1970.

Lindsay, Vachel. *The Art of the Moving Picture,* New York: Macmillan, 1915.

Lockspeiser, Edward. *Debussy,* London: J. M. Dent, 1951.

Logue, Christopher. *An Extract from Christopher Logue's Screenplay for Ken Russell's Savage Messiah,* Films and Filming, November 1972, pp. 28–9.

Savage Messiah, unpublished shooting script. January 1972.

Lyons, Charles R. *The Futile Encounter in the Plays of John Whiting,* Modern Drama, II (December 1968), 283–97.

Mahler, Alma. *Gustav Mahler: Memories and Letters,* Ed. Donald Mitchell. New York: Viking, 1969; London: John Murray, 1973.

Manvell, Roger. *You Can Go to The Devils,* Humanist, 86 (November 1971), 331–3.

Marek, George R. *Richard Strauss: The Life of a Non-Hero.* New York: Simon and Schuster, 1967; London: Gollanz, 1967.

Mezan, Peter. *Relax, It's Only a Ken Russell Movie,* Esquire, May 1973, pp. 167–71 and 198–202.

Milne, Tom. *The Devils,* Monthly Film Bulletin, 38 (August 1971), 161–2.

Moore, Harry T. *D. H. Lawrence and the Flicks,* Literature/Film Quarterly, 1 (January 1973), 3–11.

Moynahan, Julian. *The Deed of Life: The Novels and Tales of D. H. Lawrence,* Princeton, N. J.: Princeton Univ. Press, 1963.

Newmarch, Rosa. *Tchaikovksy: His Life and Works, with Extracts from His Writings and the Diary of His Tour Abroad in* 1888, London: Grant Richards, 1900.

Nicolson, Marjorie Hope. *Mountain Gloom and Mountain Glory,* New York: Norton, 1963.

O'Brien, Glenn. *Ken Russell in the Port of New York,* Interview, November 1972, pp. 9–11.

Phillips, Gene D. *An Interview with Ken Russell,* Film Comment, 6 (Fall 1970), 10–17.

Pound, Ezra. *Gaudier-Brzeska: A Memoir,* 1916; rpt. New York: New Directions, 1970.

Reisz, Karel. *The Technique of Film Editing,* New York: Hastings House, 1953; London: Focal P., 1974.

Richardson, Robert. *Literature and Film,* Bloomington: Indiana Univ. Press, 1972.

Robbins, Fred. *The Savage Russell,* Gallery, May 1973, pp. 105–6 and 126–7.

Rose, Tony. *Other People's Pictures,* Movie Maker, May 1971, pp. 300–3 [rev. of *The Music Lovers*].

Other People's Pictures, Movie Maker, October 1971, pp. 650–2 [discussion of religious themes in *Lourdes* and *The Devils*].

Other People's Pictures, Movie Maker, April 1972, pp. 244–7 [comparison of Kubrick with Russell].

Rossetti, Dante Gabriel. *The Complete Poetical Works of Dante Gabriel Rossetti,* Ed. William M. Rossetti. Boston: Little, Brown and Co., 1898.

Rosten, Murray. *Biblical Drama in England,* Evanston, Ill. Northwestern Univ. Press, 1968.

Russell, Ken. *The Angels,* unpublished first draft of script, July 1972. TS.

Discussion Between Ken Russell, Alexander Walker and George Melly, Film Night—Confrontation, BBC telecast on 28 February 1971.

Gargantua, unpublished screen treatment, January 1973. TS.

Ideas for Films, Film, January–February 1959, pp. 13–15.

Interview discussion with Joseph A. Gomez, London, June 19, 1974.
Ken Russell Interviewed by Colin Wilson: Part 2, CBS telecast on Camera Three, 30 September 1973.
Mahler, unpublished early draft, TS.
Mahler, unpublished post-production script, TS, January 1974.
Mahler the Man, Mahler Brochure, London: Sackville Publishing, 1974.
Music Music Music, unpublished screen treatment, August 1972. TS.
Tommy, unpublished shooting script, April 1974. TS.
Tommy, unpublished working draft of shooting script. TS.

Russell, Shirley. *Costume Fantasia,* Mahler Brochure. London: Sackville Publishing, 1974.

Samuels, Charles Thomas, ed. *Encountering Directors,* New York: Putnams, 1972.

Sarris, Andrew. *The American Cinema: Directors and Directions 1929–1968,* New York: E. P. Dutton & Co., 1968.

Schickel, Richard. *Great Lives on TV,* Harper's, January 1971, pp. 28–33.

Selznick, David O. *Memo from David O. Selznick,* Ed. Rudy Behlmer. New York: Viking, 1972.

Simon, John. *Citizen Ken,* Times Literary Supplement, 8 November 1974, p. 1253.

Sirkin, Elliot. *Women in Love,* Film Quarterly, 24 (Fall 1970), pp. 43–7.

Sjoman, Vilgot. *I am Curious (Yellow),* New York: Grove Press, 1968.

Spilka, Mark. *The Love Ethic of D. H. Lawrence,* Bloomington, Indiana: Indiana Univ. Press, 1955.

Starr, William. *Editorial,* Film Critic, 1 (September–October 1972), 7.

Sterritt, David. *Whole Film Is "One Flash" In His Mind,* Christian Science Monitor, 2 June 1975, p. 27.

Taylor, John Russell. *Anger and After,* Harmondsworth, England: Penguin, 1966.

Tchaikovsky, Modeste. *The Life and Letters of Peter Ilich Tchaikovsky,* New York: John Lane Company, 1906.

Trussler, Simon. *The Plays of John Whiting,* Tulane Drama Review, II (Winter 1966), pp. 141–51.

Vivas, Eliseo. *D. H. Lawrence: The Failure and Triumph of Art,* Evanston, Ill.: Northwestern Univ. Press, 1960.

Walker, Alexander. *Hollywood UK: The British Film Industry in the Sixties,* New York: Stein and Day, 1974; London: Michael Joseph, 1974.

Walker, John. *Ken Russell's New Enigma,* Observer, 8 September 1974, Magazine Section, pp. 51–6.

Warrack, John. *Tchaikovsky,* New York: Charles Scribner's Sons, 1973; London: Hamish Hamilton, 1973.

Waugh, Evelyn. *Rossetti: His Life and Works,* New York: Dodd, Mead, and Co., 1928.
Weightman, John. *Trifling with the Dead,* Encounter, January 1970, pp. 50–3 [rev. of *Women in Love*].
Weinstock, Herbert. *Tchaikovsky,* New York: Alfred A. Knopf, 1966.
Whiting, John. *The Devils,* New York: Hill and Wang, 1962; London: Heinemann Educational, 1972.
John Whiting: An Interview with Tom Milne and Clive Goodwin, Theatre at Work: Playwrights and Productions in Modern British Theatre. Ed. Charles Marowitz and Simon Trussler. London: Methuen, 1967, pp. 21–35.
Wilson, Sandy. *The Boy Friend,* 1955; rpt. Harmondsworth, England: Penguin, 1972.
Woodcock, George. *Dawn and the Darkest Hour: A Study of Aldous Huxley,* New York: Viking, 1972; London: Faber, 1972.

Zambrano, Ana Laura. *Women in Love: Counterpoint on Film,* Literature/Film Quarterly I (January 1973), 46–55.

WORKS CONCERNING RUSSELL WHICH WERE CONSULTED BUT NOT CITED

Anon. *Film Guide,* Sight and Sound, 41 (Autumn 1972), 240.
Film Star Russell?, "Tommy" Publicity Release (1974), pp. 1–2.
Films: Women in Love, America, 25 April 1970, p. 456.
The First Ken Russell Film Festival, TLA Winter–Spring Film Schedule: January 18–April 16, 1974. Philadelphia, 1974. n. pag.
Ken Russell, BFI 40th Anniversary (program for the National Film Theatre from September–November 1973), pp. 16–21.
Ken Russell and Savage Messiah, After Dark, 21 November 1972, p. 38.
Ken Russell: Biography, "Tommy" Publicity Release (1974), pp. 1–7.
Salute of the Week: Kenneth Russell, Cue, 30 May 1970, p. 1.
The [sic] Savage Messiah, Cinema TV Today, 23 September 1972, p. 18.
The Television Russell, "Tommy" Publicity Release (1974), pp. 1–4.
What Directors are Saying!, Action, 7 (January–February 1972), 36.
Armstrong, Marion. *Spirited Creatures,* Christian Century, 16 September 1970, p. 1099 [rev. of *Women in Love*].

Bazarov, Konstantin. *Women in Love,* Monthly Film Bulletin, 38 (March 1971), 53–4.
Blume, Mary. *Director Russell with Boy Friend: Ogre in a Nursery?* Los Angeles Times, 19 September 1971, Calendar Magazine, p. 18.
Bryson, Robert D. *Glascow and The Devils,* Cinema TV Today, 27 May 1972, p. 8 [censorship of *The Devils*].

Cocks, Jay, *Madhouse Notes*, Time, 26 July 1971, p. 50 [rev. of *The Devils*].
Combs, Richard. *Savage Messiah*, Monthly Film Bulletin, 39 (October 1972), p. 217.
Comuzio, Ermanns. *Ken Russel* [*sic*]*: L'altra Faccia Dell'amore*, Cineforum, July–August 1971, pp. 109–17.

Davis, Peter G. *Ken Russell's Film Studies of Composers—Brilliance Gone Berserk*, New York Times, 19 October 1975, Arts and Leisure Section, p. 1, cols. 3–5 and p. 13, cols. 1–6.
Doyle, Brian. *Production Notes,* "Tommy" Publicity Release (1974), pp. 1–24.

Evans, Peter. *Ken Russell Finds His Own Act Is Hard to Follow,* The Hollywood Reporter, 4 October 1971, pp. 1 and 6.

Fisher, Jack. *Three Paintings of Sex: The Films of Ken Russell,* The Film Journal, 2 (September 1972), pp. 33–43.

Gow, Gordon. *The Devils,* Films and Filming, September 1971, p. 49.
The Music Lovers, Films and Filming, March 1971, pp. 47–8.
Savage Messiah, Films and Filming, October 1972, p. 45.
Women in Love, Films and Filming, January 1970, pp. 49–50.

Kahan, Saul. *Ken Russell: A Director Who Respects Artists,* Los Angeles Times, 28 March 1971, Calendar Magazine, p. 18.
Kauffmann, Stanley. *Stanley Kauffmann on Films,* New Republic, 18 April 1970, p. 20 [rev. of *Women in Love*].
Knight, Arthur. *Liberated Classics,* Saturday Review, 21 March 1970, pp. 50–2. [rev. of *Women in Love* and *Tropic of Cancer*].
Knoll, Robert. *Women in Love,* Film Heritage 6 (Summer 1971), pp. 1–6.

Lerman, Leo. *Catch Up With . . .,* Mademoiselle, May 1970, pp. 128 and 203. [rev. of *Women in Love*].

MacDonough, Scott. *Britain's Volatile Oliver Reed: "I Only Bully Bigger Bullies!"* Show, April 1972, pp. 32–7 [Reed discusses his work with Russell].
Manvell, Roger. *New Cinema in Britain.* London: Studio Vista, 1969.
McKee, Allen. *Why Can't the English Make a Masterpiece?*, New York Times, Arts and Leisure Section, 24 December 1972, p. 17, cols. 1–8.

Phillips, Gene D. *The Movie Makers: Artists in an Industry,* Chicago: Nelson-Hall Co., 1973

Reed, Rex. *Rex Reed at the Movies,* Holiday, June 1970, pp. 20–2 [rev. of *Women in Love*].

Rose, Tony. *On the Set With Ken Russell,* Movie Maker, September 1972, pp. 618–19.

Russell, Ken. *The Devils He Did,* Cinema TV Today, 5 August 1972, p. 4 [ans. to David Robinson's letter on the cost of *The Devils*].

Extract from 24 Hours, BBC-1 telecast on 22 July 1971 [discussion with Ludovic Kennedy about *The Devils*].

Ken Russell Reminisces, "Tommy" Publicity Release (1974), pp. 1–4.

Ken Russell Talking, "Tommy" Publicity Release (1974), pp. 1–3.

Ken Russell Writes on Raising Kane, Films and Filming, May 1972, p. 16.

This is Money Thrown Away, Cinema TV Today, 15 July 1972, p. 10 [letter about BFI Production Board].

Schickel, Richard. *A Past Master in the Hands of a Future One,* Life, 6 March 1970, p. 14 [rev. of *Women in Love*].

Schlesinger, Jr., Arthur. *Movies: Women in Love, "Fascinating Try",* Vogue, 1 March 1970, p. 32.

Simon, John. *Madness, Watchable and Unwatchable,* New York, 27 October 1975, pp. 76–7. [rev. of *Lisztomania*].

Smith, Howard, and Brian Van Der Horst. *See Me, Hear Me, Hype Me,* Village Voice, 10 February 1975, p. 18, cols. 1–2.

Stewart, Bruce. *Russell's Devils,* Month, October 1971, p. 122.

Taylor, John Russell. *Billion Dollar Brain,* Monthly Film Bulletin, 35 (January 1968), pp. 2–3.

Tessier, Max. *Entretien Avec Ken Russell,* Cinéma, 71 (December 1971), p. 119.

The Music Lovers: La Vie Privée Sexuelle de Piotr Illytch, Cinéma, 71 (March 1971), pp. 131–4.

Tucker, Martin. *Lawrence's Women,* Commonweal, 15 May 1970, pp. pp. 223–4 [rev. of *Women in Love*].

Warga, Wayne. *Kramer Scripts Thinking Man's Women in Love,* Los Angeles Times, 3 May 1970, Calendar Magazine, pp. 1 and 12–13.

Warner, Alan. *The Boy Friend,* Films and Filming, April 1972, pp. 49–50.

Weightman, John. *How Not to Love Music,* Encounter, May 1971, pp. 48–50 [rev. of *The Music Lovers*].

Zimmerman, Paul D. *Portrait of the Artist,* Newsweek, 20 November 1972, pp. 124–5 [rev. of *Savage Messiah*].